se.

olets

ysuckle

sum

rever I am.

strength

call Life.

to shoulder

nce of your eye

a sympathetic heart.

d's gracious bounty.

Wherever I am,

at for big florists' offerings

cover thy poor bier

love & Christ's unspeakable Prayer

e another

of sweet understanding

ntly & kindly

the Fall Opening' Anna Pope, Aug 10, 1940

Presented to St. Mark's Library,

the General Theological Seminary

1983

by the Episcopal Women's History Project

This biography of Anna Cooper is a prototype of those hitherto-unrecog-
nized Episcopal churchwomen whose lives are being 'excavated' in the present
interest in women's history. Anna Cooper, though an unusually visible public
figure for Episcopal Women in the late 19th and early 20th centuries, was
typical in that her major achievements as educator and leader were in addition to her taken-for-granted work as the wife of an Episcopal clergyman and
herself a devout churchwoman. The references to her activities in the Episcopal Church are incidental to the author of the biography, but of immense
interest to those interested in uncovering evidence of the way women in past
generations lived out their Christian calling.

ANNA J. COOPER: A Voice from the South

The problem may be that Washington, the seat of history, fails to understand what history really is.

—ADA LOUISE HUXTABLE
March 17, 1974
The New York Times

ANNA J. COOPER

BY LOUISE DANIEL HUTCHINSON

Published for the
ANACOSTIA NEIGHBORHOOD MUSEUM
OF THE SMITHSONIAN INSTITUTION
by the
SMITHSONIAN INSTITUTION PRESS
CITY OF WASHINGTON

A Voice from the South

LIBRARY OF CONGRESS CATALOGING IN PUBLICATION DATA

Hutchinson, Louise Daniel.
    Anna J. Cooper, a voice from the South.

    Prepared in conjunction with an exhibit at the
Anacostia Neighborhood Museum, Washington, D.C.
    Bibliography: p.
    Includes index.
    1. Cooper, Anna Julia Haywood, 1859-1964.
2. Afro-Americans—Washington (D.C.)—Biography.
3. Teachers—Washington (D.C.)—Biography.
4. Washington (D.C.)—Biography. I. Anacostia
Neighborhood Museum. II. Title.
F205.N4C664   370'.92'4 [B]   81-5323
                                  AACR2

DEDICATED TO MY PARENTS,
VICTOR HUGO DANIEL
AND CONSTANCE ELEANOR HAZEL DANIEL—
PIONEER EDUCATORS—WHO,
LIKE ANNA JULIA COOPER,
BELIEVED IN THE POWER OF EDUCATION.

Contents

Foreword

ANNA JULIA COOPER, THE SUBJECT OF OUR PRE-
sentation, was born into a multi-ethnic and plu-
ralistic society in the late 1850s. Presenting the
facts as we know them, the story moves from the
ugliness of slavery—with all of its baseness—to a
higher moral plateau. This, after all, is in keeping
with the character of our subject. For it is her story
and her life—just as she chose to live it—that set
the course and gave direction and form to this book
and the exhibit that accompanies it.

Anna Cooper was a stoic, but not a static figure
in our history. She is one whom Booker T. Washington would have called "a doer of the word, not
a speaker of the word." She kept her counsel in the
face of adversity and negative criticism from her
detractors. Yet her deeds point to a woman whose
abilities and human compassion had great depth.
Her life had meaning and purpose, and her omission from published accounts of our history until
recent years is to be regretted. Had she lived at
another time, and in another society and culture,
she would have been applauded for the strides made
from a humble and unpretentious beginning as the
daughter of a black slave mother to the position of
a respected educator and scholar.

The significance of Anna Julia Cooper's life and
contributions must be examined against the background of that long period of history through
which she lived and worked. For it is because of our
knowledge of her work and struggle to attain *in spite*
of adversities, and the conditions of the social environment into which she was born, that we assign
significance to her life. Without this knowledge, a
recital of Anna Cooper's accomplishments and
achievements would be only empty platitudes. The
hardships, the adversities, and the struggles of her
life tested and proved the mettle and resoluteness
that command our attention and respect.

While it is indeed noteworthy that Anna Cooper
earned the highest degree attainable in Western
civilization, the accomplishment takes on even
greater meaning for us when we learn that this
success came only after fifty-seven years of painstaking work, sacrifice, self-denial, and preparation.
She counseled with some of the best minds of the
day, and her prowess as a scholar and lecturer, and
her proficiency as an educator, are also worthy of
our consideration. Anna Cooper's value as a contributing member of our society is predicated on
this, and much, much more, for her striving to
succeed was neither self-seeking nor self-serving.

Nothing came easy or was ever given to Anna
Cooper, and every reward was earned. The uncom-
pensated toil of her mother and brothers in slavery
earned her no inheritance rights to family wealth,
status, influence, or extraordinary opportunities.
Instead, her achievements were the direct result of
her own desire, initiative, drive, and tenacity.
Anna Cooper had the vision and the ability to see
life as it could and should be, in a free and democratic society. Seeking fuller participation for all its
members, at every level, she struggled to bring into
focus and into being her view of the world around
her.

Not one to succumb to egotistical vanity, Cooper
dedicated her life, time, talents, and resources to
the service of others. This trait of selfless giving is
discernible in our subject's personal and professional life. She had an indomitable will and strength of
character, seemingly indefatigable energy, high
moral principles and standards of conduct. Cooper's
life is a study of contrasts. Born into bondage, she

had a free spirit. Impregnated with the desire to learn, she taught in exchange for her own schooling. She was a woman of natural grace and bearing, whose accomplishments by the beginning of the twentieth century gained her admission into the very pleasant society of Washington, D.C. By choice, she identified with and her affection remained with those who had had few or no opportunities for educational attainment or social advancement.

Space does not permit me to dwell much longer on our subject, who, after meeting defeat at the hands of detractors and antagonists, described life as having "just enough opposition to give zest to the struggle. . . ." Such a woman deserves our attention, for among us are those for whom denial and oppression (overt or covert) have become "faits accomplis," and past transgressions by others have become excuses and crutches for present-day inertia. For them in particular, we believe the life and work of Anna Julia Cooper holds a message.

JOHN R. KINARD
Director,
Anacostia Neighborhood Museum

Acknowledgments

THE STAFF HISTORIAN ALONE MUST ASSUME THE reponsibility for the correct usage and interpretation of the large body of information that is assembled and presented in this publication. And it is with a deep sense of gratitude and appreciation that the invaluable assistance and support of individuals and contributing institutions is acknowledged. There are those to whom we owe a very special debt of gratitude. They are: the late Dr. Leona C. Gabel, whose curiosity about Anna Julia Cooper was aroused after receiving Cooper's doctoral dissertation, a gift from a friend and colleague at Smith College; Dr. Sidney Kaplan, whose continued friendship and interest in the Anacostia Museum made it possible for this story—described by Gabel as a "story in search of an author, a tale waiting to be told," to reach Washington, D.C., the site of many of Cooper's struggles and accomplishments; the staff of the Moorland-Spingarn Research Center (Howard University) and the Department of Archives and History (Raleigh, North Carolina), without whose assistance a difficult project would have been an impossible task—for fragments of the records of Cooper's life and life's work rested in many and often obscure places. Therefore, thanks must be given to Thomas Battle, Mrs. Esme E. Bhan, Mrs. Maricia Bracey, William J. Scott; also to George Stevenson—for without his suggestions, general good will and "esprit de corps," much rich primary source data, located in Raleigh, would have been irretrievable and not available for use in either the exhibition or this book.

Much of our searching was carried on either by correspondence or telephone, and many graciously endured the pressure of our queries and urgent pleas for assistance and information. Among them were W. E. Bigglestone, Oberlin College Archives; Robert W. McDonnell, W. E. B. Du Bois Papers, the University of Massachusetts; and the Smithsonian's own Jack Marquardt.

From the inception of this exhibit and publishing project, Mrs. Mary Gibson Hundley, Mrs. Betty Culpepper, Dr. David L. Lewis, Perry Fisher, and Dr. Paul Phillips Cooke have been supportive; each reviewed the Gabel manuscript, assisting in determining its appropriateness for use and adaptation as an exhibit presentation, reviewing each phase of the scripting. Dr. Cooke reviewed much of the manuscript, all of the captions, and thoughtfully prepared the Introduction to this offering. Dr. Henry S. Robinson shared family records, and Robert Scurlock made photographs from the collection of his father, Addison Scurlock, available for research and publishing. Too, the generosity of Mr. and Mrs. Burton Lewis made possible the loan of paintings by Thomas Watkins Hunster.

Others whose kindness and support must be acknowledged are Mrs. Ella Howard Pearis, Mrs. Phyllis Terrell Langston, William N. Buckner, Jr., Dick Hulbert, Paul Sluby, Sr., Mr. and Mrs. Benjamin T. Layton, the Honorable John D. Fauntleroy and Mrs. Fauntleroy, the late Mrs. Georgia R. Lawson, James J. Lawson, and Mrs. Anna Rosetta Lawson Prescott; also Joseph F. Edwards and the family of Conard and Marion Demby Edwards, Ronald V. Taylor (The Barbados Museum and Historical Society), and Lewis Saben. We also thank the Library of Congress Conservation Laboratory and Mr. Bellamy of the Photo and Prints Division; Dr. Mildred P. Cooper and Mrs. Ericka Robinson, D.C. Public Schools Office of Research and Development; Robert L. Byrd, Duke University; Mrs. Susan L. Boone, Smith College; Daniel T. Williams, Tuskegee Institute; Robert Bartram, George Peabody Department of the Enoch Pratt Free Library (Baltimore); Fritz Malval, Hampton Institute (Virginia) Archives; and Charles L. Blockson.

Public recognition must be given to Mrs. Dorothy B. Porter Wesley, who over the years assembled and curated the rich collection of black Americana available today at the Moorland-Spingarn Research Center, and who acquired the small yet important Anna J. Cooper Manuscript Collection; and to Anna Cooper's descendants, Mrs. Regia Haywood Bronson and Miss Regina Smith, whose courtesies to our staff made possible the use of Cooper photographs, writings, and memorabilia located in the LeDroit Park home.

Finally, a special thanks is expressed to all staff, whose energies and skills supported the development of the Cooper exhibit and this book. They are Hazelene E. Evans, secretary; Carolyn J. Margolis, research assistant (now with the Library of Congress); John C. Harris, project editor (now with the Smithsonian Institution Press); and research assistants Brenda Case-Frazier and Cassandra F. Smith. It was "Sandy" Smith who provided us with our lighter moments, when reporting on her "fearless" inspection of burial grounds, in Raleigh. Each contributed significantly to the successful conclusion of this project.

The immeasurable assistance of others not cited here is no less appreciated.

Introduction

Anna J. Cooper: teacher and high school principal . . . scholar and college professor . . . graduate of the Sorbonne (Paris) with an earned doctorate and yet a product, too, of St. Augustine's College . . . author and speaker . . . organizational leader and community worker, president of an institution of higher education. Each of these is an accomplishment of some distinction. And when taken all together as the work of one person they constitute unusual and substantial achievement. An additional note: whether the accomplishments of man or woman they have tremendous merit. It is thus reasonable to judge Anna Cooper as a person of great accomplishment—not simply as a fine black woman but rather as a splendid human being.

Both the Anna J. Cooper Exhibit of the Anacostia Neighborhood Museum (Smithsonian) and the exhibit book, *Anna J. Cooper: A Voice from the South,* are exceedingly effective in bringing to life a rather extraordinary woman. Both show her in her time as a young woman and teacher, as the leader of a renowned high school, as the scholar in French, and the teacher of Cicero and Virgil.

The Anacostia Museum's Cooper exhibit and book are equally effective in presenting Anna Cooper as a leader in postsecondary continuing education, as a contributor in other ways to the Washington community and to the National Association of Colored Women's Clubs, and as a person willing to accept the responsibilities of guardianship of young children. The Anacostia's Cooper exhibit is superior, I have concluded, from looking for more than a year at its painstaking creation.

Both the exhibit and this book present carefully and appropriately this woman against the history of the several decades before and after the turn of the twentieth century. Anna J. Cooper is three dimensional—has depth—is a real individual in a full setting of time and place.

In a long and active life a generation longer than the allotted Biblical span, there are a number of "high" points, unusually significant happenings, in the life of Anna Cooper: the M Street High School period; the Dunbar years; earning her Ph.D. at the Sorbonne; and even after retirement, heading Frelinghuysen University.

However significant was *A Voice from the South: By a Black Woman of the South* (1892), her major publication; however striking was her accomplishment of a Ph.D. in French from a foreign university at age sixty-five (or possibly older); and however important is her heading Frelinghuysen University, Anna J. Cooper's major service and achievement, I again conclude, lay in her preparation of high school youth through a sound curriculum and good teaching, including those who made their way in Ivy League institutions. With the exception of her four years at Lincoln University, 1906-1910, Anna Cooper was an integral part of the Washington high school scene from 1887 to 1930.

As noted at the outset, Anna Cooper was a person of real achievement, a black woman of solid stature. The Anacostia Cooper exhibit appropriately focuses on the major services of her life in five "Unit Designs" and places them in the perspective of the Negro movement of her time. Likewise, the Cooper exhibit book by Louise Daniel Hutchinson effectively presents and coordinates her life in broad context.

Anna Cooper may be considered along with Mary McLeod Bethune and Mary Church Terrell and Nannie Helen Burroughs.

A Voice from the South, Cooper's most important writing, showed her well ahead of her time in arguing for women's rights and the importance of a role for the black woman.

Her leadership in the Washington Colored Woman's League was important because that group was one of the three organizations that merged to form the National Association of Colored Women's Clubs, which in 1980 held in Washington, D.C. its forty-second biennial meeting in its eighty-fourth year.

That Anna Cooper could occupy the rostrum with Booker T. Washington (the Hampton Conference in 1892), represent black American men and women at the Pan African Conference in London in 1900, hold membership as the only female in the American Negro Academy (along with Kelly Miller, W. E. B. Du Bois, Francis Grimké, Carter G. Woodson, and Arthur A. Schomburg) can only add to her importance.

For the Anacostia Museum, Mrs. Hutchinson has based both the exhibit and this book on solid research—using resources of the Library of Congress and the National Archives, of statehouses and courthouses, of university and local libraries (for example, the Washingtoniana Division of the District's Martin Luther King Memorial Library), of city directories, and of the Smithsonian Institution itself. (It was also my good fortune late last year to examine resources in the Barbados (B.W.I.) Museum and Historical Society for information on the Heywood family, of which Anna Julia Haywood was a descendant.) The reproductions of rooms in the Cooper home at T and Second Streets, of an M Street High classroom, and photographs and captions in the exhibit book all tell us a great deal.

The splendid audio-visual experience of the exhibit and the service of the book as a vivid reading experience have an important common element: they set off Anna J. Cooper both as an individual and as a person in a period of history, in a social and cultural setting, in a changing political and racial climate. The reader can better understand why Anna Cooper should deny any gains from her white parent as the reader learns of the slave environment of the 1850s and 1860s, the time of her birth and early years. The reader can understand in the steadily increasing national, regional, and local measures of segregation and subjugation, and other forms of discrimination against the Negro—which *Anna J. Cooper: A Voice from the South* effectively relates—that Anna Cooper's acts were transgressions against a system and could not be tolerated.

This introduction might end on a note of creation of milieu—the social and cultural setting—to understand Dr. Cooper and what happened to her. The conclusion better might be two assessments of Anna Cooper, the first by the District school board, written in 1905, the second by a Raleigh attorney (white) asked by the school board to appraise her.

> *We believe that the principal, Mrs. A. J. Cooper, is a woman of good intellectual attainment, of high moral character, and of excellent reputation among her people.—School Board.*
> *Her character has always been high . . . she became a successful teacher . . . and always had the reputation of being a successful teacher. . . . as a girl, she was studious and industrious. . . .—Charles Busbee, Attorney, Raleigh.*

Our best recollection of Anna Julia Haywood Cooper might be that of the able teacher, kind human being, and person of good and respected character.

PAUL PHILLIPS COOKE

ANNA J. COOPER: A Voice from the South

Yours sincerely
& AJCooper.

I.

The Early Years

The part of my ancestors that did not come over in the Mayflower in 1620, arrived, I am sure, a year earlier in the fateful Dutch trader that put in at Jamestown in 1619. . . . I believe that the third source of my individual stream comes . . . from the vanishing Red Men, which ought . . . to the manner born and "inheritor of the globe" [make me a] genuine F.F.A. (First Family of America).

ANNA J. COOPER, n.d.
The Washington Tribune

ANNA JULIA COOPER—FEMINIST, HUMAN RIGHTS advocate, educational reformer—was also a teacher, lecturer, scholar, and the author of essays, vignettes, and poems. Born Annie Julia Haywood, about 1858, in Raleigh, North Carolina, she died in her Washington, D.C., home in 1964—more than a century later. The daughter of a slave woman, Hannah Stanley Haywood, Anna was born at a pivotal time in the country's history: on the eve of the Civil War and at the time of the birth of the Republican Party. Facts concerning her paternity are both hazy and inconclusive, yet Anna wrote that presumably her father was her mother's master, concluding that "if so I owe him not a sou and she [her mother] was always too modest & shamefaced ever to mention him. . . ."

Anna Cooper was an extraordinary woman. At first glance her accomplishments may not seem to be so remarkable. However, when we consider that she, as a nineteenth-century black woman, began her life under the most adverse circumstances, and at a time when the mental capacity of blacks and women was questioned and disparaged, her achievements take on a greater significance. For at that time women and blacks were engaged in a daily struggle to attain full citizenship rights, and the dignity that these rights accorded.

First, in order to appreciate fully the life and work of Anna Cooper, it is important that the reader know something of the socio-economic and geographic-political environment into which she was born and in which she grew up. For an event, or a series of events, may well impinge on an individual's life with such dramatic suddenness and profoundness that the outcome is inevitable. Too, such an experience may affect the personality and

Anna Julia Cooper in the early 1890s. From *A Voice from the South: By a Black Woman of the South.*

3

I was born in Raleigh North Carolina. My mother was a slave & the finest woman I have ever known. Tho untutored she could read her Bible & write a little. Tis one of my happiest childhood memories explaining for her the subtle differences between q's & g's or between b's & l's. Presumably my father was her master, if so I owe him not a son & she was always too modest & shamefaced ever to mention him.

I was born during the Civil War & served many an anxious slave's superstition to wake the baby up & ask directly "Which side is goin' to win de War?" "Will de Yankees beat de Rebs & will Linkum free de Niggers." I want to say that while it may be true in infancy we are nearer Heaven, if I had any vision or second sight in those days that made my answers significant to the troubled souls that hung breathless on my cryptic answers, such powers promptly took their flight with the dawn of intelligent consciousness. In the later struggle for existence I could not have told you how the simplest rencounter with fate would end.

An undated autobiographical account of her birth by Anna J. Cooper. Courtesy Moorland-Spingarn Research Center, Howard University.

psyche with such intensity that it leaves an indelible impression. Confronting slavery in her early, impressionable years, Anna Cooper also experienced freedom and its aftermath during the first decade of her life. Thus, in that setting, the precocious Anna Cooper made a decision about her life and future years that was irreversible. It was then that she decided to become an educator, and to work among her people.

Although we are left with only fragmentary reminiscences of Anna Cooper's early years, we may still gain retrospective glimpses of her history. One such story concerns a slave, Jacob Stanley, who might have been the father of Hannah Stanley Haywood, and the maternal grandfather of Anna Cooper, who wrote:

Hannah Stanley Haywood (1817–1899), the mother of Annie Julia Haywood Cooper. Courtesy Mrs. Regia Bronson and Miss Regina Smith.

The home of Fabius J. Haywood, Sr., is seen in Jacob Marling's painting, *Old State House.* The canvas dates from between 1818 and 1831.
From *North Carolina's Capital, Raleigh.*

Dr. Fabius J. Haywood, Sr. Courtesy North Carolina
Department of Archives and History.

Jacob Stanley was a broad chested upstand-
ing black man. Family tradition has it that he
took part in planning & construction of the
State Capitol, at the South Central entrance to
which, heading Fayetteville Street, stood the
stately brick mansion of Dr. Fabius Haywood,
Stanley's owner. For Jacob Stanley was a slave.
I don't know how—come [sic].

Fact is so substantial, so notable was his
contribution to the public exchequer that expert economists volunteered friendly advice:
"you should make that Nigger support you &
your whole family. Just his production alone."

Whereat the good humored Master with
characteristic drawl & aristocratic profanity replied: "If Jacob supports me, who the
H . . . 'l's going to support Jacob & his brats?
Damn 'f I yam. . . . !"

Entitled "Grapes From Thorns," the manuscript
relating this all-too-brief encounter discloses a
number of interesting facts. While undated, it was
written in Anna Cooper's later years, when her
eyesight had begun to fail and her fine script had
become larger. It was also written at a time when,
through her memories, Anna Cooper had retreated
to her early years in Raleigh. Several histories of
North Carolina attest to the accuracy of her facts.

The residence of Dr. Fabius J. Haywood, Sr., did
head Fayetteville Street, and the State House could
be seen from that vantage point. The original State
House had been razed following a fire in 1831, and
the one in Anna Cooper's account had replaced it.
If her story has veracity (and I believe that it has),
then Jacob Stanley, Hannah Stanley Haywood, and
her children—Rufus, Andrew Jackson, and Annie
Julia—were all the property of Dr. Haywood. Not
wishing to rely on conjectures or mere coinci-
dences, I have located expert testimony (that will be
discussed later) that irrefutably identifies Dr. Haywood as the slave master of Andrew J. Haywood—
thus of the family of Anna J. Cooper.

With the present interest in family and oral histories, still other aspects of Anna Cooper's account
are engaging and worthy of consideration. Here,
the mention of "family tradition" implies that the
story of Jacob Stanley was handed down in the oral
tradition so prevalent among black slave families.
And the reference to "Jacob's brats" causes us to
believe that there were other siblings in Hannah's
family, though they remain unknown to us. Too, it
is important to note that Jacob did have a marketable skill. Although not compensated for his labor,
Jacob Stanley made a significant contribution to his
community.

Some historians believe that the institution of
slavery did not flourish in North Carolina, and
therefore did not significantly influence the lifestyle that developed there. Yet there is new evidence that suggests that just the opposite is true.
While it is generally true that the state's unique
topography did not support a large slave population
and plantation economies, other viable alternatives
were developed. And Haywoods were among those
who sought more favorable conditions elsewhere for
establishing plantations that were worked by black
slave labor. In addition, slaves made up the bulk of
the household servants who took care of the large
and commodious homes that were built in Raleigh
after its founding. As the legislators and their families moved to the new capital city, they continued
the same plantation life that they had enjoyed in
Edgecombe and other surrounding counties. A description of this early lifestyle is found in *A Sketch
of the Haywood Family* (1956) by Dr. Hubert Benbury Haywood, Sr. Picturesque and noted for its
fine appointments, the home of one member of the
Haywood family included

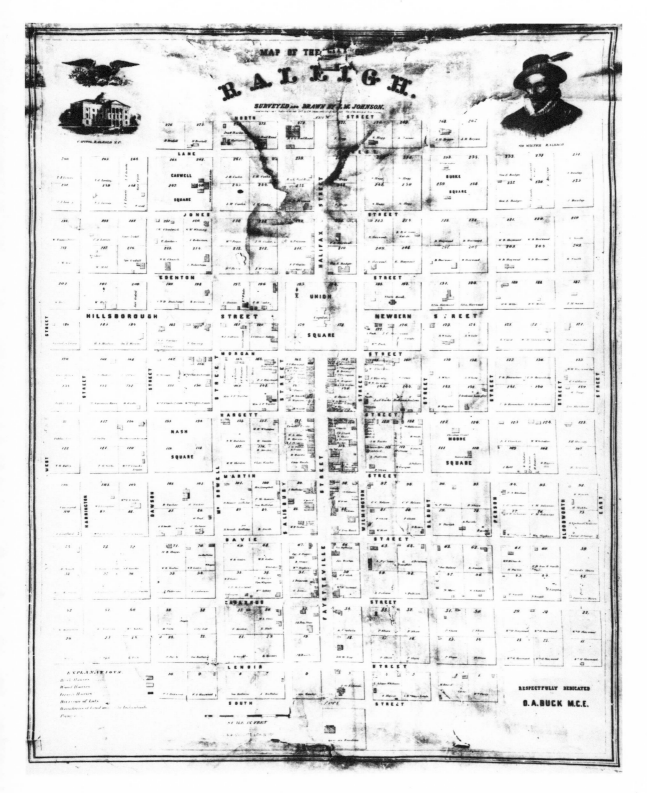

Map of the city of Raleigh, surveyed and drawn in 1847. Courtesy North Carolina Department of Archives and History.

Elmwood, shown here as it appeared about 1870, was built in Raleigh on land purchased from John Haywood, state treasurer and father of Fabius J. Haywood, Sr. From *Raleigh: A Pictorial History*. Courtesy North Carolina Department of Archives and History.

Dunbar Plantation, located in Edgecombe County, was the ancestral home of the Haywood family. From *Sketch of the Haywood Family in North Carolina*. Courtesy Duke University Library.

. . . stables, barns, a carriage house, and slave quarters. A flower garden, vegetable gardens, and fruit trees were planted for household and family use. Beyond the flower garden there was a family cemetery. With its own private ballroom and in close proximity to the State House, Haywood Hall virtually bustled with activity. The scene of social and political gatherings, the slaves were kept busy caring for the house and its master and mistress, grooming the horses, keeping the carriage in good repair, milking the cow, tending the gardens, and preparing the "sumptuous breakfasts."

A description of Dr. Fabius Haywood's home has also been preserved in Elizabeth Culbertson Waugh's *North Carolina's Capital, Raleigh*. The third story of the home, built from bricks made by the slaves on the site, was set aside for spinning by the slave women. Here silk was made from cultivated silkworms. According to Anna Cooper, her mother's entire life was spent in Raleigh until she moved to Washington, D.C., in her declining years. Therefore, it is quite possible that as a young slave woman Hannah Stanley Haywood was employed as a domestic servant in the Raleigh home of her master. According to the 1860 Slave Schedules of Raleigh, North Carolina, none of the slaves of Dr. Fabius J. Haywood, Sr., had been granted manumissions, and it is possible that as the needs for their services diminished within the master's household, the slaves were hired out to work in the city. For at the time of Anna's birth, Hannah Stanley Haywood was employed as a nurse for Charles M. Busbee (later a Raleigh attorney), and the infant girl was named for his mother, Annie Busbee.

While the smaller farmers and planters might only have had one or two slaves, who worked alongside the family in the cultivation of marketable commodities and food for the family table, larger planters, like the Haywoods, maintained a larger retinue of servants. This was true both in the urban setting and on the outlying plantations. And while the market for slaves had greatly diminished by 1860, according to the Slave Schedule for Raleigh in that year, thirteen members of the Haywood family held a total of 271 slaves. These resided within the city limits, and fourteen who were owned by Dr. Haywood were reported to be in the employ of G. H. Davis. Most of these slaves were owned by R. H. Haywood, who provided six dwelling places for forty-six slaves, twenty-nine males

Haywood Hall—built in Raleigh by John Haywood, state treasurer. Drawing by Edwin Hodgins from *Raleigh: A Pictorial History*. Courtesy North Carolina Department of Archives and History.

The home of Dr. Fabius Haywood, built by slaves in 1812. From *North Carolina's Capital, Raleigh*.

The will of Elizabeth E. A. Haywood, dated "the 12th day of July A.D. 1832." Special instructions provided that a slave called "House Jacob" be sold to a family member or to his former owner, should this become necessary to pay debts. Courtesy North Carolina Department of Archives and History.

and nineteen females. R. B. Haywood had thirty-one slaves, sixteen males and fifteen females, who ranged in age from four months to seventy-eight years. They were housed in four dwellings.

Earlier, mention was made of the development of viable alternatives to offset the difficulties inherent in the establishment of productive plantations in North Carolina. Thus it was that by the 1830s, Fabius J. Haywood, Sr., had extended his interest in slaves and the development of plantations into the states of Tennessee and Alabama. This extention was achieved through inheritance and purchase, and he was joined in this venture by other family members. Fabius's assumption of the role of head of the Haywood family was implied in the terms of his mother's will. Left the family homestead, a two-acre lot purchased by his father in the

1790s, Dr. Haywood also gained the controlling interest in the following named slaves: "Davy and Lewis . . . Mary (called Mary Jincy or Gincey), Mary (called Mary Dick), Hannah, Zilpha Anna, William, Kizzy, Frederick, Henry and John." If the Hannah cited here (surnames were not included in the document) was later to become the mother of Rufus, Andrew, and Annie, she was born in 1819 and would have been a young woman in her mid-to-late teens at the time that Fabius Haywood received his inheritance. With his brothers, George Washington and John Steele Haywood, a cousin, Alfred Williams, and other business acquaintances and residents of Raleigh, Fabius also entered into partnerships and established businesses.

Fabius Haywood amassed a sizable fortune through the inheritance of land and slaves, and with a fair amount of business acumen, he increased his wealth through the purchase of additional land and slaves; the lending of money; the holding of promissory notes; the assumption of debts of family members and others; and through his several other business ventures. One plantation combine was called the "Alabama Venture." Another business was the merchandising and pharmaceutical drug company of Williams & Haywood. Still another was the corporation of John R. Harrison and Fabius J. Haywood, Tanners of Leather. These enterprises helped to support one another. Through the merchandising business, supplies needed for the plantation were obtained at a cheaper rate. The tanning business provided harnesses for farm animals and shoes for the slaves. The slaves, in turn, produced commodities and foodstuffs for the marketplace.

In August 1834 Fabius Haywood benefited from the inheritance of his wife, Martha Whitaker Haywood, and her brother, Joseph A. Whitaker. Through the will of Thomas Banks of Smith County, Tennessee, they came into the possession of several slaves. Although Martha Haywood was the legatee, Fabius, as her husband and guardian, took control of them. According to the Deed of Transfer, "Fabius J. Haywood [would] have and hold as his property all the right [,] title and interest . . . in the following Negroes viz. Hardy, Swail, John, Antony, Rachel and child, Helen, Yellow Gilly, Barrell, Allen, Henry, Calvin, James, Lucinda, Riney, Betsy, Susan, Jinny and child, Polly, Charlotte and Jerry." The slaves remained in Tennessee, where they were re-employed under a leasing arrangement, and Fabius Haywood was compensated for their labor.

The interest of the Haywoods in slavery and the further expansion of plantations is apparent from a survey of the correspondence of family members. In 1833 Dennis O'Bryan of Warren County, North Carolina, was contacted about the possibility of renting or leasing one of his plantations on Swift Creek. In the spring of 1835, the Haywoods expressed interest in the potential influence of Texas on the cotton market, and the advantages to be gained there through emigration to this new region, "as soon as the land opened up." Thus, it is more than evident that those North Carolinians with the financial resources to do so developed alternatives that permitted their active participation in the slave economy of the South. As noted earlier, although it has been believed that the peculiar geography of the state lessened the interest of these planters in slavery, this seems not to have been the case. The belief has been expressed that the laws of North Carolina were less harsh, as regards slavery, and that the attitudes of the people there were more conciliatory. Yet the facts do not seem to support

A bill of sale for "a certain Negro woman named Patsy" to Fabius J. Haywood for $200, dated January 1, 1836. Courtesy North Carolina Department of Archives and History.

Mary Whitaker inherited slave Lear and her four children (ranging from infancy to six years of age) from her husband, Cyrus Whitaker. On May 12, 1852, she sold them to Fabius Haywood for $1,125. Courtesy North Carolina Department of Archives and History.

such a generalization. Before a correct assessment can be made of the involvement of North Carolinians with the development of slavery and a plantation economy, new studies must be undertaken, using the data and records that are available today. Only then can it be determined to what extent planters like the Haywoods exercised their options and held land and slaves outside of their state. It seems entirely unlikely that others did not also benefit from the arrangements that the Haywoods found to be so profitable.

Since Anna Cooper and her ancestors all seem to have originated from the immediate environs of Raleigh, she left no account of the lifestyles of the outlying plantations. It is fortunate, then, that a biographical account of Lunsford Lane, another Haywood slave, is extant. This narrative, *Lunsford*

Lunsford Lane. From *Lunsford Lane: Another Helper from North Carolina*. Courtesy Afro-American Collection of Charles Blockson.

Lane: Another Helper from North Carolina (1864), provides a description of plantation life in Raleigh's neighboring counties. Admittedly, Lane lived at an earlier time; his reminiscences are of the first forty years of the nineteenth century. Yet I believe that his observations are germane.

Lunsford Lane and his parents, Edward and Clarissa Lane, were purchased at auction from the estate of Joel Lane, upon whose land the city of Raleigh was built. Following the death of their master, the family was purchased by John Haywood, who for more than forty years was the state treasurer. The Lanes served John Haywood as household servants, and following his death they were willed to Sherwood Haywood. As a young slave, Lunsford often accompanied his father, who also served as a coachman, when he and the driver, Sam, carried their master on inspection trips of his outlying plantations. One was as near as three miles from the Raleigh city limits. Another, the most feared plantation, was seventy-five miles and a day's drive away. Lunsford was also assigned to help in the kitchen, where he overheard conversations among

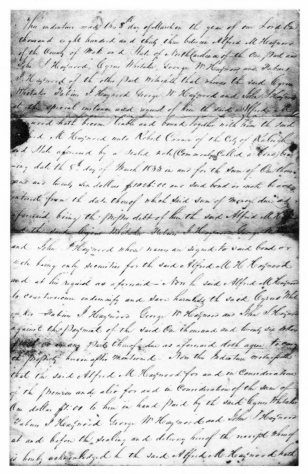

An 1833 indenture between Fabius J. Haywood, Sr., and other Haywood family members for a loan of $1,026. Property, including slaves, was used for collateral. Courtesy North Carolina Department of Archives and History.

the servants of the several Haywood households. Citing the importance of this, Lane observed that "the two senses of seeing and hearing in the slave are made doubly acute by the very prohibition of knowledge." Thus his account contains impressions gained from the sights and events that he himself witnessed, as well as those acquired from talk among the household slaves and the kitchen help.

Sherwood Haywood had three plantations that were populated with about two hundred and fifty slaves. All were within a day's ride of his Raleigh estate; the largest, with one hundred and fifty slaves, being near Tarboro, in Edgecombe County. Each spring the master made a three-day inspection tour of his plantations. At such times Lunsford saw the slaves engaged in raising cotton, corn, and hogs. The master inspected the books, and was advised of matters concerning infractions of slaves and the discipline meted out, and the condition of the land and the crops. At harvest time another tour was made. Then was the time to arrange for shipment of the crops, some of which were sent to Washington, D.C., in flatboats. Upon arrival, the crops were transferred to larger vessels and shipped on to New York. Corn stalks left standing became feed for the swine that were turned out to the fields for fattening. After hog-killing time, the bacon was stored in the plantation smokehouse for curing, and for distribution throughout the year. With the coming of the next spring the slaves fished in the Tar River for herring and shad, both plentiful in season and sold to the local fisheries.

Sherwood Haywood employed overseers, bound by contracts, who were directly responsible for the productivity of the land and the slaves. Plantations, after all, were businesses, and projections were made concerning the amount of crops the land could yield and the amount of labor the slaves could produce. To meet these quotas, overseers controlled and regulated the slaves. Infractions resulted in whippings, and runaways were retrieved by trained dogs. Overseers who were either too zealous or too lenient were dismissed. In Lunsford Lane's judgment:

> The wretched condition of the slaves on [Sherwood Haywood's] plantation was owing, in a great measure to [the] master's residence in Raleigh, and his inability, from other engagements, to supervise matters personally. Their improvidence led to much sickness and to frequent deaths. The house servants of Mr. Hay-

Sherwood Haywood of Raleigh, the master of Lunsford Lane. Courtesy North Carolina Department of Archives and History.

wood dreaded nothing so much as the threat of being transferred to [the outlying] plantations.

It was equally as difficult for slaves in North Carolina to gain freedom through manumission as in other southern states. An owner who might wish to release a slave from bondage could only do so legally by producing evidence in court that the deserving slave had rendered the state meritorious service during the Revolutionary War. Although archaic, the law was still being enforced at the time of Anna Cooper's birth. Such a law guaranteed that few black slaves would achieve manumission through the court system, and it increased the number of runaways and fugitive slaves who sought asylum outside of the state. Still, some masters "winked" at the law, and were guilty of aiding and abetting their slaves in their efforts to gain freedom. And, according to Lunsford Lane, the spread of Methodism and the work of the Quakers helped to soften the attitude of some slavemasters, and had a favorable effect on their moral fiber.

Lunsford Lane petitioned the North Carolina Assembly for permission to remain in the state as a free man while working to purchase his family. From *Lunsford Lane: Another Helper from North Carolina*. Courtesy Afro-American Collection of Charles Blockson.

In the nearly two years after Anna Cooper's birth, among the 271 slaves owned by members of the Haywood family, only one was manumitted, in 1860. In the absence of records to the contrary, and since she, her mother, and brothers first appear in the census of 1870, it can be assumed that Anna and her family were freed by the Emancipation Proclamation, on January 1, 1863. Lunsford Lane, on the other hand, had obtained his freedom through self-purchase as early as 1829. Following the death of his master, and with no written agreement to substantiate his claim, Lunsford paid the last fifty dollars to his mistress, Eleanor Hawkins Haywood. Describing her as "a woman of churlish temperament and an avaricious spirit," Lane notes that it was only through the intercession of Haywood's daughters, who prevailed upon their mother to honor his master's verbal agreement, that he succeeded in becoming free.

In spite of laws to the contrary, Lane remained and lived in the city of Raleigh as a free man. While this violation did not go unnoticed, for a period of time the law was not enforced. And later, when it was, some of the townspeople, including members of the Haywood family, petitioned the General Assembly to pass a resolution permitting Lane to live and work in Raleigh as a free man, unmolested, until he could earn the purchase price of his family.

It was several years before Lane was able to

achieve his goal. Martha Lane had been sold to Benjamin B. Smith, "a merchant, and a member and class-leader in the Methodist Church," the year following her marriage to Lunsford, in May 1828. During the intervening years, while Lunsford Lane worked and saved to secure his family's freedom, he was afraid that they would be sold away from him. His family was finally released from slavery in 1842, after he paid his wife's master the last installment due on seven promissory notes that totaled $3,500. At the same time, with the promise that he would send her $200 when he could, Lane obtained the release of his mother from Eleanor Haywood. Unable to obtain freedom papers in their native state, the family of Lunsford Lane left Raleigh on April 16, 1842. They traveled to New York, where their freedom was recorded; then settled in Massachusetts. Their final move was to Oberlin, Ohio, where they relocated among the abolitionists.

Around the time of Anna Cooper's birth, many changes were taking place in the city of Raleigh and, indeed, throughout the nation. The question of slavery was very much alive. The now famous Lincoln-Douglas debates, which concerned the extension of slavery into the free territory of America, were held in 1858, the probable year of Anna's birth. The early months of 1861 witnessed the inauguration of Abraham Lincoln as President and the formation of the Confederate States of America in Montgomery, Alabama. With the attack on Fort Sumpter, on April 12, 1861, the Civil War began. On May 20, 1861, North Carolina became the next to the last state to secede from the Union. While many North Carolinians voted for secession with some feeling of ambivalence, the sentiments of the majority prevailed.

Anna Cooper's reminiscences of the Civil War period were found on a single sheet among her papers, and are perhaps her very earliest memories. Written in her later years, when the mind tends to recall the events of the past with great clarity, she remembered that

During the Civil War, [I] served many an

In 1839 the Wake County Court charged Lunsford Lane "for going at large as [a] free[man] and hiring [his] own time." From *Minutes for Wake County Court of Pleas and Quarter Session*, 1837–1842. Courtesy North Carolina Department of Archives and History.

State
vs
Lunsford Some &
Isaac Hunter

The Defendants slaves of Benjamin B. Smith being presented by the Grand Jury at the last Term of this Court for going at large as freemen and hiring their own time. It is Ordered by the Court that a Writ issue to the Sheriff of this County to take the said Negroes into his Custody and them safely secure so that he have them before the next court.

Edmund Barker &c
vs
Thomas Kirks

Alfred Fordd security for the appearance of the Defendant brings into court the body of the said Thomas Kirks and surrenders him in discharge of himself — On Motion the said Thomas Kirks is proved into custody &c.

Upon Motion Seven Justices being present it is Ordered that Augustin Horton be permitted to have licence to peddle in this County for twelve Months it being satisfactorily shown to the Court that the said Augustin Horton is a man of good Moral Character &c.

Upon the recommendation of the Board of Commissioners of the City of Raleigh, it is Ordered that Messrs Freeman & Stith be appointed Auctioneers for the County of Wake, who thereupon enter into Bonds in the sum of Two Thousand Dollars, with Haywood Little &c as their Securities and are then qualified according to law.

A paper writing purporting to be the Last Will and Testament of Willie Robertson is produced in Open Court and offered for probate and the execution thereof is duly proved by the oath of Jacob Hunter a subscribing Witness thereto. and the said Will is Ordered to be recorded, John Ligon the Executor therein named comes into court and is qualified as such according to law.

State
vs
John Williams

Bastardy
In this case it is Ordered and adjudged by the Court that the Defendant John Williams is the Father of an illegitimate Child begotten on the body of Mariah Clements single woman, it is further Ordered that the said Defendant enter into bond with security for the support of said child; that he pay ten dollars for lying in fee and ten dollars a year for five years to the said Mariah Clements; and thereupon said Defendant enters into bond in the sum of two hundred Dollars with David T. Mayton Willie P Williams and Stephen Williams as his securities,

State
vs
Stance Lassiter

Bastardy
In this case it is Ordered and adjudged by the Court that the Defendant Stance Lassiter is the Father of an illegitimate Child begotten on the body of Polly Poole single woman, it is further Ordered that the said Defendant enter into bond with security for the support of said Child; that

Dr. E. Burke Haywood, a surgeon in the Confederate Army, was in charge of Pettigrew Hospital. From *Sketch of the Haywood Family in North Carolina.* Courtesy Duke University Library.

Confederate General Joseph E. Johnston (1807–1891), fourth-ranking officer in the Confederate Army, surrendered to General Sherman in North Carolina on April 26, 1865. From *North Carolina as a Civil War Battleground.*

Union General William Tecumseh Sherman (1820–1891). After his famous march through Georgia, Sherman turned his attention to North Carolina. From *North Carolina as a Civil War Battleground.*

anxious slave's superstition to wake up the baby & ask directly "Which side is goin' to win de war? Will de Yankees beat de Rebs & will Linkum free de Niggers."

Continuing, Anna Cooper provided a footnote to this recollection:

I want to say that while it may be true in infancy we are nearer Heaven, if I had any vision or second sight in those days that made my answers significant to the troubled souls that hung breathlessly on my cryptic answers—such powers promptly took flight with the dawn of intelligent consciousness.

The treacherous coastal waters and the peculiar geographical features of North Carolina no more prevented the Union soldiers from carrying the war into that region than had the unfavorable topography deterred the spread of slavery. Much of the eastern portion of the state was captured during the early campaigns of the war. Yet the port at Wilmington, near the mouth of the Cape Fear River, remained open to Confederate supply ships until

An artist's sketch of "negotiations between Generals
W. T. Sherman and Joseph E. Johnston, April 18,
1865, at the Bennett House near the present city of
Durham." Drawing from Frank Leslie's *The American
Soldier in the Civil War*, published in *North Carolina as
a Civil War Battleground*.

January 1865. More than ten battles took place in
North Carolina, the bloodiest occurring at Ben-
tonville (in the southern portion of Johnston
County, and in the Coastal Plain region), in March
1865. On April 26, the 125,000-strong Army of
North Carolina, under the command of General
Joseph E. Johnston, surrendered to Union General
William T. Sherman near Durham.

This, then, is the environment into which Anna
Cooper was born, and in which she spent the first
two decades of her life.

II.

The St. Augustine, Oberlin, and Wilberforce Years

When hardly more than kindergarten age it was my good fortune to be selected for a scholarship by Dr. J. Brinton Smith, founder of St. Augustine's Normal School at Raleigh, N.C. . . . in the nucleus he was planning to train as teachers for the Colored people of the South. That school was my world during the formative period, the most critical in any girl's life. Its nurture & admonition gave . . . shelter and protection. "My lines have fallen in pleasant places & I have a goodly heritage."

ANNA J. COOPER, n.d.

Anna Cooper—from the Oberlin College 1884 class album. Courtesy Oberlin College Archives.

BY 1865 SOUTHERN BLACKS HAD BEGUN TO organize around political and economic issues. In May of that year, the free blacks of North Carolina widely publicized and circulated a petition to President Andrew Johnson. Their appeal concerned the issue of suffrage, and reasoned that men who had loyally "carried the Republic's musket in time of war [should be] permitted in the days of Peace . . . to carry its ballots." The petition reminded the President, himself a native of North Carolina, that free blacks in North Carolina had enjoyed and exercised the right of franchise until the State Constitutional Convention of 1835.

Annie Haywood would have been about seven years of age then. A bright and precocious child, she must have sensed and observed the changes that were beginning to take place in her native state and capital city, although she might not have fully comprehended them. Raleigh was alive with activity, and there was much talk of establishing a popular government.

North Carolina was now a state in transition, and the question of equal suffrage—to be achieved by an amendment to the Constitution—was to be decided by a constitutional convention called by the state legislature. With 50,007 votes for and 19,397 votes against, the balance of power had begun to shift away from the west and to the east. The small farmers of the state's Atlantic coastal plains were gaining political control from the landed aristocracy, and with the farmer's newly won powers, the Democratic Party emerged. The results of the balloting, however, did not restore voting rights to

Anna Cooper's account of her entry into St. Augustine's Normal School. Courtesy Moorland-Spingarn Research Center, Howard University.

writing and reading of the Bible. Annie, however, was in school and at her very young age was teaching others to read. It is possible that one of the circulars found its way into the Haywood home and there was given proper notice, since all but Jane, Hannah's daughter-in-law, had had the benefit of at least the rudiments of education.

Chaired by the Reverend James W. Hood of New Bern, the delegates to the convention were counseled to be assertive in future relationships with their government and in all matters pertaining to their "full manhood and citizenship rights." Hood acknowledged that they had demonstrated faith and patience, and had acted with moderation—yet the Constitution of the United States guaranteed them

the right to give evidence in the courts . . . the right to be represented in the jury box. . . . [and] the right to put votes in the ballot box.

The 1870 census for Raleigh, Wake County, North Carolina, included Annie Haywood (age twelve), her mother, Hannah, and brother Andrew, with his wife, Jane. Courtesy North Carolina Department of Archives and History.

North Carolina's free black population. More than any other group of people in the state, the white population farthest down the economic ladder resented the progress of free blacks.

Beginning on September 29, 1865, a "Convention of the Colored Citizens of North Carolina" was held in Raleigh. Perhaps it was coincidental that the State Constitutional Convention was also convening in that city at the same time. Still, preparations were made to accommodate the 500 black delegates who would assemble there. This activity must have created some attention, even among the young, for hundreds of circulars were being distributed throughout Wake County, calling attention to, and urging attendance at, a local mass meeting and rally that would precede the convention. The census for 1870, the first in which former slaves were counted as citizens of the United States, cited Hannah Haywood and her son, Andrew, as literate. However, by Annie's own testimony, we know that her mother's abilities were limited to a minimum of

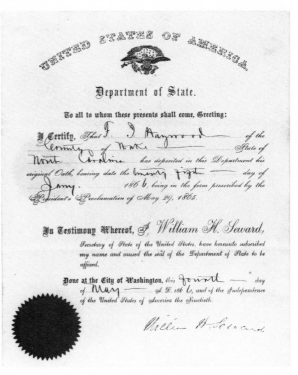

Only months after North Carolina's free blacks petitioned President Andrew Johnson, in an effort to obtain suffrage, Fabius Haywood received "Executive clemency" and "a full pardon and amnesty." Courtesy North Carolina Department of Archives and History.

Continuing, the Reverend Mr. Hood proclaimed:

These rights we want, these rights we contend for, and these rights, under God, we must ultimately have.

No longer supplicant slaves in the house of bondage, blacks in North Carolina—as elsewhere—turned to the schoolhouse to remove the vestiges of slavery. They believed that once black people were armed with the benefits of education, full citizenship and manhood rights would be forthcoming. It was this climate of self-assertion, with an awareness of full citizenship rights, that nurtured Annie Haywood in her formative years. And, with the advent of the Normal School for the State of North Carolina, designed for the education of teachers for the freedmen, Annie Haywood formally entered the doors of educational opportunity in the year 1868.

When, in 1867, the Executive Committee of the

As provided by the presidential proclamation of May 29, 1865, Fabius Haywood reaffirmed his allegiance to the Union in May 1866. Courtesy North Carolina Department of Archives and History.

A view of the campus of St. Augustine's Normal School. Courtesy North Carolina Department of Archives and History.

Board of Missions of the Episcopal Church had announced its intention to establish the St. Augustine's Normal School and Collegiate Institute, Dr. J. Brinton Smith, a committee member, resigned from the commission and accepted the principalship of the new school. The prospectus for St. Augustine's was published in the *Tri-Weekly Standard* on January 11, 1868. It read:

> The Normal School for the State of North Carolina designed for the Education of Teachers for the Freedmen will be opened in the Howard School House, on the Fair Grounds on Monday next, January 13th, at 9 o'clock A.M. Pupils admitted any time on satisfactory examination. Persons at a distance wishing either to become pupils in this school, or to obtain more particular information concerning it, will address the undersigned.
>
> J. BRINTON SMITH, Principal

Annie Haywood was about nine and a half years of age when St. Augustine's opened (some accounts say eight years), and was among the first group of pupils enrolled by Dr. Smith. In her essay "The Higher Education of Women" (published in *A Voice from the South: By a Black Woman of the South*, 1892), a mature Annie Cooper recalled those early days:

> When a child I was put into a school near home that professed to be a normal and col-

legiate, i.e. to prepare teachers for colored youth, furnish candidates for the ministry, and offer collegiate training for those who should be ready for it. Well . . . after a while I had a good deal of time on my hands. I had devoured what was put before me, and . . . was looking for more. I constantly felt (as I suppose many an ambitious girl has felt) a thumping from within unanswered by any beckoning from without. . . . A boy, however meager his equipment and shallow his pretensions, had only to declare a floating intention to study theology and he could get all the support, encouragement and stimulus he needed. . . . A self-supporting girl had to struggle on by teaching in the summer and working after school hours to keep up with her board and bills, and actually fight her way against positive discouragements to the higher education. . . . And when at last [in 1881], that same girl announced her desire and intention to go to college it was received with about the same incredulity and dismay as if a brass button of one of those candidate's coats had propounded a new method of squaring the circle or trisecting the arc.

As a "scholarship" pupil, Annie Haywood received an annual stipend of $100 for board and tuition. Some writers have used the term "teacher" in describing her duties at the school while still a young girl. Annie, however, was a "coach," or tutor, who assisted other students. For while the first students who entered St. Augustine's were admitted on "satisfactory examination," the academic prerequisites are not known, and it is unclear at what level of preparedness the school began its classes. It has been speculated, however, that Annie might have had the benefit of some schooling before she entered St. Augustine's. The Episcopal Church had operated a sabbath and parochial school, and Annie, no doubt, received encouragement and support from her mother. Many years later, in 1930, in response to a questionnaire sent to "Negro College Graduates" by Dr. Charles S. Johnson of Fisk University, Anna Cooper wrote: "My mother's self-sacrificing toil to give me advantages she had never enjoyed is worthy [of] the highest praise & undying gratitude." Yet we know from her own testimony that her mother would not have been able to satisfactorily instruct her young daughter, who had an insatiable appetite for learning. The other members of the household—her brother Andrew and his wife, Jane—were unable to help her. Andrew was only able to read a little, and, as shown on his 1867 marriage application, when he made "His Mark,"

he was unable to write. Jane could neither read nor write.

The Howard Schoolhouse, where St. Augustine's first classes were held, had served as an army barracks known as Camp Russell during the Civil War, and then was used as the Confederate Soldier's Home. On the first day, four pupils were enrolled in the school, which was located nearly one mile from the home of the Reverend Mr. Smith. The building, which was in a field with one or two barrackslike structures, was not visible from the street, and was unfinished inside, with no plaster to cover the walls to protect the young pupils from the elements. But according to Cecil D. Haliburton, who in 1937 published *A History of St. Augustine's College: 1867-1937*, the room was furnished with comfortable chairs and desks, and maps and blackboards covered the walls. Also according to Hali-

An aerial view of St. Augustine's campus. Courtesy North Carolina Department of Archives and History.

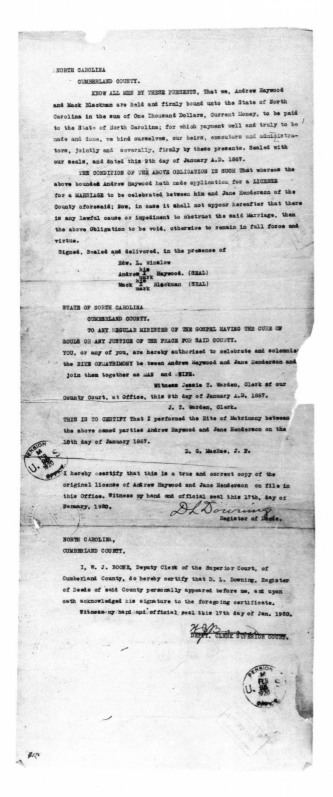

The marriage application and license issued in Cumberland County, North Carolina, on January 9, 1867, for Andrew Haywood and Jane Henderson (McCracken). Courtesy North Carolina Department of Archives and History.

burton, the trustees of the school wished to purchase a more suitable tract upon which a permanent school plant might be built. The selected land, with nearly 110 acres, had been owned by the Haywood family of Raleigh, and was known as Seven Springs. (Haliburton cites *Spirit of Missions*, May 1868, as the source of this information.) However, another source believes that the site of St. Augustine's was once a part of Willie (pronounced Wily) Jones's plantation, and that his remains today are in an unmarked grave on the grounds of the school. But even here the name Seven Springs persists. Contributions and gifts from the Freedmen's Bureau, and the estate of Charles Avery of Pittsburgh, made the purchase of the property and the erection of a two-story building possible. The bureau contributed $6,243; the gift from the Avery Fund was $25,000.

The original incorporators of St. Augustine's were Bishop Thomas Atkinson, the Reverend R. S. Mason, the Reverend Joseph B. Cheshire, the Reverend Albert Smedes, the Reverend E. M. Forbes, Gen. William R. Cox, Dr. Kemp P. Battle, Dr. A. J. DeRossett, Richard H. Smith, John Wilkes, and the Reverend J. Brinton Smith. Most were clerics of the Protestant Episcopal Church. The articles of incorporation were signed by the governor of North Carolina, Jonathan Worth, and dated July 19, 1867.

Annie Haywood remained at St. Augustine's for almost fourteen years, and during this time the school had two principals: the Reverend Jacob Brinton Smith (1867-1872) and the Reverend John E. C. Smedes.

The school opened amidst a climate of racial tension. The day after the opening, the Constitutional Convention (required under the Reconstruction Act) convened in Raleigh. At the same time, the Convention of the Colored Citizens of North Carolina was holding a mass meeting and rally, to urge self-assertion, and to petition the state government for full citizenship rights. Moderation and patience had not won for black North Carolinians the rewards hoped for. Now their convention leaders were planning new strategies and developing a petition of demands to achieve those long-awaited manhood rights.

The following year the report of H. C. Vogell, the Freedmen's Bureau superintendent of education in North Carolina, was included in the *Eighth Semi-*

General Oliver Otis Howard, commissioner of the Bureau of Refugees, Freedmen and Abandoned Lands. From *An Era in Progress and Promise, 1863–1910.*

Annual Report of Schools. Compiled by John W. Alvord, the bureau's general superintendent of schools, it was transmitted to General Oliver O. Howard. (Howard had been Abraham Lincoln's choice, and was President Andrew Johnson's appointee to the position of commissioner of the Freedmen's Bureau.) Vogell observed that "the progress of education among freedmen awakens the liveliest interest. . . . From servile degradation and debasing ignorance . . . awakened to a life of earnest and successful improvement." Yet in the report, so full of promise and optimism, Vogell also wrote:

Much disrespect has been exhibited toward teachers who have had the courage to face the

opposition to the education of these freedmen. . . . But though ignored for work's sake, and denied the civilities of life, they have faithfully pursued their labors. . . . As long as the work continues under the patronage of the [national] government there is hope. . . . If this ceases while public affairs are in the present condition, the cause will languish. It will not be safe to trust these schools to local patronage while the general sentiment of the whites is against them.

While many argued the wisdom of states and local governments paying to educate "other people's children," and looked upon the Freedmen's Bureau as a charity agency, the record of its work among blacks and some whites in the field of education was creditable. For in the District of Columbia and the five military districts of the South, it is clear that public educational systems would have been even slower in developing schools for blacks, had the bureau not taken certain initiatives and provided assistance. Still, recognition must be given to the freedmen themselves for the substantial efforts they made to gain education for themselves and their children. In North Carolina alone, there were thirty-eight schools supported entirely by freedmen. (This does not mean schoolhouses; most often more than one school met in a facility.) There were 240 schools supported in part through tuitions paid by black parents. Also, black benevolent societies raised money for teachers' salaries and books. (Vogell complained about the bureau's lack of authority to furnish books, and cited instances of ten to twelve children sharing one book and passing it around the room when called on to read.) These societies owned 111 school buildings across the state, and collectively, in the first six months of 1869, they paid a total of $4,509.78 in school tuitions. On the other hand, the bureau, which owned 157 buildings in the state, supported the salaries of nine teachers brought from outside of the state. During the same six-month period it spent $8,508.40. Thus, the schools were supported through shared resources and with blacks bearing nearly one-third of the expense; the state contributed nothing from its coffers. The number of children who benefited was 6,069, and of this number 57 were white. However, the full impact of the work of the bureau and its army of workers cannot be fully told by these statistics alone. This was only

Andrew J. Haywood (1848–1918), brother of Anna Cooper. A slave of Dr. Fabius J. Haywood, Sr., he later served in the Spanish-American War. Courtesy Mrs. Regia Bronson and Miss Regina Smith.

the beginning, and its spreading influence would later become a catalyst for new fields of endeavor.

The Eighth Semi-Annual Report sounded a note of optimism and expressed the bureau's belief that once the value of its work among the freedmen had been correctly assessed, "it must silence the most skeptical and arouse the most lukewarm" to work on behalf of the "education and elevation" of the black population. Too, it was noted that in North Carolina there had never existed "a greater field or opportunity for Christian philanthropy and benevolence than [was then] offered among the freedmen," for there were still problems to be solved. There were children in rural and remote areas who had not been reached. In addition, there were children whose education was being interrupted. Through no fault of their own, many had to return to their homes to help with the spring planting. Again, when it was time to harvest the crops additional time was lost, and the school year often began late. Thus the development of the educational system was closely tied to the economic system of the state.

Then there was the size of the state, the condition of the roads, and the available modes of transportation which made it difficult for the bureau's superintendent to meet the needs and demands of all who wished to have a school for their children. It was not at all uncommon for pupils and some teachers to walk five miles to reach the nearest school. Others traveled by water in flat-bottom boats. Then there were the large families with few or no resources. These had to make the painfully difficult decision as to which of their children could be spared to go to school—if in fact any would be able to go at all. Unfortunately, but inevitably, some did have to stay behind and contribute to the struggle for survival, for their labor was needed to help the family eke out a day-to-day existence. Fortunately, however, this was not the situation in Annie Haywood's family.

By the end of the Civil War, Hannah Haywood's children were twenty-nine, seventeen, and seven years of age. (These are approximate ages, based on the use of census records, death certificates, and Anna Cooper's recollections.) The sons, Rufus and Andrew, were already working in the city. In 1867 Andrew Haywood had married Jane Henderson (also known as Jane McCraken), of Cumberland County, North Carolina. Presumably his brother Rufus had married while still a slave. The brothers were musicians, but each earned his living in the trades, Andrew as a bricklayer and Rufus as a carpenter. The 1880 census for the Southwest Division of Raleigh reported Rufus Haywood residing in that city, with his wife, Nancy, and their children, Maggie, Mary, Love (or Lovie), Rufus, George, and John. Annie, then, was the only school-age child at home with her mother when the opportunity to acquire an education presented itself. She knew that her mother and brothers had been denied the opportunity that was now hers, and from the beginning was determined to succeed.

A letter published in the July 1873 issue of *Spirit of Missions* acknowledged the receipt of scholarship funds, as well as money for teachers' salaries, that had been sent by the Freedmen's Bureau to St. Augustine's. Annie Haywood, Jane Thomas, and John W. Perry were among the students who received financial assistance. The two young women, who remained friends throughout their lives, became in 1873 the first female students regularly employed as teachers at St. Augustine's College. By

Rufus Haywood (1836?–1892), another brother of Anna Cooper. Born a slave, he became a musician, the leader of "Stanley's Band." Courtesy Mrs. Regia Bronson and Miss Regina Smith.

that date, the school had received more than $30,000 from the Freedmen's Bureau. Nineteen other schools also benefited from the work and contributions of the bureau; Oberlin College, which received $5,000, was among them. Later, General Howard was brought before the Congressional Committee on Education and Labor to answer charges, brought by the Honorable Fernando Wood, that alleged misappropriation of certain bureau funds. The twelfth and thirteenth points of the charges are of particular interest and relate specifically to St. Augustine's College.

In the bill of particulars, Howard was charged with "caus[ing] or knowingly allow[ing] lands in this city [Washington, D.C.], owned by an officer of the bureau, to be transferred to a freedmen's school in North Carolina, the officer taking the money appropriated for that school and the school [taking] land in this city; thus perpetrating a fraud both upon the government and the freedmen." The school in question was St. Augustine's College, and the transaction involved a purse of two hundred

The 1880 census for Raleigh included Rufus Haywood and his family, and Hannah Haywood, his mother, who then lived with him. Courtesy North Carolina Department of Archives and History.

pounds sterling (about $1,000 in United States currency) that friends in England wished to be used to establish homestead sites for the freedmen. The gift was sent through J. M. McKim, secretary of the Freedmen's Union Commission. The alternative plan was to invest the money in "some agricultural operation connected with them." But Howard encountered difficulty in obtaining land in Washington for resale to freedmen. He deferred taking any action on the homesteading plan until first consulting with the benevolent group in England. Then it was decided to invest the initial gift in land that could be immediately sold to freedmen for homesteading lots under a deferred (installment) payment plan. As the freedmen began to make repayments, this money would then be placed in a special account, reinvested in more land, and the interest earned would be allocated for the school fund. Although this plan was called a "fraud" and a "scheme," Howard believed that he could thereby offer two opportunities where only one had existed before.

When the owner refused to sell land near the Navy Yard for a homesteading community for freedmen, another site had to be located. With the assistance of a select committee headed by Senator S. C. Pomeroy of Kansas, Howard successfully negotiated the purchase of the Barry's Farm tract in Anacostia, D.C. (then in Washington County and outside the city limits of the nation's capital). The 375-acre tract was bought for $52,000. In the interim, the principal of St. Augustine's College, the Reverend J. Brinton Smith, agreed to invest the money his institution was to receive from the bureau's educational fund, and purchased five acres in the Southeast section of Washington City at five cents a square foot. Land prices in the District of Columbia had spiraled at such a rapid rate that two years later, when offered $13,000 for his parcel, Smith refused to sell. Later, a land speculator testified that the five-acre tract was worth as much as $35,000, which explains Smith's refusal. When the land was finally sold for eighteen cents a square foot, the school realized a profit on its investment.

In 1869 the settlers on the Barry's Farm tract were faced with an especially hard winter, and, rather than offer alms, Howard hired the men to clear the land owned by St. Augustine's College. This raised a charge of fraud and collusion. When the investigating committee asked about an expen-

Anna Julia Cooper. Identified by Anna Cooper as a photograph of herself, it might have been taken about the time of her marriage in 1877. Courtesy Moorland-Spingarn Research Center, Howard University.

diture of $32,000, Howard gave the following explanation:

> There should be work done in grading that piece of ground belonging to the school at Raleigh, and instead of giving money to these people to feed them during the season of want they should be given work and paid wages. . . . From early in March until September, 1869, they worked on the ground. . . . Some $30,000 out of $32,000 in all had been paid for the labor of these colored men, and horses, and carts, the difference being all that he [the contractor] received . . . which was only a fair and reasonable remuneration.

Neither General Howard nor others associated with the homesteading project believed that they had betrayed the public trust, nor did the majority of the members of the Congressional investigating committee.

Annie Haywood Cooper completed the prescribed course of study at St. Augustine's Normal and Collegiate Institute in 1877. There were no graduations in her day, nor were diplomas awarded. But Annie had set her goals, and soon she would leave St. Augustine's and Raleigh with memories of her student days—and her marriage.

In the brief glimpse that Anna Cooper has left of her life at St. Augustine's, one cannot help but detect a note of sarcasm and feel her ire at the preferred treatment the institution accorded its theology students. In 1873, when the new principal, the Reverend Dr. Smedes, made changes in the school's curriculum and organized the first Greek class "for the candidates for the ministry," Anna lashed out at sexism and lost no time in registering a complaint. She was then permitted to enter the class. But when first advised that only theology students would be enrolled, Anna's retort to the principal had been that "the only mission opening before a girl in his school was to marry one of those candidates." Little did she realize that one day she would do just that, for at that time George A. C. Cooper enrolled in the school, and in 1874 began to teach the Greek class begun by Dr. Smedes.

That Smedes relaxed the rules and permitted Annie's enrollment in the class proved indeed fateful, for a close friendship developed between the young woman and her teacher. At the close of the school year, on June 21, 1877, Annie Julia Haywood and George A. C. Cooper were married. The simple ceremony was performed at a regular chapel exercise at St. Augustine's.

George and Annie Cooper continued their studies while each taught at St. Augustine's. Giving thought to what each would do in the future, they planned their life together, and the marriage gave strength to both husband and wife. Annie's commitment was to teaching, preferably in the South. George Cooper had been a tailor in his native Nassau in the British West Indies. Now at the age of thirty, his life was dedicated to the ministry as he prepared to become an Episcopal priest. Ordained a deacon the year prior to his marriage, Cooper was now nearer to achieving his goal. The second black to be ordained in the Episcopal Church in the state of North Carolina, Cooper assisted Dr. Smedes in the chapel exercises held twice daily at the school. He also assisted at the services held at St. Augustine's Church in the city of Raleigh. In July 1879 George A. C. Cooper was admitted into priests' orders in the Protestant Episcopal Church.

While there is no written account of this period

The application and certificate of marriage issued to George A. C. Cooper and Annie J. Haywood in June 1877. Courtesy Wake County Register of Deeds.

St. Augustine's Church, where Annie Haywood married George Cooper in 1877, and where the Reverend Mr. Cooper assisted Dr. John E. C. Smedes, rector. From *Raleigh: A Pictorial History.*

St. Simon of Cyrene by Frank J. Dillon, the window presented to St. Augustine's by Anna Cooper in memory of her husband. Courtesy St. Augustine's College.

serving his parish." George Cooper was buried in the "Colored Section" of the City Cemetery, in Raleigh. The inscription on the headstone reads: "His life was gentle and the elements so mixed in him that nature might stand up and say to the world, This was a man." In 1931, to commemorate the devotion of the Reverend George Cooper to his work, Anna presented a memorial stained glass window to their alma mater. The subject of this work by J. Frank Dillon is St. Simon of Cyrene, the black man who helped Christ carry His cross to Mt. Calvary.

Now a young woman of twenty-one, Anna Cooper again threw herself into her studies and began to think about the possibility of gaining higher education. Without the encouragement of Dr. Smedes, she began to write letters to Oberlin College in Ohio. In the fall of 1881 Anna Julia Cooper left St. Augustine's College and Raleigh to begin the "Second Step" that would determine her future.

Ohio, the first state formed out of the Northwest Territory region, was called the "Gateway State" because of the thousands of blacks who had traveled there via the network of underground railroad routes. Bounded then on the south by the slave states of Virginia and Kentucky, Ohio was bounded on the north by the Great Lakes—where many fugitive slaves "crossed over" into Canada to begin new lives. The village of Oberlin, in the northeastern part of Ohio, is not far from Lake Erie. In this rather remote area, which attracted freethinkers and abolitionists, a town and a college grew. The history of their development presents a comingling of facts, often making it difficult to distinguish one from the other, for Oberlin village and Oberlin College influenced each other's development.

Anna Cooper arrived at Oberlin College in the fall of 1881, and by that time, through its graduates, the school had earned an enviable reputation for the quality of its work. Its involvement in controversial issues, as well as some townspeople and students who had been with John Brown at Harper's Ferry, added a certain luster to the name of Oberlin. It was to this environment, alive with stimulus that fostered personal and intellectual growth, that Anna Cooper went to continue preparation for her career as a teacher.

In her essay, "The Higher Education of Women"

of Anna Cooper's life, no doubt it was full of expectation, as the marriage partners prepared for the future. Both were intelligent, energetic, and dedicated to service to their race in their professions. Those who knew him said he was "a man of great energy and enthusiasm, unfailing good nature, patience, and self-control." He was probably just the kind of balance wheel that this very intense young woman needed in her life. But the shared plans for the future were not to be realized, for George Cooper died on September 27, 1879.

Anna Cooper attributed her husband's untimely death to "hard work and exposure suffered while

(cited earlier), Anna Cooper also wrote a retrospective and rather provocative assessment of American thought on the subject of education for women at the turn of the nineteenth century. She questioned the credibility of a literary work that had appeared in Paris at the beginning of that century. Entitled *Shall Women Learn the Alphabet?* this volume seriously questioned the wisdom of educating women, and proposed a law that, if enacted, would have prohibited teaching the alphabet to women (regardless of their race, creed, or station in life). Noted authorities were quoted to give credence to the thesis "that the woman who knows the alphabet has already lost part of her womanliness." Ridiculous, and of little consequence? Unfortunately not, for as Anna Cooper, who did not consider herself to be a feminist, wrote:

> In the year 1833, one solitary college in America decided to admit women within its sacred precincts, and organized what was

Tappan Square at Oberlin College as it appeared in the 1880s. The chapel, Tappan and Council Halls, and First Church were located there. Courtesy Oberlin College Archives.

called a "Ladies Course" as well as the regular B.A. or Gentlemen's Course. It was felt to be an experiment—a rather dangerous experiment—and was adopted with fear and trembling by the good fathers, who looked as if they had been caught secretly mixing explosive compounds and were guiltily expecting every moment to see the foundations under them shaken and rent and their fair superstructures shattered into fragments.

But the girls came, and there was no upheaval. They performed their tasks modestly and intelligently. Once in a while one or two were found choosing the gentlemen's course. Still no collapse; and the dear, careful, scrupulous, frightened old professors were just getting

31

John Mercer Langston, who defended Edmonia Lewis against witchcraft charges at Oberlin, is shown in an 1853 daguerreotype as he appeared when completing studies at the Oberlin College Seminary. Courtesy Oberlin College Archives.

their hearts out of their throats and preparing to draw one good free breath, when they found they would have to change the name of those courses; for there were as many ladies in the gentlemen's course as in the ladies', and a distinctively Ladies' Course, inferior in scope and aim to the regular classical course, did not and could not exist.

But by the time Anna Cooper entered Oberlin College, the fear and timidity spoken of in earlier times, and that had influenced matriculation policies, had diminished. For early in its history, in 1834, after a poll of its student body and faculty, Oberlin College had dealt with its policy concerning the admission of blacks. It was only after exposure to and contact with blacks as students, however, that some who had at first expressed an objection to their presence changed their attitudes. Yet the school did experience some racial incidents, as in the case of Edmonia Lewis, who became the foremost black woman sculptor of her time. She was

charged with practicing witchcraft and attempting to poison a white classmate.

The purpose of the Oberlin experience has perhaps been best expressed by Henry Churchill King, a president of the college, who wrote:

> Oberlin seeks the education of the entire man,—physical, intellectual, aesthetic, moral and religious. It seeks an education looking preeminently to the service of community and nation,—the indubitable obligation of the privileged. It means to foster the spirit of a rational, ethical and Christian democracy. It aims to train its students personally to share in the great intellectual and spiritual achievements of the race, to think in world terms, to feel with all humanity, to cherish world purposes.

Finding the goals of the school compatible with her own, Anna Cooper had wirtten to President Fairchild, on July 27, 1881, from Haywood, North Carolina, where she was engaged in teaching for the summer. With her characteristic directness and candor, she had asked if Oberlin would accept her under the condition of "free tuition." She added that she would need assistance in finding summer teaching opportunities, and suitable housing accommodations at reasonable rates.

The letter from Cooper to Fairchild is an important and valuable one. It permits us greater insight into the conditions of her life and world, and is presented here in its entirety:

Haywood, N.C. July 27, 1881

President Fairchild,
  Oberlin, Ohio:

  Dear Sir,

  You have, I presume, already been informed through Mrs. Clarke, who spoke to you at the solicitation of a friend of mine, that I desired to enter Oberlin College next term. Four years ago, I completed the course at St. Augustine's Normal School, Raleigh, which included besides the English branches & Latin: Caesar, seven books; Virgil's Aeneid, six books; Sallust's Cataline and Jugurtha; and a few orations of Cicero;—Greek: White's first lessons; Goodwin's Greek Reader, containing selections from Xenophon, Plato, Herodotus and Thucydides; and five or six books of the Iliad:—Mathematics: Algebra and Geometry entire. I have since been engaged in teaching at the same school, and during the term just

President James Harris Fairchild of Oberlin College (1866–1889). Courtesy Oberlin College Archives.

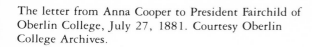

The letter from Anna Cooper to President Fairchild of Oberlin College, July 27, 1881. Courtesy Oberlin College Archives.

ended, I have filled the post of both matron and teacher there.

I am the widow of an Episcopal clergyman (Colored), Rev. G. A. C. Cooper, who died in Sept. '79. I have, for a long time, earnestly desired to take an advanced course in some superior Northern college, but could not see my way to it for lack of means. However, I am now resolved to await no longer, if there is any possibility of my accomplishing my purpose. I am now teaching a two months summer school in Haywood: Southern schools pay *very meanly*, but I expect to have money enough to keep me one or two years at your College, provided I can secure a favor mentioned by Mrs. Clarke, of free tuition and incidentals. . . . Please let me know if you think it likely that I can get any way of keeping myself after I come, by teaching, or something

A letter from Dr. Smedes to the Reverend Henderson Judd of Oberlin, September 10, 1881. Courtesy Moorland-Spingarn Research Center, Howard University.

The letter from the Reverend John E. C. Smedes of St. Augustine's to President Fairchild, September 10, 1881. Courtesy Moorland-Spingarn Research Center, Howard University.

similar, during vacation. I desire to remain to be able to complete the course, if possible.

Please let me know the lowest rate at which I can get suitable accommodations; also the examinations required for entering.

I am extremely anxious to accomplish this long cherished wish, and will feel grateful for any kindly interest taken in my behalf.

Yours respectfully,
ANNA J. COOPER.

Anna Cooper's career goals are in the letter of reference sent from Dr. Smedes to President Fairchild on September 10, 1881. He wrote, "she voluntarily resigns this post of tuition, and applies for admission to Oberlin College, that she may by the further prosecution of liberal studies—be better qualified to take part in the great work now going forward in the South for the Christian education of its colored people." He emphasized that her "pecuniary means" were very limited, but such money as she had was from "the fruit of her own labor and self-denial." Further, he recommended that Anna Cooper be admitted to an advanced class; perhaps sophomore or even junior. Dr. Smedes assured President Fairchild that "she [would] work with great zeal, diligence, and ability" and more than meet the requirements of his faculty. Writing to effect a transfer of Anna Cooper's church membership to an Oberlin Episcopal congregation, Smedes described her as "a Christian woman of unusual culture and intelligence, and of unfeigned zeal and piety." The unusual abilities often assigned to Anna Cooper were present and recognized in her home community of Raleigh, even before she departed for Oberlin. One of the most revealing accounts of her accomplishments while a teacher at St. Augustine's is included in a letter written by the Right Reverend Thomas Atkinson on September 2, 1878, about the school's two women teachers (who must have been Annie Haywood and Jane Thomas). He wrote:

> It may be said, without any exaggeration, that they might be compared favorably with the pupils of any female school in the country, not only in their knowledge of the branches of a good English education, but of Latin, certainly, and I believe of Greek, and also the higher mathematics. . . . They are much superior not only to the young women [in the school], but to the young men generally; but they serve to indicate what may be attained, under good instructors, by young persons of their race.

That Anna Cooper was so well prepared was due largely to her own initiative.

As a student, Anna made friends and did well at Oberlin, where she was accepted into the family of Professor Charles H. Churchill. Older than most of her classmates, with a stated purpose and limited funds, Anna spent her time prudently and did not engage in much frivolous activity. She had no inter-

Mary Jane Patterson (1845–1895). Courtesy Oberlin College Archives.

among the first Afro-American women to earn B.A. degrees from an American college. (Mary Jane Patterson is believed to have been the first.) Mary Eliza Church had been sent by her parents, Robert and Louise Church, from Memphis, Tennessee, to Yellow Springs, Ohio, at an early age. There she attended a grammar school connected with Antioch College and lived with a couple whose name was Hunster—and whom she affectionately addressed as "Ma" and "Pa" Hunster. Leaving Yellow Springs, she enrolled in the high school at Oberlin and then in the preparatory department at Oberlin College. After completing the requirements there, she entered the two year literary program for "Ladies." She completed this course, and with her father's assurance that she "might remain in college as long as [she] wished, and he would foot the bill," Mary Eliza Church continued in the Classical Course, more familiarly called the "Gentlemen's Course." Mary Church and Ida Gibbs had been friends before they entered Oberlin College, for the Gibbs family lived in Oberlin and Mary and Ida attended the preparatory department together. They also shared a dormitory room during their freshman and senior years. Perhaps the difference in their ages and family background and lifestyles accounts for the fact that seemingly no close friendship developed among these two young women and Anna Cooper, who were the only black female members of their class. Even though the professional lives of Mary Church Terrell and Anna Julia Cooper closely paralleled one another after their graduation from Oberlin, Terrell made no mention of Cooper in her autobiography many years later. Both were attractive, intelligent, and competent in their chosen life-work, yet, while not spoken of, it is as if a chasm had developed between the two.

Ida Gibbs (later Ida Gibbs Hunt) was the daughter of Judge Mifflin Wistar Gibbs, who, soon after the Civil War, moved his family to Oberlin so that they might benefit from the educational opportunities there. After settling his business affairs in Victoria, Vancouver, Gibbs rejoined his family in 1869, and, according to Carter G. Woodson's account, "The Gibbs Family," he then "took a course in the law department of an Oberlin business college." Earlier, while a member of the Common Council of Victoria (1866), he had "read law" with an English barrister. In 1872 the family moved to Little Rock, Arkansas, and Gibbs began to practice

est in "catching a beau," for, again, unlike her classmates, she had been married and was then a widow. Thus it may be assumed that she adopted a much more serious countenance. An interesting account of these years, but written from quite another perspective, is to be found in the autobiography of Mary Church Terrell—then Mary Eliza Church—A Colored Woman in a White World.

Mary Eliza Church and Ida A. Gibbs were Anna Cooper's classmates, and the three were members of the Oberlin graduating class of 1884. Preceded by Mary Jane Patterson, also of Raleigh, and a member of Oberlin's class of 1862, these three women were

Mary Eliza Church (Terrell)—from the Oberlin College 1884 class album. Courtesy Oberlin College Archives.

Ida A. Gibbs (Hunt)—from the Oberlin College 1884 class album. Courtesy Oberlin College Archives.

law. Ida Gibbs had enrolled at Oberlin as a boarding student at the time, and the absence of her family might have cemented her friendship with Mary Church, to the exclusion of Anna Cooper. Throughout their adult lives, however, the three Oberlin graduates of the class of 1884 seem to have maintained at least an outwardly cordial relationship.

By her own account, Anna Cooper's home life with the Churchill family was both pleasant and intellectually stimulating. Certainly for Anna, these three years must have been a study of contrasts. She had grown up in a household where reminiscences were of "slavery days," and where an older brother was the father figure; where no books lined the shelves of a library; where there was no carefree conversation about the day's activities; where the mother, without the shelter of a husband's love and concern, took care of other people's homes and children in order to make opportunities for her own. And we know that for Anna there had been no loving grandmother to reign over the skinned knee and bruised feelings department—or to dispense that special kind of love that only

grandmothers know about. The Churchills had shown her another lifestyle, and the fierce determination of her mother and the cultured environment of the Churchills were to become role models that she would remember when, many years later, she would raise the orphaned children of Mr. and Mrs. John L. Love of Ashville, North Carolina, and the five Haywood children, the grandchildren of her brother Andrew.

Much of what Anna Cooper felt about life, her educational philosophy, and her attitude about racial issues, she later recorded in response to some sixty-seven select questions in the "Negro College Graduates' Questionnaire." Some of the answers were cryptic and brief, while others were quite detailed. Here, too, we get a glimpse of Anna Cooper's response to the Oberlin experience. It is from this questionnaire that we learn that the faculty members she found to be most stimulating were President Fairchild, Professor Churchill, and Tutor King, also an Oberlin president. The most positive influences on Anna's life there were Mrs. Adelia Johnston's weekly young people's meetings, the music, the sermons, and the companionship.

The Churchill family home at Oberlin College, where Anna Cooper resided while a student there. From *The Churchills of Oberlin.*

When asked about extracurricular activities, she answered, "I taught advanced Algebra in Oberlin Academy. The students were white." Clearly, this was an indication of how Anna Cooper spent her free hours. When questioned about the school's religious training, she responded, "I entered Oberlin a bigoted 'Churchman' I felt not the slightest attempt to proselytizing & yet altho I continued to attend the little Episcopal Church religiously the breadth & real Catholicity of the Oberlin spirit, the friendly contacts & wider study had the inevitable result which I consider humanizing. . . ." And, again, Anna Cooper expounded on her unshakable belief in her chosen profession—teaching. Clearly and without equivocation, she wrote, "Teaching had always seemed to me the noblest of callings &

I believe that if I were white I should still want to teach those whose need presents a stronger appeal than money. . . . It is human to be stimulated by appreciation where it is genuine." Here Anna Cooper's response is fully in keeping with her philosophy of life and of education; it is also in keeping with the Oberlin credo: education for personal growth and a life dedicated to service. Neither Anna Cooper nor Oberlin believed in self-serving platitudes or self-glorifying philanthropy and charity.

With her Oberlin years now drawing to a close, it must have been with a sense of wonder and pride that Anna looked back over the long but satisfying road she had trod, and the distance traveled since 1868 when she first entered St. Augustine's. Nearing her twenty-sixth birthday, she was now about to step from the threshold of academic preparedness into the broad arena of educational challenges and opportunities as a teacher. With what she called her

The Churchill family, about 1890. Anna Cooper and the Churchills remained close friends throughout her life. From *The Churchills of Oberlin*.

"pluck and energy," she no doubt saw the immediate future as yet another plateau to be reached as she satisfied her desire to obtain even more education. With the signature of "Jas. H. Fairchild" and the Oberlin seal affixed to her diploma that attested to her preparedness, Anna Cooper left Oberlin in 1884.

A friend and a member of the graduating class, Leonard Garver, corresponded with Anna during the year 1884, and about her he wrote:

Thine is a wealth of womanhood:
A mind of might: a heart of good.
We feel that in the future thine
A mission is almost devine.

After graduation, Anna Cooper had planned to return home to Raleigh and to St. Augustine's faculty—but "there was as hitch & [I] went to Wilberforce instead." As she explained, Dr. Smedes had engaged her services before graduation and had promised a professorship. In the interim, however, he prepared to retire, and the administration of St. Augustine's was turned over to the Reverend Robert Bean Sutton, who did not feel obliged to honor the contract. Rather, he offered Anna Cooper the position of "teacher in charge of girls," and she refused!

Mrs. Adelia A. Field Johnston (1837–1910), an Oberlin College graduate (1856) and history instructor. Courtesy Mrs. Regia Bronson and Miss Regina Smith.

The Oberlin College class of 1884 on the steps of
First Church. Anna Cooper is at right rear, Ida Gibbs
(Hunt) two rows below her, and Mary Church
(Terrell) is in the third row at right. Courtesy Oberlin
College Archives.

Instead, she went to Wilberforce College, in
Xenia, Ohio, in September 1884, where she was
able to earn $1,000 annually. She had left St.
Augustine's College at a salary of $30 per month,
and it was not until she announced her intention to
leave to continue her education that Dr. Smedes
offered to double her income. Now at Wilberforce,
in charge of the "department of modern languages
[and] science," she found the work both rewarding
and challenging.

Apparently Anna's decision not to return to St.
Augustine's and her home in Raleigh was the cause
of disappointment and concern for her mother. A
postcard addressed to "Mrs. Hannah Haywood,
Care [of] Mr. A. J. Haywood, Raleigh, North
Carolina," was sent from Wilberforce on October 7,
1884. Found among Anna Cooper's books many
years after her death, it was obviously intended to
reassure Hannah Haywood, who wished that her
daughter would write more frequently. In her fine
script Anna wrote, in part:

Dear Mother: Today is Monday—our recre-
ation day—a very busy one. . . for me as
almost all days are now & I suppose are likely
to continue so for sometime yet. . . .I have
been reading French all the morning & as my

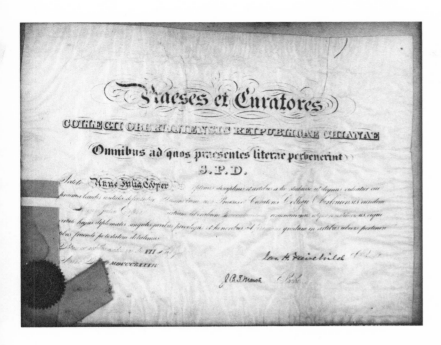

Anna Julia Cooper's diploma from Oberlin College, 1884. Courtesy Mrs. Regia Bronson and Miss Regina Smith.

The diversity of Wilberforce University's academic program is shown in this illustration. From *How to Solve the Race Problem*. Courtesy Mr. James J. Lawson.

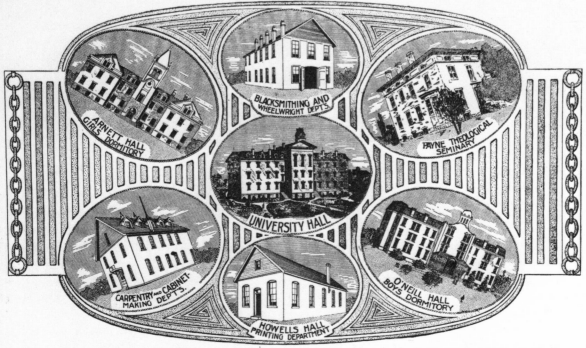

WILBERFORCE UNIVERSITY,
WILBERFORCE, GREENE CO., OHIO.

Joshua H. Jones, A. M., D. D., President.   Horace Talbert, A. M., Secretary.

ARNETT HALL GIRLS DORMITORY

BLACKSMITHING AND WHEELWRIGHT DEPTS.

PAYNE THEOLOGICAL SEMINARY

UNIVERSITY HALL

CARPENTRY AND CABINET MAKING DEPTS.

HOWELLS HALL PRINTING DEPARTMENT

O'NEILL HALL BOYS DORMITORY

COURSES:—Classical, Scientific, Law, Music, Academic, Theological, Normal, Military, Business, Art, Sewing, Carpentry, Printing, Cooking, Shoemaking, Blacksmithing.

Catalogues sent on application.   Students admitted at any time.   School opens first Tuesday in September.   Vacations in December and March.   Commencement, third Thursday in June.

A postcard from Anna Cooper to her mother, Hannah Stanley Haywood, sent from Wilberforce University in 1884. Courtesy Mrs. Regia Bronson and Miss Regina Smith.

eyes were tired I turned to pen you this line to ask you not to worry ever about me. I will try, that is it is my intention to write you regularly. If I don't you may be sure I am well & hard at work for if I were sick I would have all the time to write you regularly.

Having relieved her mother's concern, Anna then turned her attention to family and more personal matters at home, and she continued:

Heard from Mrs. Harris last week who tells me that she has written you. I hope she will come to Raleigh soon & see you. We are having it very warm now in fact it seems as if summer did not set in this year till September. Glad to hear of Georgie's going to Hampton. I shall write to him in a few days. How is Rufus conducting himself? & Johnny —is he in school? I don't understand your allusion to the house near the church. What about it? Is Jane Thomas's mother at the school this year & does Dr. Sutton have charge at St. Augustine's? I wish you would tell me if any one has bought & built near that lot of mine. Does your little house keep comfortable? Where do you spend most of your time? I have quite a pleasant little room & a nice girl to help me with room work. So on the whole I am quite comfortable. I drink the water from the stone spring & suppose it is healthful. Love to all.

Affectionately, ANNIE
Wilberforce

October 6, 1884

The boys George and Rufus inquired about in the message were the sons of Rufus and Nancy Haywood. Johnny was John R. Haywood, the adopted son of Andrew and Jane Haywood; all were the grandsons of Hannah Stanley Haywood, and Anna's nephews.

By September 1885, Anna Cooper had been away from Raleigh for nearly four years. For a year she had taught modern languages, literature, and mathematics at Wilberforce; that summer she also worked as Bishop Benjamin W. Arnett's secretary. Now returning home, and at a lesser salary than that earned at Wilberforce, she rejoined St. Augustine's faculty and taught mathematics, Latin, and Greek. It seems possible that it was now Anna's intention to remain in Raleigh and settle among her family, for according to the records of the Recorder of Deeds, she began the construction of a four-room house on her building lot. By her own account, her brother Rufus had died in 1882, and left a widow and six children. While the eldest of these children was employed as a seamstress in Raleigh, most were still of school age. Nearing seventy, Anna's mother had done domestic work almost all of her free adult life. Now that she was reaching advanced years, it is almost certain that Anna wished Hannah to stop working. While at home, Anna assumed more and more of the responsibility for the care of her mother and her brother Andrew and his family. The construction of a home of her own, together with her level of involvement with family and community affairs, all seem to suggest that she planned to remain in her native state.

In 1886, with the assistance of others on the faculty, Anna Cooper began an out-reach program to extend the work of St. Augustine's College into the community of Raleigh. She helped to establish a Sabbath school and mission guild. A similar program had begun under the direction of Gertrude Haywood (later Mrs. Trapier) before the founding of St. Augstine's, and it might have been there that Anna had first received the opportunity to attend school. Now she was extending a helping hand to her neighbors; those who had invested in her early education had indeed "cast bread upon the waters!"

Important among Anna Cooper's community activities was her membership in the North Carolina's Teachers' Association, and she was a signer of that organization's "Resolutions on Normal and Collegiate Institute and Report No. 1." This report was sent as a "Memorial" to the North Carolina State Legislature, and it was resolved that:

1st. . . . We, the colored educators and friends of Negro education in North Carolina, do hereby express our opinion that it is the duty of our State to make reasonable and just provisions for the training of the colored youth.

2nd. . . . That the State may be induced to do its duty to the colored teachers and youth of the State.

3rd. . . . That the present Normal School provisions are inadequate and do not justify the educational boast of the State.

Bishop Benjamin W. Arnett of the African Methodist Episcopal Church was greatly admired by Anna Cooper for his support of the cause of black women. In 1892 she dedicated her book, *A Voice from the South*, to him. Courtesy Mr. James J. Lawson.

4th. . . . That the State should make appropriations for the establishment and management of a State Normal and High School Institute for its colored citizens which would be a reasonable offset for the University, largely encouraged and supported by public patronage and State money, and used exclusively in the interest of its white citizens.

5th. . . . That we offer these resolutions in all candor and prompted by a consciousness that there is not at present adequate provisions for the demands which the importance of the profession among the colored citizens of the State justifies.

In the year 1887 Oberlin College awarded Anna Cooper an M.A. degree in mathematics. While she had demonstrated great competency and interest in the romance languages and literature, mathematics was her major subject in college, and, as she noted, she had taken "all branches." The degree was awarded on the strength of Anna Cooper's three years of teaching experience on the college level.

III.

Washington, D.C.: New Challenges

Who does the best his circumstance allows need have no qualms in judging results. The world changes & if I had my story to start now, I should surely have to meet other problems & conditions from those of 50 years ago; but I doubt not I should adjust myself to them with the same pluck & energy that I believe to be an unchanging part of me. I should miss perhaps a friendly interest & even a surprised applause on the part of whites who are now concluding that N.[egroes] are best educated in N.[egro] schools.

ANNA J. COOPER
"Negro College Graduates' Questionnaire,"
1930

Anna Julia Cooper at her desk in the M Street High School. Courtesy Moorland-Spingarn Research Center, Howard University.

IN SEPTEMBER OF 1887 ANNA JULIA COOPER LEFT her home in Raleigh to accept yet another opportunity and challenge. During a visit to Washington, D.C., the previous year, she had addressed the Convocation of Clergy of the Protestant Episcopal Church on the subject "Womanhood A Vital Element in the Regeneration and Progress of a Race." This would be an often-repeated topic when later she began to lecture around the country. Anna was the house guest of Dr. Alexander Crummell (revered as the dean of the black clergy) and his wife, and while in the city must have come to believe that the nation's capital presented a unique opportunity and climate in which she could experience growth—both as a person and as an educator. When, in 1887, Superintendent George F. T. Cook of the Colored Schools of Washington City and Georgetown encouraged Dr. John R. Francis, a member of the Colored Trustees, to write to Oberlin College and make inquiry about a recent graduate of that institution who might be capable of teaching mathematics and science in the Washington Colored High School, Anna J. Cooper was recommended for the position. At the beginning of the next school term, and at a starting salary of $750, she entered upon her new duties.

By the time Anna Cooper became a teacher in the District of Columbia's only black high school, Tuskegee Institute—with its program of vocational and industrial education—was emerging as *the* model for black education. Even though Tuskegee was patterned after Hampton Institute, the charisma of Booker T. Washington soon caused it to overshadow his alma mater and brought attention both to himself and his school. His was the Horatio Alger success story, although institutions like

George F. T. Cook, an Oberlin graduate, was the only black superintendent of the Colored Schools of Washington City and Georgetown between 1868 and 1900. Courtesy Moorland-Spingarn Research Center, Howard University.

Wilberforce College (later Wilberforce University), founded in the 1850s, and St. Augustine's had earlier successfully offered programs of industrial training along with classical education.

Not only did Booker T. Washington set the pattern for the future development of educational programs for blacks, but following his ascendancy to power, after the 1895 Atlanta Address, he also tried to set the tone for race relations in America. Washington's first major address (often called the Atlanta "Compromise") and his figurative analogy of the closed fist and the separate five fingers,

demonstrating how black and white Americans might now economically and socially co-exist, ushered in a new era of black-white relations. The new leader of America's four million blacks declared amid cheers from whites who listened to him at the Atlanta Cotton Exposition that the struggle for full equality had shifted from the philosophy of "agitation," espoused by the fallen leader Frederick Douglass, to his own philosophy of accommodation. The death knell for the cause of equal rights had sounded; the era of reconstruction had ended. The atmosphere and spirit of cooperation and amelioration, which had begun to emerge during that period, was losing ground and deteriorating. Now the hard line of racial discrimination and segregation was emerging, and these twin evils, bolstered by sexism, were becoming the foundation that would undergird second-class citizenship for black Americans. It mattered not whether they lived in the North or South, whether their lifestyles were urban or rural, or whether their academic credentials were from a one-room school house in the Delta region of the South or the Ivy League colleges of the Northeast. The bottom line, of course, was the exploitation of a laboring class readily identifiable by color. Among the northern captains of industry there were some who were no more sympathetic to black aspirations and hopes than were southern planters. In both groups some agreed that education would ruin the best laborer (a sentiment carried over from slavery), and make those assigned menial tasks for low wages dissatisfied with their lot. To fill the void and attract the money of white philanthropists, after the withdrawal of support by Freedmen's Societies and benevolent organizations, many southern black colleges began to reorganize or modify their instructional programs along the lines of the preferred Tuskegee model.

According to Donald Spivey (*Schooling for the New Slavery*), when the Civil War ended blacks faced a neo-slave system. Labor was needed to tend the crops for the marketplace and for the new industrial combines of the South, which represented northern exploitation of southern resources. Required to release its forced labor supply at the end of the war, the South showed great ingenuity in developing alternative employment systems that were not limited to debt peonage and sharecropping. Other means were used to terrorize and intimidate blacks, and return them to the soil and the control of white

Dr. John R. Francis, a D.C. Public Schools trustee (1885–1888). From *Twentieth Century Negro Literature*.

When Anna Cooper began teaching in the Preparatory School and later the Washington Colored High School, then headed by Francis L. Cardozo, classes were held in the Miner Building, located at the corner of Seventeenth and Church streets, NW. The school building was appropriately named, for the Preparatory School had been organized in the basement of the Fifteenth Street Presbyterian Church, and its first money had come from the Miner Fund. Established in memory of Myrtilla Miner, the fund commemorated her efforts on behalf of Washington's black female students, for whom she had established a school in 1854. At that time the Fifteenth Street Presbyterian Church was pastored by the renowned abolitionist Henry Highland Garnet, who a few months before his death would serve as minister resident and consul-general to Liberia, where he died.

Historically, the school had attracted some of the best-trained black teachers in the country, and before Anna's arrival two women had served as its principal. The first was Emma J. Hutchins of New Hampshire, who possibly had come to Washington

planters and overseers. One system that was employed was that of industrial education—designed with an explicit function and goal: the resubjugation of blacks by providing them with educations that would severely limit their participation in the economic arena, except as menial laborers, and that would prepare them both psychologically and philosophically to accept and know their place in the socio-economic-political system of the "New South."

During the last two decades of the nineteenth century black educational institutions witnessed an erosion of their programs. Money was needed for the expansion of their physical plants and to attract better teachers. The competition among these institutions to acquire the needed fiscal resources became keener, while the allocations from state legislatures—as in the instance of Land Grant Colleges—were either withheld or inadequate and begrudgingly given. Later the Washington Colored High School would feel the impact of the new political climate and the educational philosophy that it promulgated.

Francis L. Cardozo, principal of the Washington Colored High School (1884–1896). Courtesy Association for the Study of Afro-American Life and History.

47

The Miner Building, site of the Preparatory School and later of the Washington Colored High School (1877–1891). Courtesy Mr. William N. Buckner, Jr.

under the auspices of the New England Friends Mission. This group continued its support of the District's black public schools through 1872. The second was Mary Jane Patterson (1849–1894) of Raleigh, North Carolina, and Oberlin, Ohio. According to Hallie Q. Brown in her volume *Homespun Heroines*, Miss Patterson's father had been a fugitive slave, who relocated his family from Raleigh to Oberlin about 1854. Completing the Oberlin College four-year course in 1862, Miss Patterson had taught in Philadelphia for about seven years before coming to the District of Columbia. Serving two appointments as the Preparatory School's principal (1871–1872 and 1873–1884), she continued as a member of the school's faculty until her death. Her tenure was interrupted for one year, when, in 1873, Professor Richard T. Greener, the first black graduate of Harvard University, served as the school's principal. Then the Preparatory School was moved

to the Charles Sumner Elementary School at its present location, the corner of Seventeenth and M streets, NW. According to a bit of Washington folklore, the name "M Street" became attached to the school while it was in the Sumner building. An elementary school was also housed there, and to distinguish the one from the other, the Preparatory School was called "M Street" because it occupied rooms on that side of the building.

In 1891 the Preparatory School moved into new quarters that had been designed specifically for its use. A sunlit auditorium and classrooms were located on the top story of the building, and the school could boast of a well-equipped science laboratory. Although built on a shallow lot, between New Jersey and New York avenues, large rooms in the basement provided space for recreational and physical education programs. In addition, there was a well-appointed office for the principal and a combination conference room-lounge for the teachers. While familiarly known as the M Street School, the institution's diplomas continued to carry the name "Washington Colored High School." The newly located school, the only high school for the District's black student population at that time, continued under the administration of Francis L. Cardozo. Students were admitted on the basis of qualifications and performance, and the school maintained a full enrollment. There was always a waiting list, for the school attracted students from neighboring jurisdictions of the District and from several states where there were no high schools for blacks.

The M Street School records for 1891 are extant, and clearly attest to the socio-economic mix present among the student population. No student who wished to gain an education was knowingly turned away, and many teachers sacrificed their time and personal lives to assure the preparedness of these students. Most of the teaching staff were women, and those who wished to marry were required by law to leave their profession. Since the law excluded married females from the classroom until 1923, a sizable spinster teacher population arose. However, widows like Anna Cooper were allowed to teach. In the school year 1890–1891 alone, the District's

A page from Superintendent George F. T. Cook's report to the school trustees, 1874–1875. Courtesy District of Columbia Public Schools.

public school system employed a total of 265 black teachers, and of this number 40 were male and 225 were female.

Under Dr. Cardozo's guidance, the District's first trade and business curricula for black youth were developed at the M Street School. The programs were designed to give students alternatives, for the principal and teaching staff were pragmatists and realized that not all of their students would either want, or be able, to go on to college. The school's philosophy was that those who would enter the trades and business courses should be "educated," and not just become "skilled hands." Those students who elected the vocational and business courses participated fully in all other school activities. An outstanding example of such a student was Nannie Helen Burroughs, who, in 1899, was the class valedictorian. She had hoped to receive an appointment as a Domestic Science teacher, but because the District's public school system only appointed twenty black graduates a year (with or without normal-school training), she was one

Caroline Eliot Parke, an early teacher at the Preparatory School also taught at the M Street High School during Anna Cooper's tenure there. Courtesy Dr. Henry S. Robinson.

The M Street High School as it appeared in 1900. From *A History of the City of Washington.*

among many who received their training in Washington who were obliged to seek employment in other school districts. As in the case of Wilhelmina Patterson of Anacostia, D.C., who, with the help of Mary Church Terrell, gained a teaching position in Texas, some had family concerns that made the acceptance of appointments a great distance from their homes difficult to handle. An orphan, Miss Patterson had the responsibility of a younger brother, Frederick Douglass Patterson, who in later years succeeded his father-in-law, Robert Russa Moton, as the third principal of Tuskegee Institute. In the District, however, priority was given to students

Nannie Helen Burroughs (1883–1961), founder of the National Training School for Women and Girls in Washington, D.C., as she appeared in 1909. From *The Dream and the Dreamer.*

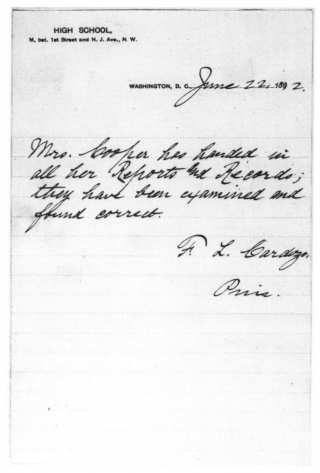

The cover of Anna Cooper's M Street High School record book, 1891–1892. Francis L. Cardozo certified that the records were "examined and found correct." Courtesy District of Columbia Public Schools, Division of Research and Evaluation.

who completed the Normal School Program. Normal School No. 2 for Washington's blacks was then headed by Dr. Lucy Ellen Moten, an outstanding educator who also earned a medical degree from Howard University, in 1897.

Anna Cooper found the M Street School and its students stimulating. She took a special interest in the cadet corps, and each year the winning battalion of the intramural competitive drill was invited to her home for tea. The young men wore their very handsome uniforms that were purchased through the combined efforts of themselves and their instructors. The cadet corps had first been organized by Christian A. Fleetwood, a Civil War Congressional Medal of Honor winner. Originally from Baltimore, Fleetwood had remained in Washington after the war. Before teaching military science at the M Street School, he had been a clerk with the Freedmen's Bureau and the Freedmen's Bank.

Anna Cooper believed that the cadet corps instilled pride and a sense of patriotism, and was one of its ardent supporters. The cadets were a source of community pride as they marched in inaugural parades and performed at special functions on the White House lawn. They were noted for their gentlemanly conduct and decorum. Fiercely competitive and completely loyal to the ideals of their school, members of the corps would become the nucleus for the first Colored Battalion of the National Guard, and would later earn great respect during the Spanish-American War.

The Cadet Corps was founded the year after Anna Cooper's arrival at the M Street School. Along with Fleetwood, its founder, the instructors of military science were Edward L. York, Orestus K. Kincaid,

A winning company of M Street High School performing a military drill. From *Self-Educator for a Rising Race.* Courtesy Mr. Benjamin T. Layton.

Arthur J. Brooks, Milton Dean, and Edward L. Webster. Some of the winning student company commanders organized into a social group called "The Officers." Among them were James Walker, Albert Ridgley, Frank Allen, Benjamin Washington, John C. Payne, and Arthur Newman. Newman later became an administrator and an instructor of military science in the District's black schools. In 1893 Louis Cornish, Jr., was chosen to be one of the official honor guards to escort outgoing President Benjamin Harrison and in-coming President-elect Grover Cleveland. Another corps member, Major Walter Howard Loving, organized and directed the world-famous United States Philippine Constabulary Band, which was commissioned in 1902 by William Howard Taft, who then served as governor-general of the Philippines. In

1904 Loving took the band to the St. Louis Exposition, where it was awarded second prize in an international band competition. The first prize went to the Le Garde Republicain Band of France. When inaugurated President of the United States in 1909, Taft ordered the United States Philippine Constabulary Band and its director to Washington to perform and participate in the inaugural parade. Loving remained in the Philippines for more than forty years, and his devotion to duty and love of country were praised by General Douglas A. MacArthur, then supreme commander of Allied forces in the Southwest Pacific. Anna Cooper and others, who had watched Loving's progress and accomplishments with pride, were saddened when it was learned that the Japanese invaders of the Philippines had ruthlessly executed him in one of their concentration camps. During the period of his incarceration, "the little man with the magical baton" had been inspired to write two pieces of music, "Exaltation"—an ode to the Philippines—

Louis Cornish, Jr., an M Street School student and an official presidential honor guard. Courtesy Mr. Paul Sluby, Sr.

and "Victory March," dedicated to General Mac-Arthur.

Robert N. Mattingly (class of 1902) commanded the winning battalion in the first Inter-High Competitive Drill between the M Street High School and the newly formed Armstrong High School. An outstanding student in mathematics, Mattingly was a Phi Beta Kappa member and a graduate of Amherst College (1905), where he completed the four-year course in three years. Later he would become a D.C. Public School administrator and organize the Cardozo Senior High School, in 1928, and continue as its principal until his retirement in 1954.

Anna Cooper served under the administration of Dr. Winfield Scott Montgomery, principal of the M Street High School from September 1896 until April 30, 1899. As noted by G. Sumner Wormley in the article "Educators of the First Half Century of the Public Schools of the District of Columbia," Montgomery "held every position in the public

Major Walter Howard Loving, director of the United States Philippine Constabulary Band, 1909–1945. Courtesy Library of Congress, Daniel Murray Papers.

Robert N. Mattingly, a graduate of M Street High School and Amherst College, was the winning commanding officer of cadet Company B, 1901–1902. Courtesy Association for the Study of Afro-American Life and History.

schools . . . from teacher to assistant superintendent with equal efficiency and dignity." Born near Vicksburg, Mississippi, Winfield Scott Montgomery and his brother, Henry Percival, were runaway slaves. During the Civil War they attached themselves to the Union Army, and later were taken to Vermont as contrabands of war. Separated and raised by different families (the Catans and Gilettes), both Winfield and Henry made their way to Washington and followed teaching careers. Each made a significant contribution to the progress of those schools assigned to Washington's black community.

The Montgomery brothers were typical of many who came to M Street as teachers. Most were well educated for the times, and all were armed with tenacity and determination; determined that in spite of the imperfections of the school system—hampered by segregation and inadequate funding—the children would learn. The successes so often

spoken of are proof that the children *did* learn. In addition to Anna Cooper, others who taught at the M Street School included Parker Nell Bailey, Harvard University; Laura Frances Barney, High School of Philadelphia; Percival Drayton Brooks, D.C. Public Schools; Julia Waugh Mason, D.C. Public Schools; Mary Elizabeth Nalle, D.C. Preparatory High School and Minor Normal; Mary Jane Patterson, Oberlin College; Harriet Elizabeth Riggs, Calais, Maine; and Professors Storum and Thompson. (The 1891 record books for all named are extant.)

By 1891 Anna Cooper was teaching "last year" Latin, and among the students who entered the new M Street School building with her were Grace Addison, Addie Beckwith, Mary Burrell, Ida Brown, Bertha Edwards, Hattie Franey, Annie Frazier, Carrie Gaines, Winifred Hansborough, Beatrice Johnson, Lillie Johnson, Minnie Lucas, Lillie Mason, Teresa Marshall, Gertrude Merritt, Lula Peters, Estelle Pinkney, Sadie Piper, Leonora Randolph, Eleanor Robinson, Julia Shipperson, Geneva Shorter, Isabel Smith, Lucy Shepherd,

Officers from the regular army and the District of Columbia National Guard serve each year as judges in the annual contests; and the names of the successive commanding officers, winning Company, winning Captain and winning school are as follows:

School Year	Commanding Officer	Winning Company	Winning Captain	School
1891-92	Capt. Albert Ridgley			
1892-93	Capt. Louis A. Cornish	2nd Pltn.	Lieut. Benj. Washington	M Street
1893-94	Maj. Chas. M. Thomas	2nd Pltn.	Capt. Chas. E. Minkins	M Street
1894-95	Maj. Chas. E. Minkins	A	Capt. Henry D. Burwell	M Street
18 .5-96	Maj. Chas. E. Minkins	B	Capt. C. K. Wormley	M Street
1896-97	Maj. C. K. Wormley	C	Capt. Archibald M. Ray	M Street
1897-98	Maj. Wm. O. Davis	B	Capt. J. O. Montgomery	M Street
1898-99	Maj. Leon S. Turner	B	Capt. Wm. Brown	M Street
'1899-00	Maj. Leon S. Turner	B	Capt. Wm. J. Howard	M Street
1900-01	Maj. Walter P. Ray	C	Capt. R. N. Mattingly	M Street
1901-02	Maj. R. N. Mattingly	B	Capt. Chester H. Jarvis	M Street
1902-03	Maj. Milton S. Bush	B	Capt. Hugh R. Francis	M Street
1903-04	Maj. Hugh R. Francis	C	Capt. John H. Wilson	Armstrong
1904-05	Maj. Jas. M. Saunders	D	Capt. Arthur F. Albert	Armstrong
1905-' 6	Maj. Henry C. Weeden	D	Capt. Wm. A. Henderson	Armstrong
1906-07	Maj. W. A. Hamilton	A	Capt. John R. Pinkett	M Street
1907-08	Maj. Sterling O. Fields	A	Capt. Edward B. Gray	M Street
1908-09	Maj. C. C. McDuffie	E	Capt. A. A. Taylor	Armstrong
1909-10	Maj. A. A. Taylor	A	Capt. W. W. Lawson	M Street
1910-11	Maj. Norman I. Ewing	A	Capt. Hugh B. Shipley	M Street
1911-12	Maj. John C. Woods	A	Capt. Arthur C. Logan	M Street
1912-13	Maj. Arthur A. Dyer	A	Capt. Rayford W. Logan	M Street
1913-14	Maj. R. W. Reynolds	F	Capt. Arthur C. Payne	M Street
1914-15	Maj. Wm. J. Barnes	C	Capt. Robert O. Powell	Armstrong
1915-16	Maj. William Lewis	B	Capt. Lorimer D. Milton	M Street
1916-17	Maj. Earl R. Alexander	E	Capt. Sterling A. Brown	Dunbar
1917-18	Maj. Sterling A. Brown	D	Capt. George W. Davis	Armstrong
1918-19	Maj. Charles Lewis	B	Capt. Ralph W. Scott	Dunbar
1919-20	Lt. Col. W. M Cook	K	Capt. William B. Mason	Dunbar
1920-21	*Maj. C. S. Scott, 1st Bt. Maj. G. Newsome 2d Bt. Lt. Col. T. L. Dulany *Maj. A. Booker, 1st Bt. *Maj. S. Blackwell 2d Bt.	C	Capt. Claude R. Terrell	Armstrong
1921-22	Lt. Col. C. A. Wells *Maj. M. Johnson, 1st B. Maj. B. Branson, 2d Bt.	L	Capt. Powell F. Allen	Armstrong
1922-23	L*. Col. J. S. Carroll Maj. T. W. Boyde, 1st B. * Maj. H. Shamwell, 2d B.	B	Capt. Lowell C. Wormley	Dunbar

*Winning Battalion.

The roster of winning cadet companies, officers, and schools competing in the Annual Competitive Drill between 1891 and 1923. From *Dunbar High School Yearbook*, 1923. Courtesy Mrs. Ella Howard Pearis.

Dr. Winfield Scott Montgomery, principal of the M Street High School (1896–1899), was also assistant superintendent of the D.C. Colored Schools. Courtesy Association for the Study of Afro-American Life and History.

Henry Percival Montgomery (1852–1899), principal of the Hillsdale and John F. Cook schools, was supervising principal of the Seventh School Division from 1882 to 1899. Courtesy Association for the Study of Afro-American Life and History.

Maggie Scott, Julia Tibbs, Jessie Wormley, Mattie White, and Estelle Wilkinson. Also, there were Oliver Arnold, Alexander Coleman, Thomas Palmer, Albert Ridgely, Cyrus Shippen, and Harry Williams. These students came from Washington City and from the neighboring communities of Kendall Green, Brightwood, Mt. Pleasant, and Hillsdale (Anacostia), D.C., in Washington County—where there were no schools beyond the grammar grades. According to Anna Cooper's record book, the occupations and skills of parents included laundress, porter, caterer, fireman, farmer, steward, grocer, waiter, barber, government messenger, dairyman, plasterer, shoemaker, assistant librarian of the United States Capitol, teacher, clergyman, and housekeeper.

On May 1, 1899, Robert H. Terrell was named principal of the M Street School, and he continued in that post until December 31, 1901. Although his tenure was brief, he made a favorable impression upon the students, who remembered him with re-

spect and affection. One such student was Robert Mattingly, who in May 1974 privately published his *Memories 1897–1954 of the M Street-Dunbar High School*. He recalled that Terrell, during his second year as principal, had volunteered to teach the beginner's course in Greek, and was an excellent teacher. Here we are also told that Terrell was able to hold the interest of his young scholars by interlacing course work with humorous accounts of his own student days at Harvard. Terrell apparently enjoyed his students and established a good rapport with them. During that time he discretely courted a teacher in the school's language department—and the romance did not go unnoticed by his students, who one day penned the following sentiment on the blackboard: "Mr. Terrell is certainly getting good. He used to go to dances, but now he goes to *Church.*" A play on words, the reference was obviously to the close relationship that was developing between Robert H. Terrell and Mary Eliza Church.

Robert H. Terrell (1857–1927) was born in Or-

55

ange County, Virginia, the son of Harrison and Louisa Coleman Terrell. He was sent at an early age to be educated in the District of Columbia, and later attended Lawrence Academy in Groton, Massachusetts. After receiving a B.A. degree from Harvard in 1884, he went on to earn law degrees from Howard University in 1889 and 1893. Before accepting the position as principal of the M Street School, Terrell had been chief of a division in the Treasury Department, and in 1893 was admitted to the D.C. bar. For five years he was a partner in the law firm of John M. Lynch & Terrell.

Robert H. Terrell (1859–1927), principal of the M Street High School (1899–1901) and President Theodore Roosevelt's appointee as the District's first black municipal judge. From *An Era in Progress and Promise, 1863–1910.*

A page from Anna Cooper's M Street High School record book, 1891–1892. Courtesy District of Columbia Public Schools, Division of Research and Evaluation.

Anna Cooper followed Terrell as the principal of the M Street School, and while the dates of her administration are most often given as 1901–1906, her appointment did not become effective until January 2, 1902, as reported in *The Women's Tribune* of April 5, 1902. This weekly paper was printed and published by feminist Clara Bewick Colby, who said of the promotion:

> It is a great pleasure to record the promotion of Mrs. Anna J. Cooper to the principalship of the Colored High School of Washington—in the place of R. H. Terrell, who resigned to occupy a position as a justice of the peace for the District. Mrs. Cooper has been assistant principal for some time and her promotion was made in strict accord with the merit system. . . . During the last year as assistant principal Mrs. Cooper instituted a course of week-

ly lectures to the girls on topics relating to personal and social improvement which have proved very beneficial.

As principal, Anna Cooper inherited a tradition, for when Superintendent Cook had presented his first report to the school trustees, in the early 1870s, he stressed that a major goal of the Preparatory School, in which he took great pride, was "to present to the pupils . . . incentives to higher aim in education." Under the administration of well-trained and dedicated principals and teachers, the school had succeeded in meeting this goal. The groundwork for the school had been laid by Emma J. Hutchins, the first principal, who resigned at the end of the first year and accepted a position in Oswego County, New York. She relinquished the principalship believing that among the corps of newly trained black teachers in the District, there were those able to carry on the work first begun under the auspices of the Freedmen's Bureau. As indicated by the curriculum, the school was now much advanced and rapidly progressing as new courses were added.

During Anna Cooper's tenure, the tradition of providing incentives to encourage higher aims in education continued. The school was administered under the rules of the board that was organized by new congressional authority, effective July 1, 1900. The only discernible difference between it and the other high schools in the system at that time was the complexion of the student body. Admission to the M Street School required the successful completion of public grammar school. Students who had not completed formal instructions, but were able to pass the entrance examination, were also permitted to attend. The examination included English grammar and composition, history, the United States Constitution, basic arithmetic, and algebra. The school had seats for 530 students, who, unlike those at the elementary level, had to pay for books and supplies. Since seats were at a premium, students were only admitted, withdrawn, or reinstated upon the application of their parents or legal guardians, and their attendance and progress were strictly monitored.

By 1902 the M Street School had a four-year liberal arts (or classical) program and a two-year business education program. Students enrolled under either curriculum were eligible for admission into the normal school program available for blacks,

Julia Evangeline Brooks, an M Street graduate and faculty member, later became Dunbar High School's assistant principal and dean of girls. From *Dunbar High School Yearbook,* 1923. Courtesy Mrs. Ella Howard Pearis.

and could pursue teaching careers in their area of specialty. Starting in 1902, and through voluntary enrollment, the business students at M Street became the first to enter the new Armstrong Business High School, later the Armstrong Technical High School. M Street teachers also shared the teaching load at the new school, and Julia Evangeline Brooks (the daughter of the Reverend Walter H. Brooks) voluntarily organized the first Spanish classes in the Armstrong High School. A former M Street student, she had continued her education at Howard University after completing Normal School No. 2, and later returned to the faculty at M Street where she gained an enviable reputation as the dean of girls.

While Anna Cooper was principal, first-year M Street students were required to take English, history, algebra, Latin, and physics or chemistry. English and Latin were the only required subjects for third- and fourth-year students. Among the several

The Abbé Felix Klein. From *In the Land of the Strenuous Life*. Courtesy Mrs. Regia Bronson and Miss Regina Smith.

electives were French, German, Spanish, Greek, history courses, trigonometry, advanced geometry, chemistry, physics, and political economy. The students who attended this school were extraordinary only in the sense that they were taught to believe in themselves—and to believe that they could achieve. Although the course of study seems imposing, there was no preselection of students, and most were the children of working-class parents; those whose parents could afford tuition or private instruction were in the minority. But these parents fully appreciated the quality of education that was obtainable from their public school and they enthusiastically supported it.

In 1903 Father Felix Klein, a professor at the Catholic Institute of Paris, visited the M Street School, and an account of the visit as well as his impressions of the principal and the students he met and observed have been preserved in his book *In the Land of Strenuous Life*. To establish the objectivity of the Abbé Klein's remarks, it is well to note that his visit was spontaneous and by chance, and according to him, it was among his most interesting experiences while touring America and Canada. He had come as a guest of the American government, wishing to study educational and religious institutions in North America. An interesting aspect of his account is that it is presented in juxtaposition to his encounter with Tuskegee Institute, for while visiting President Theodore Roosevelt, Father Klein was encouraged to visit Tuskegee in order to see at first hand the role model for black education in America. Tuskegee Institute was then perceived to be the model in black education; it was the panacea and made white Americans feel less threatened. Later, the District's school superintendent would find it imperative to visit Tuskegee, and recommend that Washington's schools be reorganized along more "satisfactory lines."

Excerpts from the Abbé Klein's observations will provide the reader with some insight into the daily operation of the M Street School during the tenure of Anna Cooper as its principal:

I arrived then, one morning, about ten o'clock, at "the colored high school." I rang several times; no answer. I had only to push the door; everything was open, as usual. Although . . . I could easily see the classes working, there was no one to whom I could speak. . . . Fortunately, I espied, near a staircase, this notice: "Principal's room on the second floor." I went upstairs, and [saw] seated in an office . . . a negress, pretty, young, and intelligent looking. I addressed her [and] explained the object of my visit. "I am the Principal," she said; and she gave me an outline of the courses of study, answered my questions, and offered most graciously to show or to explain anything that might be of interest to me. The school has a registry of 530 pupils, from fourteen to eighteen years of age, 130 boys and 400 girls, all colored. We entered the different classes without interrupting the work other than by a short introduction to the professors. The teaching staff whom I met comprised only women—all, like the students, more or less black. There were all shades of color, from olive to ebony; but not a single white face, although many approached it. . . . These young people seemed attentive, wide-awake, and intelligent.

I could do no more than hurry through the science classes, which they were anxious to show me on account of the very fine laboratories; but I stopped in an English class where one of George Eliot's novels was being explained, and where I heard some very satisfactory answers. I then asked to hear a lesson in Latin. The Principal replied that there would be one in a few minutes, but that it was she who must give it. "All the more reason why I should like to hear it," I made bold to say.

The Latin class contained sixteen pupils, of whom three were young girls. As soon as I had been introduced, she began to explain the first part of the Aeneid. Those called upon to recite acquitted themselves so creditably that I suspected a recent previous acquaintance with the passage; at any rate, the explanation must have been followed with the closest attention and well remembered. But there was one thing certain, and that was the excellence of the explanations which the Professor gave, in my presence, of the subject of the poem in general, of Virgil's aim, of the historical and mythological allusions, of the metre, of the grammatical rules, and the matter of the text. For my own part, I should have been incapable of such accurate knowledge and such pedagogical ability. We spent the entire hour on the first eleven lines of the poem; and without being aware of it I stayed to the end, deeply interested. It is not every day that one has occasion to sing the Trojan hero (the teacher strongly recommended "hero" as a translation of *virum*), or the fabled beginnings of Rome, in the society of American negroes under the direction of a woman of their own race.

Coming out from our Latin lesson, I had the pleasure of seeing the entire troupe, coming from the different classes, file by in ranks, two by two, in absolute silence. Seeing that I appeared surprised at this military gait, the Principal remarked, "With such a large number of pupils, this is necessary for good order and for rapidity." We then saw a short exercise in gymnastics, which takes the place of recess, and during which the boys and girls are separated. . . . We continued talking. My amiable guide was happy to tell me that the previous year she had been able to obtain for one of her students a scholarship at Harvard University; and this, she thought, with good reason, would be a splendid encouragement for the others, and a means of increasing the number of leaders who seek to elevate her race.

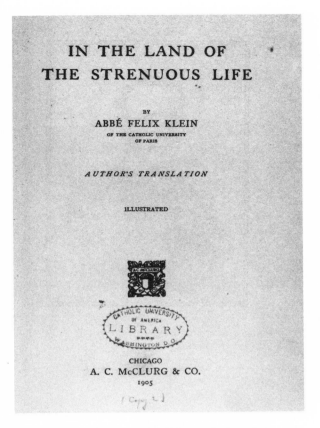

IN THE LAND OF
THE STRENUOUS LIFE

BY
ABBÉ FELIX KLEIN
OF THE CATHOLIC UNIVERSITY
OF PARIS

AUTHOR'S TRANSLATION

ILLUSTRATED

CHICAGO
A. C. McCLURG & CO.
1905

The title page from the English translation of the Abbé Klein's book. From *In the Land of the Strenuous Life.* Courtesy Mrs. Regia Bronson and Miss Regina Smith.

I learned also that the school is nonsectarian, admitting Protestants and Catholics on the same footing. But for all that, it is not without religion. Every morning at nine o'clock, before class recitations begin, a portion of the Bible is read, a hymn is sung, and "Our Father" is recited. . . .

To see these 530 young negroes and negresses, well dressed and well bred, under teachers of their own race, pursuing the same studies as our average college students, who would dream of the existence of a terrible race-question in the United States?

The Abbé Klein proved to be a keen observer who gave thoughtful consideration to all that he had witnessed on that eventful morning, when, by chance, he visited the M Street School. His insightful passages tell much of the competency and preparedness of the students and their teacher-principal. In addition, we learn something of Anna

Cooper's attitudes and philosophy as an educator and race leader, for she was imbued with the belief that the purpose of education was to prepare her students for service to their race, since southern white colleges would not take them, and most southern black colleges at that time were not accredited. And with the exception of some like Fisk and Atlanta University, the black colleges had begun to reorganize along the lines of Hampton and Tuskegee institutes to compete for available funds, and their curriculums were severely limited. (Tuskegee Institute did not become an accredited college until 1935.) Thus, there would be little hope of getting black students into the professions of medicine, law, and the social sciences unless they could first gain admission to the large, endowed northeastern colleges. The object was not prestige; the object was black survival! The subjects to be pursued were utilitarian. Anna Cooper, not that many years removed from Raleigh, North Carolina, where the only hospital for blacks had been founded by the wife of the president of St. Augustine's College, knew the statistics only too well. She knew firsthand that the illiteracy rate among southern blacks was still in excess of 60 percent, and that the population growth of blacks was disproportionate to that of whites because of the high rate of infant mortality, even though black women became pregnant more frequently. She knew that black women worked harder and died sooner, and that their black babies were born weaker because prenatal care was not available. She did not need actuarial charts and graphs; she had been there and had spent her summer months teaching poor blacks in North Carolina's rural communities. She had not forgotten— and because she had not she imbued her students with the philosophy of education for service. These students, then, would become the "bootstraps" by which the race would be uplifted. Too, Anna Cooper was pragmatic in her understanding that blacks needed the benefits to be derived from both a classical and a vocational education, and she took a stand on this very controversial issue before Booker T. Washington's ascendancy to power in 1895, and before the ideological differences between Washington and W. E. B. Du Bois had escalated to the level of the now historical controversy. Her declaration was made while attending the Second Hampton Negro Conference on May 25, 1894.

Robert Russa Moton (1867-1940) was a disciple of General Samuel Armstrong and Booker T. Washington, and after twenty-five years of service to Hampton Institute he succeeded Washington as the second principal of Tuskegee Institute. In his autobiography, *Finding A Way Out,* Moton tells us that it was at his suggestion that the Hampton Negro Conferences were inaugurated. He explains that Dr. H. B. Frissell, Armstrong's successor as president of Hampton Institute, was concerned and disturbed by what he perceived to be a misunderstanding among blacks about Hampton's goals and educational programs. At this time there was also a growing dissension, especially among Virginia's black population, concerning the real objectives and benefits of the Hampton experience. According to Moton, "After observing this condition for three or four years [I] finally came to the conclusion that this opposition to Hampton was due largely to a lack of knowledge of Hampton's methods of work and what was being accomplished by those methods." Moton then decided that it would be a good thing to invite "coloured men and women with college training, from whom most of this kind of opposition came," to attend a forum at Hampton where they would have an opportunity to have a clearer understanding of Hampton Institute's educational philosophy and program. Robert Moton also wished to dispel what he called "unwarranted antagonism."

The Tuskegee Farmer's Conference was the pattern for the Hampton Negro Conference, and Booker T. Washington presided over the first assembly, in 1893. Dr. Frissell convened the second conference, and in Moton's estimation it was the first time he could recall seeing so many Negroes of distinction gathered together for the opportunity of engaging in frank and open discussion and criticism of the Hampton and Tuskegee educational plans. To facilitate such an open discussion, the conference promoters "purposely arranged to have papers on subjects that were under criticism and from men who . . . opposed Hampton methods." Among the invited educational giants of the race were Anna Cooper, President W. S. Scarborough of Wilberforce University, Dr. Kelly Miller, Fannie Jackson Coppin, Professor Hugh M. Brown, Dr. Du Bois, the Reverend Francis J. Grimké, Archibald H. Grimké, the poet Paul Laurence Dunbar, T. Thomas Fortune, and Dr. Inman Page. It was in that assemblage that Anna Cooper publicly supported

vocational education as a choice of curriculums that blacks might pursue. She said:

> I believe in industrial education with all my heart. We can't all be professional people. We must have a back bone to the race. It was once doubted if a Negro had a soul. After it was found that he [did] . . . there was still a question [of] whether he had a brain. A little time ago, a descendent of Calhoun said that if Calhoun had known what he knew about the Negro's brain power, there would not have been the [Civil] War. There is a crisis ahead in the labor question. The foreign element is unstable, and restive, ready for strikes, and as a rule impatient of control. The people of this country will inevitably look around for a stable working class. When the time comes for the need to be appreciated and satisfied, the Negro must be ready to satisfy it; there will be

Virginia Hall at Hampton Institute, Virginia, where the opening session of the Second Hampton Negro Conference was convened in May 1894. From *An Era in Progress and Promise.*

no prejudice against the colored man as a worker.

Anna Cooper was overzealous in her optimism and did not correctly assess the mood of the country at that time. Yet even beyond preparing a people to take their rightful place in the varied marketplaces of America, she knew that the whole individual needed the full range of educational services and experiences. Later she would exclaim, "we are not just educating heads and hands, we are educating the men and women of a race." This kind of educational philosophy was not to go unchallenged for very long, and as she would later learn, the question of the kind of education that would be made avail-

William N. Buckner, Jr., in the dark room of the M Street High School's physics laboratory, about 1904. Courtesy Mr. William N. Buckner, Jr.

able to blacks was one that would be decided by politicians in collaboration with the captains of industry, who also prominently served as members of the several philanthropic educational boards and commissions. As did politics, the development of the "New South" made strange bedfellows, and the ripple that began at Hampton Roads on the James River would become a tidal wave that would reach both West and East Africa.

Generally there is little awareness of the embryonic days of first the Preparatory School and then the M Street High School, yet many of the students who came under the tutelage and influence of Anna Cooper did achieve success, lead useful lives, and make significant contributions to the society in which they found themselves. So it is to

those students that we turn to see their level of preparedness, their choices of professions or trades, and their ability to function effectively in the community setting. Among them were Sadie Tanner Mossell, class of 1915; Albertus Brown, class of 1897; Nannie Helen Burroughs, class of 1899; Joseph H. Douglass; Herman Dreer, class of 1903; Eva Beatrice Dykes, class of 1910; William Brooks Edelin and West Alexander Hamilton, class of 1904; John Hayden Johnson, class of 1894; Willard Mercer Lane, class of 1904; James Luther Pinn, class of 1896; Robert Queen, class of 1902; Willis Richardson, class of 1906; Jean Toomer, class of 1913(?); and William N. Buckner, Jr., class of 1907.

The family of Sadie Tanner Mossell (later Mrs. Raymond Pace Alexander) moved from Philadelphia to Washington early in the twentieth century, where the father was employed as a pharmacist's clerk and the mother kept a notion's store in the vicinity of Howard University. Graduating in the class of 1915, Sadie, a civil rights activist, went on to become a successful attorney and the first black woman to earn a Ph.D. in economics from the University of Pennsylvania, in 1921. Along with Eva Beatrice Dykes and Georgiana Rose Simpson, she was one of the first black women to earn a Ph.D. degree from an American college. Also M Street graduates, the Misses Dykes and Simpson later returned to teach at Dunbar High School. The son of Harrison and Caroline Hess Brown, Albertus Brown became a lawyer. During his grammar school days he had sold newspapers, and, while in high school, was employed as a messenger for United States Senator Mark A. Hanna and the Republican National Committee. Graduating from Howard University's Law School. Brown then moved to Toledo, where he was admitted to the Ohio bar, founded the Frederick Douglass Community Center, and organized the Toledo branch of the National Association for the Advancement of Colored People (NAACP).

In 1909 Nannie Helen Burroughs founded the National Training School for Women and Girls in Lincoln Heights, D.C. She succeeded in organizing this school (the only boarding school for black women north of Richmond) even though opposed by the strong and powerful Black Baptist Minister's Alliance. Joseph Henry Douglass, grandson of Frederick Douglass and the son of Charles Remond

Sadie Tanner Mossell Alexander (1899–), the first black woman to earn a law degree from the University of Pennsylvania (1927), was also the first to be admitted to the Pennsylvania state bar. From *Who's Who in Colored America*.

and Mary Elizabeth Douglass, became a concert violinist. Trained at the New England Conservatory and in Europe, he taught music in the District's public schools before his appointment as violin instructor in Howard University's music department. Invited to perform for Presidents McKinley and Taft, Douglass was the first concert artist of his race to record for the Victor Recording Company. Herman Dreer, winner of the M Street Teacher's Scholarship (1903), graduated magna cum laude from Bowdoin College in 1907. Earning a second degree from Virginia Theological Seminary at Lynchburg in 1914, he enjoyed interaction with young people and pastored a Junior Congregation in St. Louis.

The daughter of James Stanley and Martha Ann (Howard) Dykes, Eva Beatrice Dykes was educated in the District's public schools before entering Howard University, where she edited school publications and graduated summa cum laude in 1914.

She earned a second B.A. degree at Radcliffe College in 1917, graduating magna cum laude. Eva Dykes also earned master's and Ph.D. degrees from Radcliffe College in 1918 and 1921, respectively, before joining the faculty of Dunbar High School.

The family of Mary Lorraine and James Reese Europe moved from Mobile, Alabama, to Washington, D.C., when it became time for the children to enter school. Gifted and talented, the children gained attention as pianists, and while Mary trained to become a music teacher, James became a promoter of jazz. Mary L. Europe returned to the M Street School to teach, and when the school became the new Paul Laurence Dunbar High School (1917), she wrote the music for the school's alma mater. Anna Cooper wrote the lyrics. Renowned as a musician and band leader, James Reese Europe carried American jazz to France during World War I, and triumphantly led the black soldiers up New York City's Fifth Avenue when they returned from "making the world safe for democracy."

West Alexander Hamilton taught in the District's elementary schools (1907–1917), and then combined a business and military career. Hamilton, who rose to the rank of colonel, was a member of the first all-Negro battalion of the D.C. National Guard, which was federalized and then patrolled the Mexican border during the Spanish-American War. During World War I, Hamilton went to France with the 372nd Infantry, led by James E. Walker, another M Street alumnus. John Hayden Johnson, the son of the Reverend Robert Johnson and Mrs. Martha Johnson, graduated from Howard University's Medical School and became a physician in the city of Washington—where he also served on the D.C. Board of Education from 1916 until the 1936–1937 school year, when he was replaced by Col. West A. Hamilton.

Compromise, a play by Willis Richardson, was written at the request of Dr. Alain LeRoy Locke (America's first black Rhodes scholar) and was published in *The New Negro* (1926). During World War I, Richardson had taken correspondence courses in poetry and drama and by 1922 his plays had been produced in Chicago and Washington and on Broadway. Continuing to write while employed as a government clerk and mechanic, Richardson was awarded the Amy Spingarn prize for his plays, *The Broken Banjo* and *Bootblack Lover,* in 1925 and 1926. Jean Toomer was also a contributor to *The*

Former M Street High School cadets on the staff of
the First Negro Separate Battalion, D.C. National
Guard, about 1916–1917. Seated, from left to right:
John E. Smith, James E. Walker, West A. Hamilton,
Albert Ridgley. Standing: Francis J. Ennis (left) and
Enos B. Smith. Courtesy Mr. Paul Sluby, Sr.

New Negro, and was the grandson of P. B. S. Pinch-
back, the acting governor of Louisiana in 1872.
Perhaps best known for his great novel, *Cane,*
sketches of black life published in 1923, Toomer's
personal identification crisis did not prevent him
from writing clearly and with sensitivity about the
black experience in America, as shown in the following stanza of his "Song of the Son":

Major James Walker, commander of the First Negro Separate Battalion, D.C. National Guard. Courtesy Mr. Paul Sluby, Sr.

In time, although the sun is setting on
A song-lit race of slaves, it has not set;
Though late, O soil, it is not too late yet
To catch thy plaintive soul, leaving, soon
    gone,
Leaving, to catch thy plaintive soul soon
    gone.

O Negro slaves, dark purple ripened plums,
Squeezed, and bursting in the pine-wood air,
Passing, before they strip the old tree bare
One plum was saved for me, one seed becomes

An everlasting song, a singing tree,
Caroling softly souls of slavery,
What they were, and what they are to me,
Carolling [sic] softly souls of slavery.

Thus, these students who had been trained and nurtured during the embryonic days of the Preparatory School and M Street High School, and who had come under the influence of Anna Cooper, made a creditable showing that more than justified the public expenditures invested in those early days of common school education for blacks. In addition, the useful service that each rendered the community more than justified the faith of their teachers, administrators, and the public at large.

The M Street High School graduating class of 1907. Its motto was "Intelligence, Morality, Efficiency." Courtesy Mr. William N. Buckner, Jr.

MR. W. L. HOUSTON,
Of this City, who is widely discussed as the next G. M. of G. U. O. of O. F.

M STREET HIGH SCHOOL

Subjoined will be found the Action of the Board of Education.

Relative to the M Street High School Controversy. Obligation Goes With Equality.

After many delays and several postponements, the board of education last night, in special meeting, passed upon the charges against Mrs. Anna J. Cooper, principal of the M Street Colored High School. The board retained Mrs. Cooper in her position as principal, but arraigned her severely for the

Her retention was ascribed to her high intellectual attainments, her excellent reputation, and because she received the support of a large proportion of the colored race in the District. No changes were made in the curriculum of the school. All members of the board were present.

After hearing the report of the committee of the whole board on the case, the following resolution was unanimously adopted:

That all courses of study in the public schools of the District, from the kindergarten to the normal schools, adopted and enforced by the present board of education since its organization, are designed to be, and are, identical for the white and the colored schools.

That it has been the steadfast policy of the board to regard the public school system as a unit for all admin-

That the board declares that the public school system as at present organized and administered offers to every child of school age an equal opportunity to acquire a common school education in a favorable environment and under the best teachers obtainable; that the advanced courses of the high, manual training, and normal schools are open to all who are able to attain such reasonable standards of scholarship as are everywhere recognized as essential to advancement toward the higher learning; that the same text-books are prescribed, and, in the graded schools, furnished without cost to all alike; that no discrimination has ever been made by the board in the cost and completeness of new school buildings in favor of any section of .... work have received like pay, while pupils performing kindred tasks have shared kindred honors.

OBLIGATION WITH EQUALITY.

That the board believes that this equality of participation in the advantages of free education should carry with it an equality of obligation, and that no individual or class of pupils should desire or expect the rewards of scholarly endeavor without fully measuring up to the standards of attainment set for all.

That the board also believes that it is a false and hurtful manifestation of sympathy toward any class of pupils for a teacher or school officer to lower the standards in conformity to which alone pupils can be rightly advanced, and that a regard for the highest interests of the student, whatever his station in life, should withhold from

on the case was lengthy, and ce of four closely written type pages. The trouble at the sch dealt with in every detail. L report on the late Swartzell ca document was aimed to sat parties interested in the case, is the hope of the board that will be harmony at the school future

The principal was arraigned fe ting a text book not prescribed; obeying orders of the directors schools in not sending four d fied pupils back to the eighth from the first-year class, and fe ing pupils in the school by the ion of so-called "sympathetic" ods. While it was proven th tain pupils had been drinking cants in the school, the repo that the case was a single in and that there was no ground general charge that there ha drinking among the pupils.

LACK OF LOYALTY ALLEG

The report continued furt say; "We find that the princi not maintained that proper relation, that strict loyalty director of high schools that prevail in a well-organized syst

The board spoke highly o Cooper's attainments and her character, and concluded wit following:

In view of all the facts and c ions and the very strong desire large proportion of the colored this District to have Mrs. Coo

OOPER
Principal M St. High School

tained as principal, we her retention, with the exp tion, however, that the sta work, the grading of stud the recommendations of stu graduation be conducted st accordance with the policy board of education and the con of this report, and that in her conduct she shall recognize thority of her superior office director of high schools, and o her official conduct in all resp

IV.

The M Street
School Controversy

The most significant fact, perhaps, in Mrs. Cooper's contribution to education in Washington & certainly the most directly promotive of the cause of Higher Education in her own segregated group [was] the courageous revolt she waged against a lower "colored" curriculum for the M Street High School. The proposal was already in Congress to "give the pupils of this school a course of study equal to their abilities." The proposal looked innocent & benevolent, but Mrs. Cooper at the risk of insubordination . . . insisted that her pupils should have equal opportunity to choose whatever subjects might be chosen if they were in one of the other High Schools. While the discussion was at white heat she actually prepared pupils who entered Harvard, Yale, Brown & Oberlin and won for the first time a place in the list of accredited High Schools for the Washington High School for colored children known then as the M St. High School.

ANNA J. COOPER, *n.d.*

A report of the M Street High School controversy from an unidentified Washington, D.C., newspaper. Courtesy Moorland-Spingarn Research Center, Howard University.

BY THE 1904–1905 SCHOOL YEAR, ANNA COOPER had become the focal point and was center stage in a dispute that would become known as the M Street School controversy, and that, in the opinion of the black scholar Horace Mann Bond, brought "the Du Bois–Booker T. Washington controversy over 'industrial education' . . . to a head during Mrs. Cooper's principalship." In *The Negro Scholar and Professional in America,* Bond contends that Anna Cooper's real problems arose when "she aligned herself with the Du Bois group and succeeded in keeping M Street's curriculum that of the standard college preparatory school of the time." Yet it is frequently overlooked that this school did not offer or promote classical education to the exclusion of all else, and that students in growing numbers enrolled in the vocational and industrial courses—for these instructional programs had been initiated by Anna Cooper's predecessor, Francis L. Cardozo, and would continue. There was no disparity in quality among the educational programs offered at the M Street School, where many of the faculty supported Anna Cooper when she insisted upon the highest standards of preparedness and achievement and urged her students to emulate the academic success of their teachers. Perhaps what really incurred the wrath of the espousers of industrial education was the fact that in spite of concerted efforts being made to promulgate the theory and myth of black mental inferiority, and, at considerable cost, institute the preferred educational system deemed appropriate for the assumed limited abilities of blacks, Anna Cooper and her faculty had succeeded in soliciting and obtaining scholarships from their alma maters. Thus it became possible for some M Street students to attend Harvard, Brown, Oberlin, Yale, Amherst, Dartmouth, and Radcliffe. Horace Mann Bond concluded that the results obtained by Anna Cooper and her faculty "are now apparent, M Street [and] later Dunbar [did] contribute to the ranks of Negro scholars in medicine, in law, in engineering, [and] generally in the arts and sciences to a truly extraordinary degree. Yet, despite this impressive record, Anna Cooper was ousted from the principalship of the M Street High School on June 30, 1906, when the District's Board of Education failed to reappoint her.

The allegations, and later formal charges, that would lead to the Board of Education's decision not to retain Mrs. Cooper were reported in two of the city's newspapers, the *Washington Bee* and the *Washington Post*. The entire population of the city was kept informed on the progress of the dispute, as charges and countercharges were brought by each of the opposing factions. A survey of the minutes of the D.C. Board of Education for the school years 1905-1906 and 1906-1907 (some are not extant and others are not available for use) indicate a ground swell of support for Mrs. Cooper and reveal the amount of time spent by the board in trying to mitigate differences. Still, some members of that body, without the benefit of a full investigation, their judgment seemingly based entirely on the hearing the controversy had received in the press, saw their duty to be that of choosing between two employees of the school system: Percy M. Hughes, the white director of Washington high schools, who instigated and then instituted formal charges against Mrs. Cooper, and Anna J. Cooper, the "Colored" female principal of the M Street High School, who refuted them. Since the press was to play a large role in influencing public sentiment and the decision of the Board of Education (a public policy making agent), the full account that appeared in the September 19, 1905, issue of the *Washington Post* is included here, so that the reader may know the importance that this venerable newspaper attached to the matter, the tone of its reporting, and the amount of copy it devoted to the controversy over a protracted period of time. The article began with a bold headline that informed its readers that "Various Factions Are Agreed That It Will Be Better for Teachers and Pupils if Accusations Are Promptly Disposed Of. Contention Began Over Two Years Ago, and Grew Out of a Lecture." Coinciding with the opening of the school

year, the *Post* article then recapitulated the dispute as it had developed over the past months and told its readers that:

The doors of the M Street High School were opened yesterday to its several hundred colored pupils. For eighteen months complaints have abounded as to its management and for almost a year formal charges regarding the methods of discipline and the efficiency of its teaching force have been on file. The high school committee of the board of education took these charges under consideration last December. Witnesses were heard, but the investigation was not concluded. A promise has been made that the case will be reopened soon. The delay, however, has been so great that all parties concerned are crying out against the school board. This outcry is just now strong because a new school year is beginning and teachers as well as pupils are demoralized by the contention.

First of all, perhaps, this contention of which Washington people have heard occasional installments affects the efficiency of Mrs. A. J. Cooper, principal of the M Street School. She came originally from North Carolina, is a graduate of Oberlin, and has been a teacher in the District schools, in one capacity or another, for fully twenty years. She is popular. Those who question her efficiency as a teacher make no war upon her personally. But while they admit that she may be a woman of unusual intelligence, they say her personality is not impressive and that she is incapable as a disciplinarian.

BAD CONDUCT AMONG PUPILS

Incidental to this, there are rumors of disorder and absence of good conduct among the pupils. These include charges of drinking and cigarette smoking. Her critics blame Mrs. Cooper for such occurrences. Her friends assert that when fathers and mothers cannot curb the habits of their children, teachers should not be expected to do so.

The situation, whatever the merits of the respective arguments, is not without features affecting administrative officers of the District schools. One faction, which includes most of the colored preachers of various denominations, is standing by Mrs. Cooper's claim she is being persecuted. They point to the superintendent of public schools, Mr. A. T. Stuart, and the director of high schools, Mr. Percy M.

Hughes, as figuring in efforts to oust her. It is only fair to say, however, that both Mr. Stuart and Mr. Hughes are generally regarded as innocent of such intentions and are striving to elevate the standards of the colored high school. There are influential colored people here who side with Mr. Hughes. They believe he has the correct view and that the meetings of the preachers and of graduates of the colored high school in Mrs. Cooper's behalf have been instituted largely by the jealousy of colored people against any interference by white officials with their educational affairs.

Assertions are heard that the five colored teachers in the M Street High School not in accord with Mrs. Cooper have been favored by the governing authorities. It is said that recently one of these five teachers was promoted with the sanction of the board and that specific charges of insubordination against her were never investigated.

TEACHERS ACCUSED OF IMMORALITY.

The moral fitness of more than one subordinate teacher in the high school to instruct young minds is also involved in the wrangle. Two teachers, said to have been disqualified because of improper conduct, have been removed in a dilatory way within a year or two. Another teacher, now holding his position, is accused of intemperate habits which, it is alleged, he does not conceal from his pupils.

The history of the trouble dates back at least two years. Its beginning was probably in a lecture that William Edward Burghardt Du Bois, professor of economics and history in Atlanta University, delivered before the pupils of the M Street School in the winter of 1902-03. Among other things he called attention to the tendency throughout the country to restrict the curriculum of colored schools. Among the auditors of Prof. Du Bois that evening was Dr. O. W. Atwood, of high character and standing with Washington people. He was particularly interested in the statement about the restrictions of the curriculum and was not disposed to accept it without some investigation as applying to the local schools. The report of the board of education for that year, which came out a few months after Prof. Du Bois' lecture contained the following from Director Hughes.

DIRECTOR HUGHES' REPORT

In the M Street High School, which has barely to date followed the scheme of work laid down for other high schools, certain charges have been made. It was early apparent that the pupils of that school needed a surer grounding in certain lines in order to profitably do the advanced work of the high school. With this in mind modifications were made in the English and Algebra requirements of the first year with very satisfactory results. A further revision and modification of some other lines of work ought to and I believe will result in very desirable improvements.

Acting of his own motion and as a private citizen interested in seeing good educational facilities for colored children, Dr. Atwood instigated inquiries of its members as to the intention of the school board. He was assured by the late Gen. Boynton and other members that there was no intention to restrict the curriculum. It was claimed, nevertheless, that this step was in the direction of depriving District colored pupils of their opportunities for a high school training. Mr. Hughes' comment raised a storm of denunciation and criticism. A page of one annual report by the school board, containing his comments, was torn out and the copies were circulated in mutilated form. This, it has been said, was done on the motion of a colored member of the school board. Be that as it may, unexpurgated copies could be had at the Capitol, for the report was printed by the general government.

ASKED FOR AN INVESTIGATION

Matters dragged along till the winter of 1903, when Dr. Atwood asked for an investigation of the various colored schools in the District including the graded high and industrial schools. He was joined in this request by Dr. C. B. Purvis, John F. Cook [Jr.], Dr. William A. Warfield of Freedmen's Hospital; Aaron Russell, and one or two others. They were in accord with Dr. Atwood, who did not then and does not now take Mr. Hughes to task for the report he made. Dr. Atwood, one of the few colored leaders not vigorously opposing Director Hughes, held that the school official had performed his duty as he saw it and that it would be far wiser to investigate and ascertain whether pupils were receiving the best instruction possible. If there were defects, such as would be reflected in the qualifications of colored youth entering the high school, then these defects in instruction should be corrected at once.

This request led to correspondence. The school board asked for specific charges. James F. Bundy, one of the colored members, was foremost in requiring these. Charges, more or less specific, were then made. One was that drunkenness prevailed among the pupils of the M Street School. The names of two boys, which had come to Dr. Atwood in the course of his inquiries about conditions, were given.

TRACED TO SEVERAL CAUSES.

To this the board, by hand of its late secretary, W. F. Rodrick, replied in a letter dated April 23, 1904. The letter stated that the charge of drunkenness had been investigated by the principal, Mrs. Cooper, who reported that there was no evidence to sustain the charges made. The letter also dealt with charges that pupils entered the M Street School who were not ready for high school work. It said that, in the opinion of the board, deficiencies apparent in the work of many of the pupils entering the M Street School were not due wholly either to a lack of preparation in the ungraded schools or to unskilled teaching in the high school, or to the fact that some pupils attempt high school work who are incompetent to perform it, but to all these causes combined. The letter concluded with assurance that "the matter is receiving careful consideration."

Dr. Atwood started further inquiries as to accusations of drunkenness. One of the two boys, whose name had been given him, proved to be an orphan and of a family with which the doctor was well acquainted. This boy's family said he had been drinking and smoking, the boy went to Dr. Atwood's office, and eventually made a pledge to abstain, which he is said to have faithfully kept. He gave the names of comrades, described how they met in a room not far from the school building, to drink beer, how two of them spent one forenoon, when they were supposed to be at school, consuming 25¢ worth of whiskey, and how they appeared intoxicated before their principal Mrs. Cooper. As described to Dr. Atwood, these lads and six or eight others had what they called "a combine," which was a kind of school drinking club.

AFFIDAVIT TO CONFOUND MRS. COOPER.

This testimony was subsequently put in the form of an affidavit to confound the conclusion of Mrs. Cooper that the charges of drunkenness in her school were unfounded. Mrs. Cooper eventually had opportunity to reply to these and other charges made afterward by Director Hughes. It is claimed on her part that the boy made the affidavit because of his pique at having been suspended for putting talcum powder on the collar of his pal, who occupied a seat in front of him.

The boy making the affidavit is no longer in the M Street School. He would have graduated last year had it not become imperative that he go to work to help support his family. It is asserted that the drinking and cigarette smoking among the pupils of the schools continued there. However, there seems to be no specific cases in the formal charges.

The wrangle had thus far been confined to colored citizens. The high school committee, then consisting of the late Gen. H. V. Boynton, Mr. J. Holdsworth Gordon, and Mr. James F. Bundy, took the matter up a year ago last June, under directions that the colored high school be investigated. Little appears to have been done till the following December—about nine months ago—by which time formal charges against Mrs. Cooper had been preferred by the director of the high schools, Mr. Hughes. The essence of his charges were inefficiency and inability to maintain good order and decorum. The hearing of witnesses began about the middle of December, and the teachers in the M Street High School were questioned.

CEASED INQUIRY DURING SUMMER

The character of this testimony has not been divulged, but apparently was not conclusive. Members of the committee and of the school board went on their summer vacations. A few months ago Gen. Boynton's death occurred. Charles W. Needham, president of George Washington University, was appointed to the vacancy, and has been put on the committee on high schools in Gen. Boynton's place. It is this committee which has recently promised to take up the case and dispose of it as speedily as possible.

Meanwhile the agitation among the colored people is at an acute stage. A few days ago there was a meeting of Methodist preachers. Rev. Daniel Peter Seaton presided, and a pronounced stand was taken in behalf of Mrs. Cooper. Other preachers have also declared in her favor, among them Rev. Francis J. Grimké, pastor of the Fifteenth Street Presby-

The Reverend Walter H. Brooks supported a full disclosure of Anna Cooper's reply to the charges made against her. From *How to Solve the Race Problem*. Courtesy Mr. James J. Lawson.

The Reverend Sterling N. Brown, pastor of the Lincoln Temple Congregational Church, also filled one of the seats allocated to blacks as a trustee of the District's schools (1896–1900). From *How to Solve the Race Problem*. Courtesy Mr. James J. Lawson.

terian Church, one of the most intelligent and at the same time most respected colored men in Washington; Rev. Walter Brooks, of the Nineteenth Street Baptist Church; Rev. W. V. Tunnell, of King Hall Chapel, and Rev. S. N. Brown of Lincoln Memorial. These pastors and others are understood to have seen the reply Mrs. Cooper made to the charges by Director Hughes and by Dr. Atwood's committee. There was also a recent meeting by alumni of the M Street High School, but it is said that out of a thousand and more graduates of that school only twenty-seven responded to the call for a meeting.

REV. FRANCIS GRIMKE'S VIEWS.

"As a rule I do not mix in school affairs," said Rev. Francis Grimké Sunday, when he was asked his views on the M Street School management. "In this case, however, I have made an effort to get at the facts. I have satisfied myself that there is a concerted movement to persecute Mrs. Cooper. She is an estimable woman and has been doing excellent work in our schools. Those who were opposed to her appointment as principal of the M Street

School seem to have continued their opposition."

"I think it outrageous that the High school committee has not settled the controversy one way or another long before this. The cause for the delay is a mystery to me. The only explanation I can give is that thus far they have been unable to find sufficient evidence to sustain the charges, and have been awaiting events. I have known Mrs. Cooper a long time and consider her a woman of great intelligence. The reply that she made to the charges was comprehensive. I wish it were available for publication."

"The best answer to the charges of inefficient teaching in the M Street High School is found in the fact that its graduates under Mrs. Cooper's instruction go into the Northern colleges; like Harvard, Williams, and Cornell. Without conditions, Francis, a recent graduate, entered Harvard not long ago, passing the entrance examinations creditably. In fact, Mrs.

71

Anna Julia Cooper seated with Charlotte Forten Grimké. Standing (left to right) are Ella D. Barrier, the Reverend Francis J. Grimké, and Fannie Shippen Smythe. Courtesy Association for the Study of Afro-American Life and History.

Cooper is able to show that one of the pupils who graduated while deficient, did not graduate with her consent, but with the consent of Director Hughes, to whom she referred the young man's case."

Highly Regarded by Her Pupils.

"Is Mrs. Cooper capable in enforcing discipline?" was asked.

"To that I can answer," said Dr. Grimké, "that she is very affectionately regarded by her pupils, who constitute a large personal following. They say some of her pupils drink and smoke cigarettes, but I fail to see how that, if true, can be altogether charged against her, when the parents of these children are unable to restrain them. How can Mrs. Cooper be expected to enforce rules in that regard which are not enforced at home?"

"Have you any information about the alleged immoral conduct of members of the teaching force in the M Street High School?"

"I know nothing about that," was the answer. "I know that, from all appearance, there is a plot for the undoing of Mrs. Cooper. The five teachers opposed to her have been favored by Supt. Stuart and Director Hughes, and promotions have been given those teachers in preference to the teachers that have been loyal to her. Under such conditions, with all the responsibility of that large school upon her shoulders, the long delay of the school committee is unwarranted. It is a miserable situation."

John F. Cook [Jr.], who has taken an interest in the case, said that early action by the school board was expected. He added that cigarette smoking and all other vices certainly should be discouraged among school children, if such vices existed.

While the public was privileged to a discussion of some aspects of the M Street controversy, there still was not a full disclosure of all of the facts, and it seems that the board was guilty of employing questionable tactics to either frustrate or discourage Anna Cooper's supporters. Representatives of prominent groups complained that they were left to wait in a crowded anteroom at the Franklin School building, while members of the board retreated behind closed doors to deliberate personnel matters not to be entertained in open session. Too, Mrs. Cooper's supporters contended that meetings were deliberately scheduled late in the evening to dis-courage the community's participation, and they complained that the board was discourteous to some, who, in the process of giving testimony, were cut off without warning. At one such meeting, the board attempted to outsit Mrs. Cooper's proponents, rearranging its announced agenda and placing those scheduled to speak on her behalf at the end of the proceedings so that they had to wait until midnight to be heard.

On Thursday evening, September 29, 1905, the Board of Education held a business meeting with the agreement that it would hear all persons who wished to speak on the matter of the M Street controversy. Former Congressman George H. White of North Carolina (the last of the black Reconstruction congressmen), who was among the assembly that had gathered in the library of the Franklin School, waited until past 10 o'clock at night to be permitted to speak. When it was learned that all in the crowded room wished to give testimony in support of Mrs. Cooper, the board continued its business session in the hope that the crowd would adjourn and return home. When it did not, only Congressman White was admitted to give testimony that consumed a half hour. Only then did the board disclose that it had received damaging testimony, which, without proof, "cast some aspersion upon Mrs. Cooper's record in North Carolina." The informant was only identified as a "Mr. Leisenring," about whom nothing is known. If this was a ploy calculated to dissuade support, it did not work. Yet the board failed to tell the congressman about the letter sent from North Carolina by attorney Charles Busbee (cited earlier), which was dispatched eighteen days prior to this meeting and that heartily endorsed Anna Cooper and "sincerely hope[d] she may receive the confidence and support of the educational authorities in Washington." Busbee's response to the board's query had been sent via a circuitous route through the office of former Senator Jeter Connely Pritchard of North Carolina. Here one cannot help but suspect the board of subterfuge and believe it guilty of not conducting a fair and impartial investigation. Anna Cooper had been in the employ of the school system continuously for nearly two decades and had received a merit promotion, and it is absurd to think that her fitness for duty on all counts had not been checked. If, indeed, the board was looking for skeletons in the closet, it found none.

Sept. 11, 1905.

To the Board of Education of the District
of Columbia,

Washington, D.C.

Gentlemen:

I have been requested to state what I know of the character and qualifications of Mrs. Anna J.Cooper, who is, I learn,
Principal of M.Street High School. Her mother was my nurse,
and she was named for my mother.

As a girl she was studious and industrious and was always
imbued by unusually high principles. Her mother was an unlettered slave and free woman, but her daughter's respect and devotion never failed. She took a high stand in the schools and
became a successful teacher, was a wife of a colored clergyman
of the Episcopal Church, whose standing equalled that of any
man of his race, who had the respect and regard of the community. Her married life was short, and not very long after her
death Mrs. Cooper removed to Washington. Her character has been
always high, and she has in a very rare degree the confidence
and respect of the white people of Raleigh. She has always had
the reputation of being a successful teacher, my information
upon this head being necessarily by reputation. In correspondence and exhibits the proof of integrity and intelligence, and
I sincerely hope she may receive the confidence and support of
the educational authorities of Washington.

Yours truly,

The letter from attorney Charles Busbee of Raleigh to the D. C. Board of Education, September 11, 1905. Courtesy Moorland-Spingarn Research Center, Howard University.

74

While the Board of Education stalwartly held that it had no personal objection to Anna Cooper, a distasteful rumor with moral overtones had begun to circulate that was calculated to embarrass her and raise questions about fitness for duty. Her name began to be linked romantically with that of John L. Love, Jr., her foster son, who was also a teacher of English and history at the M Street High School. Anna Cooper never dignified the innuendoes with a response and they never found their way into the official record, yet the rumors persisted and gained currency among some. The instigator must have believed that the rumors would either silence Anna Cooper or drive her from her post, but as she had been known to do in other times when faced with a vexing situation, she kept her own counsel.

Charles Busbee had described Anna Cooper as "industrious and [one who] was always imbued by unusually high principles. . . . Her character [had] been always high, and she [had] in a very rare degree the confidence and respect of the white people of Raleigh." Further, Busbee informed the board that Anna Cooper "always had the reputation of being a successful teacher." Although not made public until two weeks after its receipt, on September 15, 1905, a communiqué endorsing Mrs. Cooper had also been sent to the board by the Principal's Association. Describing her as one who "in her whole life and character [presents] all that stands for the highest and purest womanhood," the association informed the board that Anna Cooper "inspires her pupils with faith and confidence in their own untried powers, and demonstrates that they possess capabilities common to all children." They concluded with the thought that "These young men and women with evolved, enlightened minds and hearts will enrich and honor the world by better and higher service." Representing the M Street Alumni Association, M. Grant Lucas, its president, expressed confidence and faith in the M Street School and urged the board to demonstrate "characteristic wisdom, justice, judgment, and [sense] of equity," and hoped that in their deliberation "the interests of the M Street High School . . . be amply protected, and defended." Further, the Alumni Association "RESOLVED, That we do hereby reaffirm our confidence in the present administration of the M Street High School and that we do most respectfully commend to the board of education the faithful, devoted, and painstaking principal, Mrs. A. J. Cooper." When Congressman White had met with the board, he had left them with the warning that "The colored people of Washington thoroughly resent the persecution of [Mrs. Cooper] in this matter, and if the board should decide against her they [the District's black residents] are willing to appeal to a higher tribunal."

Seated in 1905, Dr. Charles W. Needham was the only member of the Board of Education to speak publicly about the M Street controversy, which now caused the community to question the board's ability to give clear and dispassionate direction to the schools. He did not believe that the allegation of widespread drunkenness among the pupils of M Street had been sustained, and if the situation was as it seemed then it hardly warranted disciplinary action against the principal for failing to report what he believed were isolated instances of student indiscretion. Further, he thought too much had been made of the allegation concerning the principal's failure to report such indiscretions, and that the "controversy with Mr. Hughes about the scholarship of the pupils [was not] sufficient [to] warrant the removal of Mrs. Cooper." In his view, "the matter should not have been allowed to race along so long, and . . . it should be finally settled as soon as possible," in an effort to restore public confidence. On Monday night, October 30, 1905, the Board of Education convened "in special meeting, passed upon the charges against Mrs. Anna J. Cooper."

According to the *Washington Post*, the board's report was a "document aimed to satisfy all parties interested in the case," and while it concluded with "the hope . . . that there [would] be harmony at the schools in the future, " the board formally announced Mrs. Cooper's retention, and then "arraigned her severely for the loose methods which [had] prevailed at the school under her administration." This lackluster vote of confidence was simply a face-saving device that did not reaffirm the board's trust in Anna Cooper, nor did it give her the exoneration she had fought to achieve. Too, the board clearly disregarded its organizational structure, decreed by Congress, and negated the duties and authority of the colored assistant superintendent, in deference to the white director of high schools. The offense for which Anna Cooper was really charged was that of being disloyal to her white superior, Percy Hughes. Thus the board established the "pecking order" and served notice that the management of the M Street School and its academic program would be closely monitored. Departing from its lengthy report and policy statement, the board went on to say:

> We recommend [Mrs. Cooper's] retention, with the express direction, however, that the standards of work, the grading of students for graduation be conducted strictly in accordance with the policy of the board of education; and . . . that in her official conduct she shall recognize the authority of her superior officer, the director of high schools, and conform her official conduct in all respects to rules of the board.

Further, the investigating committee of the Board of Education recommended that

> a strict observance be made of the work in the M Street High School, with a view of maintaining the standards and work herein set forth; preventing any improper conduct on the part of teachers tending to create disaffection, securing a strict observance of that discipline, official recognition of superior officials, and conduct essential to the best and highest educational results in this important school, and that stated reports of these observations be made to the board for proper action thereas.

Unfortunately, however, this was not to be the end of the M Street High School controversy.

Without a modicum of self-determination, Washington, D.C., in 1905 was a city of political patronage and federal appointments. Then, as now, the Board of Education was a vehicle to the political arena where—like so much chaff separated from the wheat—the losers were separated from the victors. Those who wished to gain power and have a voice in the decision-making process would first have to curry favor with those who were the power brokers and held tight to the reins. Yet in earlier years, Presidents, beginning with John Adams, had shown a willingness to have the citizens of the District of Columbia administer their municipal affairs. In the early decades of the twentieth century, however, Congress was determined to exercise its rights of "exclusive jurisdiction" over the territory, even though, in the case *Cumming v. Richmond County Board of Education* the United States Supreme Court ruled that:

> While the benefits and burdens of public taxation must be shared by citizens without discrimination against any class on account of their race, *the education of the people in schools maintained by state taxation is a matter belonging to the respective states, and any interference on the part of the Federal authority with the management of such schools cannot be justified except in the case of a clear and unmistakable disregard of rights secured by the supreme law of the land.* (Italics added.)

Since, in 1906, the comptroller of the United States Treasury would uphold the Board of Education's decision to dismiss Anna Cooper from the principalship of the M Street High School on the assumption of an implied authority, here too we may assume that the Supreme Court also implied that the intervention of Congress in the management of the District's public schools was inappropriate and improper conduct.

The transition from the era of Frederick Douglass to that of Booker T. Washington seemed complete, and the prophetic warnings of Douglass, and later W. E. B. Du Bois, had gone unheeded—for Douglass had said:

> Power concedes nothing without a demand. It never did and it never will. Find out just what any people will quietly submit to and you have found out the exact measure of injustice and wrong which will be imposed upon them, and these will continue till they are resisted with either words or blows, or with both. The limits of tyrants are prescribed by the endurance of those whom they oppress.

In 1903, in *The Souls of Black Folk*, Du Bois had warned that the problem of the twentieth century would be the problem of the color line.

In the closing months of 1904, W. Calvin Chase, the controversial editor-publisher of the *Washington Bee* had begun, through a series of editorials, warning Washington's black community of "DANGER AHEAD." Congress, he said, was seeking ways of withdrawing its annual appropriation to Howard University, and Congressman Foster of Vermont had introduced a bill that, if passed, would place all of the city's black institutions under the administrative authority of the white superintendent. Chase reminded blacks that they were losing their political influence along with seats on certain boards and commissions, where they had

William Calvin Chase, editor-publisher of the *Washington Bee*. From *Shadow and Light*.

once had a voice. He admonished them for fussing among themselves "till at last they had lost all they had gained," for blacks were no longer appointed to the Fire Commission, the Police Commission, and they had also lost control of their schools and could "hardly dictate the appointment of teachers to be appointed in their schools."

Some months before the Board of Education had formally heard complaints of the director of high schools against Anna Cooper, Percy Hughes had circumvented the office of H. P. Montgomery, the black assistant superintendent, and made a recommendation to the board that, if accepted, would have ordered the restructuring of the M Street School's curriculum. With the business courses then being taught at the new Armstrong High School, and the development of a manual and technical program underway, Hughes proposed that vocational and trade classes also be introduced in the M Street School, where through "training in the use of tools and the ability to handle them . . . they [would] be able to develop a wholesome respect for the dignity of labor and for the man who works." Clearly, Anna Cooper and the classical program at the M Street School were a "troublesome presence,"

and Hughes's disdain for both could not have been more obvious.

In February 1905 Dr. George H. Richardson, a former member of the Board of Education had addressed a meeting of the Bethel Literary and Historical Society, and he denounced certain pernicious actions of the board and warned that "jimcrowism runs rampant and rears its hideous hulk in our educational system." Such jimcrowism, he said,

widens the breach and heightens and solidifies the barriers which stand between us and the rest of the community: which crystalizes the most malignant types of prejudice, prescribes the field in which genius shall operate, and denies to us the opportunities and results of competition on account of color.

The unsettled controversy languished while the graduating exercises for the Washington Normal School No. 2, the Armstrong Business and Manual Training School, and the M Street High School were held in the convention hall on June 16, 1905. According to the *Washington Post,* the hall could scarcely hold all who wished to attend the ceremony, but those gathered there were in a festive mood and for this occasion differences were put aside. The gaily decorated hall banked with hundreds of flowers from well wishers, with the added attraction of hundreds of electric lights, made a pleasing scene as the United States Marine Band played a program of appropriate musical selections. The principals to the controversy were all on stage, while the audience anxiously awaited the arrival of the evening's orator, Dr. Booker T. Washington (Dartmouth College had awarded him an honorary doctorate in 1901). It has been said of Dr. Washington that he was a great showman, and instinctively knew how to "work" a crowd and electrify an audience, and as one considers the address that was not wasted on Congress, the District Commissioners, or the Board of Education, one gets the feeling that he indeed was equal to the task of presenting the "lesson of the hour." Following a brief introduction, the speaker of the evening rose and was greeted by cheers, thunderous applause, and the waving of handkerchiefs by the ladies in the audience (a customary greeting of affection in that day). They had come to greet and hear Washington, and he did not disappoint them. As the enthusiastic crowd quieted, Dr. Washington, "bowed his acknowledgment" and began. So rarely do we come

The Aeolian Mandolin and Guitar Club (1900) and the M Street High School orchestra (1904)—evidences of the social and cultural growth the school fostered. Courtesy Mrs. Beatrice Christopher.

Booker T. Washington. His educational philosophy significantly influenced the development of Washington's public schools. From *One Hundred Distinguished Leaders*.

upon an address by a national figure that has been prepared for the residents of the District of Columbia alone that some excerpts of the prepared remarks, though lengthy, follow:

The influence of the colored man who resides in the District of Columbia is far from local as far as concerns our race; it is national; is, in the words of another, continental, almost imperial! Perhaps it is true that there cannot be found any group of ninety thousand colored people anywhere in the world whose general average of intelligence is so high as is true of those to be found here. Nowhere else in this, or any other country, can you find a group equal in size whose educational advantages in the way of physical equipment and personnel of teachers are so complete as just here. Nowhere else, in or out of this country, is there a city where so much is expended, as a whole, per capita, on a similar group of black people. If you would realize more fully what this statement involves, let me say: For the

school year 1900-1901 there was expended for the tuition alone of your 20,000 children, $275,000, or a per capita of $13.73. This was $60,000 more than was expended for the tuition of the 287,000 negro children in one of our Southern States, where the per capita was less than $1. Thirteen dollars versus $1. One dollar yonder; $13. here!

Let not this comparison suggest that I would take one single dollar from you. Rather would I add to what you receive, for few commodities are so worthless as *cheap education*. Practically the same relative difference exists between the white communities covering the same territory. My one thought is to impress upon parents, students, teachers—all, that in proportion as you have received you will be expected to give—not alone to this community—for, let me repeat, the money expended here has a national significance and a national influence. Your unique and almost unequaled school facilities bring to you as parents, as students, as teachers a rare opportunity; bring to you at the same time a grave and far-reaching responsibility. In actual training, in high and useful service to the world, the students here must be a living demonstration of the difference between your educational equipment and that of the "black belt" to the south.

Because of your superior opportunity and duty to the race, I believe that in the home, the schoolroom, in the work of those who here to-day graduate, that you will sink all personal, local, and selfish differences, if such exist, and rise above all petty details and temporary considerations, and occupy more securely the high commanding positions which your location and surroundings justify.

You teach here not alone the 20,000 black children of this city, but set the example for and influence the training of the 3,000,000 black children of the nation. Your strong position in equipment, in teaching force, makes it literally possible for you to put into practice the command of the Teacher of Teachers—when he said "Go ye therefore and teach all nations, teaching them to observe all things whatsoever—I have commanded you!"

Having admonished the District's black community to heal itself from within, Washington very deftly dealt with the local controversy, and in the hearing of all of the parties to the dispute. Later in the address, Washington gave high praise to Roscoe

A cooking class at Miss Davis's School, Thompson Plantation near Tuskegee, Alabama, about 1902. Courtesy Library of Congress, Frances Benjamin Johnston Collection.

A trades' class in shoemaking, Tuskegee Institute, Alabama, about 1902. Courtesy Library of Congress, Frances Benjamin Johnston Collection.

Conkling Bruce, a graduate of the M Street School, Harvard University, and the head of his department of academic curriculum at Tuskegee Institute. It was no secret that Bruce (the son of B. K. Bruce, the first black United States Senator to serve a full six-year term) wished to leave Tuskegee, where he found Washington's educational philosophy perplexing and the students receiving too little academic training to make them functional either in the trades or as teachers. Still, there were those who wondered if Washington's praise of Bruce was not tantamount to his endorsement of him to replace Anna Cooper as the M Street High School's principal. The speechmaking and conferring of diplomas were followed by the benediction, and the crowd left Convention Hall wildly cheering as the Marine Band played the Star Spangled Banner.

By September 1905, community support for Anna Cooper had increased while the good feeling evident at the June commencement exercises had dissipated. The dialogue that black board members James Bundy and Bettie Coxe Francis had initiated in an effort to resolve the controversy proved futile. While W. Calvin Chase complained that the city had become a "dumping ground for broken down politicians and political tricksters," and agitated for Home Rule, the board was not dissuaded from its pending course of action and was nearing the date that it would issue Mrs. Cooper a strong public reprimand. As Chase exclaimed "Enough is enough!" the board continued to be evasive and indecisive with impunity.

The congressional *Organic Act of 1906* afforded the Board of Education power both to dismiss and to appoint new teachers, as well as the authority to continue or reappoint former teachers in the system without examinations. On the strength of this new authority with broad discretionary powers, in October 1906 the District's Board of Education chose not to rehire Anna Cooper as the principal of the beleaguered high school. As noted earlier, this decision of the board, made upon the recommendation of the school superintendent (as provided by Congress), was upheld by the comptroller of the United States Treasury. While such authority to dismiss was not explicit, it was implied.

Anna Cooper had felt that William Estabrook Chancellor, who succeeded A. T. Stuart as school superintendent, had joined the conspiracy against her, yet by law he had to support the Board of

Roscoe Conkling Bruce, a graduate of M Street High School and Harvard University (1902). From *How to Solve the Race Problem* Courtesy Mr. James J. Lawson.

Education that hired him. Following his report to the board in October 1906, Chancellor was off on an official month-long visit to the southern states, and especially to Tuskegee Institute, to acquaint himself "with the race question." Contrary to what the District's black citizens had supposed, William Tecumseh Sherman Jackson, a graduate of Amherst College and Catholic University, and a teacher of mathematics at the M Street High School, was appointed to succeed Anna Cooper as the new principal. Bruce, however, was not overlooked and was appointed to the position of supervising principal of the Colored Division on September 14, 1906.

From the beginning, Anna Cooper's tenure as principal of the M Street High School was marked by turmoil and controversy, for she had refused to compromise her convictions and principles in exchange for expediency and the approval of her superiors.

Leaving the M Street High School and the city of Washington after the board had publicly announced its decision not to rehire her, Anna Cooper went to Lincoln Institute in Jefferson City, Missouri, where she was appointed teacher of lan-

Mrs. Anna J.
⇒ Cooper ⇐

Prof. of Latin and Greek in Lincoln University, a scholar, lecturer and author, who has traveled extensively in the United States and Europe

Will Deliver a Lecture at the

1st Baptist Church
In this City, (Guthrie)

Jan. 1, 1909, at 7:30 P. M.
Under the auspices of the Excelsior Library

Her Subject: "Ideals and Reals or What do You Want?"

As to her ability as a speaker, Mr. Gitterman, President of the Education Association at Washington, says: "For the past six years I have known Mrs. Anna J. Cooper, M. A., and both professionally and personally she has my hightest regards. Her high principles and charm of address make her an inspiring lecturer and leader. It is always a pleasure to any audience to hear one who possesses that fortunate combination of learning and great modesty and lack of self conscious. ness which we term culture. I consider Mrs. Cooper a model in this as in many other respects. **A. S. Gitterman,** Pres. of Public Education Association, Washington

Senator Blair, Says: "Her superior ability as a writer and lecturer are well known, and her capacity and attainments qualify her for almost any form of literary labor.

⇒ THE ASBURY JOURNAL OF SEPT. SAYS ⇐

The Asbury Journal says of Mrs. Cooper, who addressed a Conference at Asbury Park Sept 10, 1902. "Mrs. Anna J. Cooper principal of a Washington D. C. High School is a remarkable woman. She has a vivid personality an enthusiasm that is contagious a power of expression that held her audience spellbound and a magnetism that at once communicated itself to her hearers.

She was applauded as no other speaker has been applauded during the conference. Mrs. Cooper's wide range of ideas, her wonderful command of language, and her brilliancy of thought would would make her fortune on the lecture platform."

The Excelsior Club has invited the G. A. R. to join them in this celebration of January 1st.

So let all our citizens turn out to do honor to one of our greatest women and our Old Soldiers.

ADMISSION 25¢

PROCEEDS FOR EXCELSIOR CLUB LIBRARY.

TICKETS ON SALE AT: Library; New State Drug Store; Mrs. Nicholson Restaurant.

guages. Still, she had not abandoned the struggle, and according to the minutes of the January 16, 1907, meeting of the Board of Education, she instituted a claim for reinstatement to her position and back salary. The board records only note that "On motion the same was referred to the attorney for the Board."

Miles away from the scene of the struggle, and without bitterness or rancor, Anna Cooper wrote of this epoch of her life, and her thoughts are included in the published *Class Letters '84 Oberlin College* (1909). As the class historian responsible for soliciting letters from the members of her graduating class, she also included her letter to acquaint former classmates with the important events in her life since last they communicated:

Lincoln Institute,

Jefferson City, Mo., May 1, 1909

. . . My last letter was written from Washington, D.C., where I taught in high school work twenty years. During five of this time I served as principal of the M street high school, the largest school of secondary education for colored youth in the country. In this work I had the satisfaction of believing that I was able to broaden the outlook on life for some and to encourage the effort for higher development. I can only say that my labor in this direction met with appreciative recognition from the people whom I served. But they are lowly, and for the most part, *voiceless.* The dominant forces of our country are not yet tolerant of the higher steps for colored youth; so that while our course of study was for the time being saved, *my head was lost in the fray,* and I moved west. Here I am teaching Latin and Greek eight hours to the day, with police service, rhetorical and commencement dramatics thrown in now and then for "duty work." But if the industrializing wave that threatens, reaches us here too, it is likely to be another case of "Move along, Joe!"

All of which, according to my way of thinking, is unfortunate and unfair. No people can progress, without the vivifying touch of ideas and ideals. The very policy of segregation renders all the more necessary a leadership that has been on the Mount. If any group or class

William Tecumseh Sherman Jackson, the first black to earn an M.A. degree from Amherst (1897), taught math at the M Street School (1892–1906) until appointed principal to succeed Anna J. Cooper. Courtesy Association for the Study of Afro-American Life and History.

cannot be allowed living contact through seeing, hearing, feeling the best of life in their day and generation, there is no compensation morally or socially except to let them find their thrills through the inspiration of the broadest education and generously equipped schools.

. . . As for me, I stand on the double foundation stone of our Alma Mater—*"Labor and Learning"*—unrestricted and harmonious, without clash and without cliques,—simply, for my people and for all people a man's chance to earn a living not dissociated from man's first right and highest prerogative,—to live.

Faithfully yours,

ANNA J. COOPER.

Notice of a lecture by Anna J. Cooper, 1909. Courtesy Moorland-Spingarn Research Center, Howard University, Anna J. Cooper Manuscript Collection.

V.

The Black Woman's Club Movement

"Where there is no vision, the people perish."
                                    Proverbs 29:18

A nation's greatness is not dependent upon the things it makes and uses. Things without thots [sic] are mere vulgarities. America can boast her expanse of territory, her gilded domes, her paving stones of silver dollars; but the question of deepest moment in this nation today is its span of the circle of brotherhood, the moral stature of its men and its women, the elevation at which it receives its "vision" into the firmament of eternal truth.

> ANNA J. COOPER
> September 5, 1902
> "The Ethics of the Negro Question"

Dr. Anna Julia Cooper, a portrait by Frank J. Dillon, 1938. Courtesy Mrs. Regia Bronson and Miss Regina Smith.

THE DECADE OF THE 1890S WAS AN IMPORTANT period in the development of black intellectual and political thought, and these years were especially important ones for black women in America, who during this era founded organizations that would gain national importance. While often obscured in the official histories of these organizations, Anna Cooper was in the vanguard and believed that the struggle for human rights might be waged more effectively with the perspective and balance that intelligent black women would bring to the fray.

Beginning in the mid-1890s, the emergence of a national Black Woman's Club Movement in America would be the culmination of more than a half-century of significant participation in anti-slavery societies, abolitionist groups, and women's rights organizations. In the earlier decades of the nineteenth century only one voice had articulated black women's needs, hopes, and aspirations—their own!—and so it would continue to be as the century drew to a close.

When considering the struggles and accomplishments of black women during the antebellum period, most often we hear the names of two folk heroines, Sojourner Truth and Harriet Tubman. Yet the treatment afforded each is often incomplete and severely limited, and set apart from other women of their day. Sojourner Truth is most often depicted as an itinerant preacher, while Harriet Tubman is pictured as the unlettered conductor of the Underground Railroad, who also suffered spells of somnolence. But each uniquely advanced the women's rights movement in America, where women, black and white, were equally as adamant in their belief that their destiny—as women—was intrinsically and inescapably tied to the fate of American

Fannie Barrier Williams, an articulate black clubwoman, was a delegate to the Congress of Negro Women at the 1895 Cotton Exposition in Atlanta. Courtesy Moorland-Spingarn Research Center, Howard University.

blacks. It was reasoned that through cooperative efforts designed to achieve human rights and suffrage for blacks, women might then advance their own cause.

The impetus for convening the Seneca Falls Convention of 1848 had grown from the continuing dissatisfaction and agitation of women, who eight years earlier had been denied seats as American delegates to the World Anti-Slavery Convention in London. Led by Elizabeth Cady Stanton and Susan B. Anthony, who thought it illogical that such a body as the World Anti-Slavery Convention could deny them seats as delegates solely on the basis of their sex, the Seneca Falls Convention had as its objectives to organize women nationally and to place the issue of the inequitable treatment of women on the national agenda. To dramatize and protest the plight of women, the black abolitionist Charles Remond had refused his delegate seat at the anti-slavery convention. The convention managers, however, did not relax the rules and women were required to join with visitors in the gallery throughout the ten days of deliberation.

Later, Anna Cooper would become an effective protagonist for equal opportunities for women, at a time when black women had begun to view pragmatically the feminist and suffrage movement as a tactically viable tool for gaining full civil rights for blacks. Along with Anna Cooper, women like Harriet Tubman, Fannie Barrier Williams, Ida B. Wells, Frances E. W. Harper, and Josephine St. Pierre Ruffin were counted on to mount the lecture platforms as advocates of the movement. Whether charismatic figures or articulate spokeswomen, they drew large crowds and the attention of the press.

The active role that black women played in the women's rights movement is all the more noteworthy when it is realized that because of their race, they could not become members of the very organizations whose causes they espoused. White feminists enlisted the support of black women and benefited from their participation, but many believed that black women should only organize among themselves. When admitted into white organizations at all, black women were most often enrolled in separate "Colored" units that were subordinate to the will and control of the white parent body. Yet there were some suffragettes, like Frances Dana Gage, who, when speaking of Sojourner Truth, freely admitted the important role this black woman played in the early days of their fledgling movement. According to Gage, Sojourner Truth

amid roars of applause . . . leaving more than one of us with streaming eyes, and hearts beating with gratitude . . . had taken us up in her strong arms and carried us safely over the slough of difficulty, turning the whole tide in our favor.

Starting in Colonial America, the attitude and policy of racial separateness continued into the nineteenth and twentieth centuries, and in *Century of Struggle* Eleanor Flexner noted that this attitude and policy "was in line with the practices of other groups." Indeed, Anna Cooper and her peers later found that such attitudes would persist in the operations of the Women's Christian Temperance Union (WCTU), and still later, would be adopted by the Board of Managers of the Young Women's Christian Association (YWCA). Concerned that such attitudes could be tolerated by the white women's groups, black women in the late 1800s began to withdraw their support and to organize nationally among themselves.

In 1886 Anna Cooper had written an essay, "Womanhood a Vital Element in the Regeneration of a Race"; it was a paper she would deliver many times before both black and white audiences. With fervor she proclaimed, "Only the BLACK WOMAN can say 'when and where I enter, in the quiet, undisputed dignity of my womanhood, without violence and without suing or special patronage, then and there the whole Negro race enters with me.' " Evenhanded in her ire, Cooper chided white women for presuming to speak for black women; black men were rebuked for failing to support the efforts of black women to improve themselves, and for adopting the chauvinistic attitudes of white males. She decried the notion that black women should deport themselves as pretty, empty-headed sex objects, and urged that the woman's side of truth be heard. Anna Cooper "offered a distinctively feminist argument and asserted . . . that the needs of black women were different and distinct [even] from those of black men." Her plea was for a viable partnership that would result in the blending of the voices of black men and women in the struggle for human rights.

The only man who would brave the disapprobation of his male peers in attendance at the Seneca Fall Convention, Frederick Douglass had asserted as early as 1848 that "RIGHT IS OF NO SEX!" But later, Douglass too would be chided for his failure to support the inclusion of women's rights in the language of the Fifteenth Amendment. A political pragmatist, Douglass had conceded that while voting rights for women were "desirable," these rights were "vital" for black males. Although Douglass would later be charged with abandoning the women's movement by some of his staunchest women allies, he stood his ground, noting that he had always advocated women's right to vote. But, said Douglass,

> it will be seen that the present claim for the negro is one of the most "urgent" necessity. The assertion of the right of women to vote meets nothing but ridicule; there is no deep seated malignity in the hearts of the people against her; but name the right of the negro to vote, all hell is turned loose and the Ku-Klux and Regulators hunt and slay the offending black man.

While Elizabeth Cady Stanton and Susan B. Anthony delivered stinging charges against Douglass,

Fannie Jackson Coppin, an honors graduate from Oberlin College, developed the educational programs at the Institute for Colored Youth in Philadelphia. From *Evidences of Progress Among Colored People.*

the Fifteenth Amendment to the Constitution was passed, and did promulgate sex as a criterion for suffrage. It would be some time before the breach between the old comrades would heal.

In 1893 Anna Cooper, Fannie Barrier Williams, and Fannie Jackson Coppin were invited to address a special meeting of the Women's Congress in Chicago. This international gathering of women was held to coincide with the World's Columbian Exposition, in order to assure a large audience and wide coverage in the press. The theme of this special session, designed to give black women a hearing, was "The Intellectual Progress of Colored Women of the United States Since Emancipation." Anna Cooper's thesis was one that she frequently addressed: "The Needs and the Status of Black Women." Consistent in her charge that all women, but especially black women, had been neglected and allowed to languish in virtual ignorance, she conceded that while "the majority of our women are not heroines," she did not know "that a majority of any race of women are heroines." Yet she knew that the black woman in the eyes of the highest tribunal in America [was] deemed no more than a chattel, an irresponsible thing, a dull block, to be drawn hither or thither at the volition of an owner, still the Afro-American woman maintained ideals of womanhood unshamed by any ever conceived.

Continuing, Cooper observed that

Resting or fermenting in untutored minds, such ideals could not claim a hearing at the bar of the nation. The white woman could at least plead for her own emancipation; the black woman, doubly enslaved, could but suffer and struggle in silence.

Since she herself had been a slave in America's southland, Anna Cooper claimed the right to speak for "the colored woman of the South," and she admonished her listeners that it was there in the South that millions of this country's blacks had "watered the soil with blood and tears"; too, it was in the South that black women had made their "characteristic history," and there their destiny was evolving. She crystalized the sentiments of her "constituency," and delivered it as a message to this congress of women. Nearing the end of her address Anna Cooper declared that

We take our stand on the solidarity of humanity, the oneness of life, and the unnaturalness and injustice of all special favoritisms, whether of sex, race, country, or condition. . . . Least of all can woman's cause afford to decry the weak. We want, then, as toilers for the universal triumph of justice and human rights, to go to our homes from this Congress, demanding an entrance not through a gateway for ourselves, our race, our sex, or our sect, but a grand highway of humanity. The colored woman feels that woman's cause is one and universal; . . . is sacred and inviolable; [and] not till race, color, sex, and condition are seen as the accidents, and not the substance of life; not till the universal title of humanity of life, liberty, and the pursuit of happiness is conceded to be inalienable to all; not till then is woman's lesson taught and woman's cause won—not the white woman's, not the black woman's, not the red woman's, but the cause of every man and of every woman who has writhed silently under a mighty wrong. Woman's wrongs are thus indissolubly linked with all undefended woe, and the acquirement of

Frederick Douglass (1817?-1895). Courtesy Mrs. Ann Weaver Teabeau.

her "rights" will mean the final triumph of all right over might, the supremacy of the moral forces of reason, and justice, and love in the government of the nations of earth.

While invited as a platform guest but not scheduled to speak, Frederick Douglass was so moved by the proceedings of this special meeting, that he rose to make a few impromptu remarks. Filled with emotion, he concluded with the following sentiments:

I have heard tonight what I hardly expected to hear. I have heard refined, educated colored ladies addressing—and addressing successfully—one of the most intelligent white audiences that I ever looked upon. It is the new thing under the sun, and my heart is too full to speak; my mind is too much illuminated with hope and expectation for the race in seeing this sign.

Fifty years ago and more I was alone in the wilderness, telling my story of the wrongs of slavery, and imploring the justice, the humanity, the sympathy, the patriotism, and every other good quality of the American heart to do away with slavery. . . . you can easily see that when I hear such speeches as I have heard this evening from our women—*our women*—I feel a sense of gratitude to Almighty God that I have lived to see what I now see.

Anna Cooper's views were known beyond the audiences she encountered when lecturing, for in 1892 she had privately published a collection of her essays under the title *A Voice from the South: By a Black Woman of the South.* Affectionately, she inscribed the volume to Bishop Benjamin William Arnett "with sincere esteem for his unselfish espousal of the cause of the Black Woman and of every human interest that lacks a Voice and needs a Defender . . . the primary utterance of [her] heart and pen." Even before then, through the pages of *The Southland,* a periodical that Cooper described as "the first Negro magazine in the United States," her views had gained currency. Founded in 1890, *The Southland* had attracted a large readership, and its popularity was attributed to the reputation of its founder, the Reverend Joseph C. Price, president of North Carolina's Livingstone College, who was often favorably compared as an orator with Frederick Douglass for clarity of thought, wit, and wisdom.

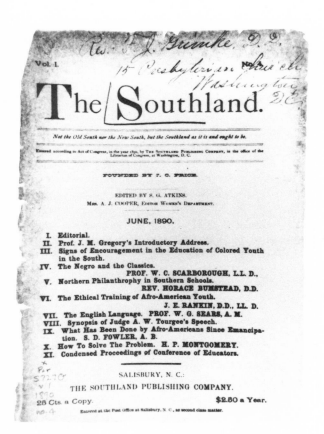

Anna Cooper was Women's Editor of *The Southland* in 1890. Courtesy Duke University Library.

The magazine was to become an important and influential vehicle, which would keep southern blacks informed about the issues and of progress that was being made around the country.

Anna Cooper was extended an invitation by the Howard University alumni to read her essay "The Higher Education of Women" before the meeting of the American Conference of Educators, held on March 25-27, 1890. Black women were a minority (within a minority) among the membership of the conference's board of managers, where they were represented by Dr. Lucy Ellen Moten, principal of the District's Normal School No. 2 (Colored), and Julia Waugh Mason (later Mrs. Layton), a teacher at the M Street High School. Cooper's was one of the few voices of black women heard by the conferees, when she exclaimed:

As individuals, we are constantly and inevitably, whether we are conscious of it or not, giving out our real selves into our several little worlds, inexorably adding our own true ray to the flood of starlight, quite independently of our professions and our masquerading; and so

Lucy Ellen Moten, a professional educator. Under her tutelage, Normal School No. 2 prepared well-trained teachers. Photograph by Addison Scurlock. Courtesy District of Columbia Public Schools.

in the world of thought, the influence of thinking woman far transcends her feeble declamation and may seem at times even opposed to it. . . .

There is, then, a real and special influence of woman. An influence subtle and often involuntary, an influence so intimately interwoven in, so intricately interpenetrated by the masculine influence of the time that it is often difficult to extricate the delicate meshes and analyze and identify the closely clinging fibers. And yet, without this influence—so long as woman sat with bandaged eyes and manacled hands, fast bound in the clamps of ignorance and inaction—the world of thought moved in its orbit like the revolutions of the moon, with one face (the man's face) always out. . . .

All I claim is that there is a feminine as well as a masculine side to truth; that these are related not as inferior and superior, not as better and worse, not as weaker and stronger, but as complements—complements in one necessary and symmetric whole. That as the man is more noble in reason, so the woman is more quick in sympathy. That as he is indefatigable in pursuit of abstract truth, so is she in caring for the interests by the way—striving tenderly and lovingly that not one of the least of these "little ones" should perish. That while we not infrequently see women who reason, we say, with the coolness and precision of a man, and men as considerate of helplessness as a woman, still there is a general consensus of mankind that the one trait is essentially masculine and the other as peculiarly feminine. That both are needed to be worked into the training of children, in order that our boys may supplement their virility by tenderness and sensibility, and our girls may round out their gentleness by strength and self-reliance. That, as both are . . . necessary in giving symmetry to the individual, so a nation or a race will degenerate into mere emotionalism on the one hand, or bullyism on the other, if dominated by either exclusively; lastly, and most emphatically, that the feminine factor can have its proper effect only through woman's development and education so that she may fitly and intelligently stamp her force on the forces of her day, and add her modicum to the riches of the world's thought. . . .

It is true that the higher education for women—in fact, the highest that the world has ever witnessed—belongs to the past; but we must remember that it was possible, down to the middle of our own century, only to a select few; and that the fashions and traditions of the time were before that all against it. . . . That the average woman retired before . . . shafts of wit and ridicule and even gloried in her ignorance is not surprising. . . . The ideal of the day was that "women must be pretty, dress prettily, and not be too well informed.". . . "woman, wine, and song," as the "world's best gift to man," were linked together in praise. . . . but duty is nearer home. The high ground of generalities is alluring but my pen is devoted to a special cause. . . . I ask the men and women who are teachers and co-workers for the highest interests of the race, that they give the girls a chance! We might as well expect to grow trees from leaves as hope to build up a civilization or a manhood without taking into consideration our women and the home life made by them, which must be the root and ground of the whole matter. Let us insist then on special encouragement for the education of our women and special care in their training. Let our girls feel that we expect something more of them than that they merely look pretty and appear well in society. Teach them that there is a race with special needs and is already asking for their trained, efficient forces. Finally—if there is an ambitious girl with pluck and brain to take the higher education, encourage her to make the most of it. Let there be the same flourish of trumpets and clapping of hands as when a boy announces his determination to enter the lists; and then, as you know that she is physically the weaker of the two, don't stand from under and leave her to buffet the waves alone. Let her know that your heart is following her, that your hand, though she sees it not, is ready to support her. To be plain, I mean let money be raised and scholarships be found in our colleges and universities for self-supporting, worthy young women, to offset and balance the aid that can always be found for boys who will take theology.

The earnest well trained Christian young woman, as a teacher, as a homemaker, as wife, mother, or silent influence even, is as potent a missionary agency among our people as is the theologian; and I claim that at the present state of our development in the South she is even more important and necessary.

A bird's-eye view of Livingstone College in Salisbury, North Carolina. From *Evidences of Progress Among Colored People.*

Let us then, here and now, reorganize this force and resolve to make the most of it—not the boys less, but the girls more.

According to Bert James Loewenberg and Ruth Bogin, "individual capacity for growth through formal schooling was the cornerstone" of Anna Cooper's belief, and as written in their *Black Women in Nineteenth-Century American Life,* "The experience of her own potentialities unfolding through a life-long career of teaching and learning reinforced the conviction with which she advocated educational opportunity for others." But for Anna Cooper the conviction was not arrived at at the end of her long and fruitful career as an educator. The subject of educational opportunities for black women had also been uppermost in her mind, when, in 1886, she addressed a convocation of black Episcopal ministers in the District of Columbia. Tailoring and measuring her remarks to fit the audience that sheaddressed, Anna Cooper maintained that:

Now I claim that it is the prevalence of the Higher Education among women, the making it a common everyday affair for women to reason and think and express their thought, the training and stimulus which enable and en-courage women to administer to the world the bread it needs as well as the sugar it cries for; in short it is the transmitting [of] the potential forces of her soul into dynamic factors that has given symmetry and completeness to the world's agencies.

Decrying the insults and ridicule heaped upon women for daring to develop their intellects, personalities, skills, and interests, Anna Cooper then entreated her audience to move away from the thinking of the past, when even renowned world scholars equated "learning" for women with "vice." As cited by Cooper, Gotthold Ephraim Lessing (1729-1781), a German critic and dramatist, thought that "the woman who thinks is like the man who puts on rouge—ridiculous." Also, Cooper quoted the French philosopher Voltaire, who said, "Ideas are like beards—women and boys have none," while the Irish author and scholar, William Maginn (1793-1842), was once heard to remark, "We like to hear a few words of sense from a woman sometimes, as we do from a parrot—they are so unexpected!" Denouncing such thinking as "vulgar" and archaic, Anna Cooper rebuked the men for assigning such little importance to the worth and work of women. Given "no work of her own to do . . . no absolute and inherent value, no duty to self, transcending all pleasure-giving that may be deemed of a mere toy," was it any wonder, she mused, "that [women's] value was purely a relative

The Reverend Joseph C. Price, president of Living-stone College, founded *The Southland* magazine. From *Evidences of Progress Among Colored People.*

one and to be estimated as are the fine arts—by the pleasure they give." Further, she warned that while these sentiments might have been popular when written, "the old, subjective, stagnant, indolent and wretched life for [women had] gone."

In 1890, when preparing to address the American Conference of Educators, Anna Cooper had surveyed American colleges that then admitted women to determine how many also admitted black women, and she was discouraged by the results of her study. The data gathered clearly indicated the need for both immediate and long-range planning to prepare for the encouragement and enrollment of black women into institutions of higher education. By 1890 Fisk University had enrolled twelve; Oberlin College, five; Wilberforce University, four; Ann Arbor and Wellesley College had each enrolled three; Livingstone College, two; Atlanta University, one; and Howard University had no black female students enrolled in the general college program. Cooper's study did not include women in the special two-year courses in pedagogy. In the same

year of Cooper's survey, however, Cornell University graduated its first black woman student from the scientific course. She was Jane E. "Nellie" Datcher, a former student from the M Street High School.

Sounding the note of alarm heard earlier, when, in 1886, she had addressed the black ministers and charged them with failing to provide scholarships and subsidies for black girls and women, Anna Cooper also reprimanded her audience of black educators and, as might be said today, accused them of being "part of the problem, rather than part of the solution." She pointed to nearly two hundred Afro-American women who, at that time, were in European colleges because American colleges either would not enroll them or were unprepared to meet their unique interests and needs.

By 1890 black Americans had just passed the quarter-century mark of freedom, and the conveners of the American Conference of Educators themselves had attended Howard University during its embryonic and fledgling years. Among them were Jesse Lawson, Furman J. Shadd, and James M. Gregory. The keynote speaker, Gregory, was also president of the conference, which was called with the hope that a permanent and national association would be founded. The biracial conference had two objectives; first, to discuss subjects that pertained only to the educational interests and needs of black people, and second, to call national attention to the progress that blacks had made, as well as to dramatize the difficulties yet to be overcome. Further, it proposed "to secure harmony of action and advance the interests of those engaged in the education of the colored youth of America."

Others who along with Anna Cooper were invited to present papers were the Reverend Horace Bumstead, president of Atlanta University; James C. Murray of Gammon Theological Seminary; W. S. Scarborough of Wilberforce University; Dr. J. E. Rankin, president of Howard University; and W. G. Sears, Lincoln University, Missouri. Issues discussed are reflected in the topics of the several papers delivered: "The Negro and the Classics," "Northern Philanthropy in Southern Schools," "The Ethical Training of Afro-American Youth," and "What Has Been Done by Afro-Americans Since Emancipation." Represented among the conferees were some of the best-trained black educators of the day.

Not one with myopic vision, Anna Cooper addressed the question of "The Higher Education of Women," her thesis considering the full range of experiences and work that she believed women should rightfully be involved with. As one who had only arrived to take up residence in the city of Washington in 1887, Anna Cooper by the early 1890s had become deeply involved with, and was a leader in, "women's" work.

In June 1892, the same year that she published her widely acclaimed book, *A Voice from the South: By a Black Woman of the South*," Anna Cooper was an organizer of the Colored Woman's League of Washington, D.C., which was incorporated on January 11, 1894, and she was a signer of that organization's articles of incorporation. Others were Helen A. Cook, Charlotte Forten Grimké, Josephine Beall Bruce, Mary Church Terrell, and Mary Jane Patterson. Committed to organizing black women nationally, this group offered a program of "racial uplift." Beginning in Washington, they instituted kindergarten teaching training for young women, rescue work among the city's poor

Dr. Furmann J. Shadd (Howard University, class of 1881) was an organizer of the 1890 American Conference of Educators. From *Howard University Medical Department: A Historical, Biographical and Statistical Souvenir.*

Helen A. Cook, an incorporator of the Colored Woman's League of Washington, D.C. Courtesy Mr. Paul Sluby, Sr.

and indigent population, and classes designed to improve women's industrial and homemaking skills. They also worked to improve the moral and social conditions among the city's alley dwellers, for among the blacks who had migrated into the District during and after the Civil War, there were those who had come from rural areas, some of whom had found it difficult to adjust to urban life. By the end of the nineteenth century, a large number of these newcomers were still existing in marginal and sub-standard conditions, and the women of the league believed that through their programs, which offered opportunities and not alms, they could help to eradicate poverty and its associated ills. Working cooperatively with churches and other benevolent societies, the league gave many of Washington's black women training that gained them marketable skills, viable alternatives, and new hope. In the vanguard, Anna Cooper chaired the league's Alley Sanitation Committee and was that organization's corresponding secretary for a number of years. The work of the Alley Sanitation

Committee would continue later under the auspices of the first Colored Social Settlement House, which Cooper would help to found, and whose work evolved from initiatives taken by the league's several committees.

After the success of the meeting of the Congress of Representative Women in Chicago (1893), the National Council of Women, in a letter addressed to Anna Cooper and dated October 9, 1894, invited the league to become a member of that organization. The council's president, Mrs. May Wright Sewell, also invited the league to send a representative to the National Council's convention to be held February 17–March 2, 1895. (Note: Frederick Douglass would make his last public appearance at the National Council's convention on the day of his death, February 25, 1895.) The invitation to join the council was predicated on the fact that the Washington league's articles of incorporation clearly stated that group of black women's intent to organize nationally, for only national organizations were eligible to join and participate as members of the National Council of Women. It seems likely, too, that Anna Cooper and the other black women who addressed the Women's Congress special session in Chicago in 1893 must have favorably impressed the members of the council. In the interim, the corresponding secretary of each group had been instructed to meet in Washington, D.C., to confer on arrangements for a joint session that would take place sometime during the convention called for 1895.

While the District's Territorial Government (1871-1874) had passed anti-discrimination laws (not enforced until the 1950s) that outlawed segregation in places of public accommodation, Washington was still a southern town and displayed attitudes that demanded the separation of the two races. While some wish to believe that women like Anna Cooper, because of culture, educational attainment, or position in the community, were accorded better treatment than the masses of blacks, such was not the case. By the 1890s the need to protest the discriminatory policies and practices of some Washington establishments, as well as to respond to their own feelings of racial identity and solidarity, gave further impetus to the development of black women's organizations.

Upon the arrival in Washington of the secretary from the National Council of Women, Anna Coop-er scheduled an appointment to meet with her. At the appointed hour, when she arrived at the designated meeting place (a local downtown hotel) and requested directions to the guest's elevator, she was informed that "Colored" persons must use the stairway. Unwilling to accept this discrimination, she left the hotel, and later penned a note of apology for failing to keep the appointment. Some would have dismissed this as an unpleasant encounter, but Anna Cooper deplored the humiliating situation that had confronted her, and said so—exclaiming her unwillingness to knowingly accept "special favoritism, whether of *sex, race, country,* or *condition.*" As observed by Dr. L. A. Scruggs in *Women of Distinction* (1893), "as learned [and] refined . . . as she is, she is still not exempted from humiliation." No doubt Anna Cooper was still smarting from another humiliating experience some months earlier, also reported by Scruggs. The incident occurred while Anna Cooper was visiting family and friends in Raleigh late in 1892. "She was *insulted* in a waiting-room at the depot, and ejected from the room. For what? Simply because she was a *colored* woman," according to Scruggs. She was

> Insulted and ejected (with a first class ticket in her hand) by a white man who [was] by far her *inferior* in every respect. . . . Indeed, *it is true* that great negro women work hard and go through much that is far from being pleasant after as well as before achieving greatness.

> However the storms, and whatever the difficulties, the women of this race have bright prospects of a better future in such pioneers and representatives as Mrs. A. J. Cooper.

Anna Cooper, Josephine St. Pierre Ruffin, and Helen A. Cook each addressed the first evening's assembly of the first National Conference of Colored Women, convened in Boston's Berkley Hall on July 29, 1895. The three-day meeting was well attended by representatives from fourteen states and fifty-three clubs. Anna Cooper delivered a paper that outlined the need for organizing black women nationally, and Mrs. Ruffin, the keynote speaker, sounded a note of urgency, reminding the women of scurrilous attacks on the character of black men and women. A letter had recently appeared in print, from the president of the Missouri Press Association to Florence Balgarnie of England, describing black women as prostitutes and black men as liars. A member and secretary of the British

Officers of the Colored Women's League of Rhode Island. Courtesy Library of Congress.

Anti-Lynching Committee, Miss Balgarnie had sent the letter to Mrs. Ruffin, who felt it time to send the "call" to black women to come to Boston and discuss issues of mutual concern. Many years later, Mary Church Terrell would remember that "Although this matter of a convention [had] been talked over for some time, the subject [had] been precipitated by a letter . . . reflecting upon the moral character of all colored women. . . . [T]oo indecent for publication . . . a copy of it was sent with [a] call to all the women's bodies throughout the country." Then, according to Terrell, black women were urged to read the document "carefully and discriminatingly" and "decide if it be not time for us to stand before the world and declare ourselves and our principles." As she noted, "The time is

The Women's Newport League (Rhode Island) Day Nursery. Courtesy Library of Congress.

95

Margaret Murray Washington. After her marriage to Booker T. Washington in 1893, she joined him in the effort to develop Tuskegee Institute. From *Who's Who in Colored America*.

short, but everything is ripe; and remember, earnest women can do anything."

Determined to found a national body that would cut across lines of special interests and regional and sectional differences, the women organized themselves into committees that would study issues and problems of concern to all and report back to the meeting to be held the next year. Concerns were assigned priorities, and a mechanism was developed for addressing them. Anna Cooper was appointed to head the Committee to Study the Georgia Convict System, the Florida State School Law, and Other Atrocities. The matter of the forced lease labor system was an issue that Booker T. Washington had addressed in a letter to the editor of the *Southern Workman* (the organ of Hampton Institute), on February 18, 1886, and the condition that Washington abhorred as a "horrible mode of treating prisoners" still commanded the attention of black people, who most frequently were the victims of it. At the conclusion of the business meeting, the floor was relinquished to Helen Cook, who delivered a plea for unity among the women.

Headed by Mrs. Cook, the Washington League was respected for the initiatives it had taken, and for its unique location "at the seat of government." The New Era Club, headed by Mrs. Ruffin, and the newly organized Federation of Afro-American Women's League, incorporated in Boston by Mrs. Booker T. Washington, were strong contenders for leadership. In the past, geographical and sectional differences, along with a rivalry among strong-willed personalities, had resulted in a polarization of these groups; also, the women in leadership roles were sometimes charged with using the clubs to advance the causes and positions of their husbands. Now, with an interim organizational structure in place, the Boston meeting adjourned on a note of unity, and Mrs. Washington was named provisional chairman and would convene the meeting to be called in the nation's capital the next year. In the meantime, Mrs. Ruffin and the New Era Club's official organ, *Women's Era*, would become the official clearing house, and through it, all convention plans and arrangements would be disseminated.

Delegates to the first Annual Convention of the National Federation of Afro-American Women met in Washington, D.C., at the Nineteenth Street Baptist Church, beginning on July 20, 1896. Here, they were challenged by the Reverend Walter H. Brooks to use the mighty force of their character, their intellect, and their history of service, "to lift up and ennoble womanhood." In response, Rosetta Douglass Sprague, the surviving daughter of Anna Murray and Frederick Douglass, said:

> While the white race have chronicled deeds of heroism and acts of mercy of the women of pioneer and other days, so we are pleased to note in the personality of such women as Phyllis Wheatley, Margaret Garner, Sojourner Truth and our venerable friend, Harriet Tubman, sterling qualities of head [and] heart and that hold no insignificant place in the annals of heroic womanhood. . . . Our progress depends on the united strength of both men and women—the women alone nor the men alone cannot do the work. We have so fully realized that fact by witnessing the work of our men with the women in the rear. This is indeed the *women's era*, and we are coming. . . .

While not mentioned in the official minutes of this meeting, Anna Cooper was scheduled to report for the Committee to Study the Georgia Convict

System, and must have been in attendance; therefore, a witness to this historical event, for she had devoted a decade to the proposition that black women—in intelligent and harmonious unison with black men—must become advocates for full equality and human dignity. Too, with her great sense of history, Cooper must have shared the thrill of the audience when it was known that their "venerable friend," Harriet Tubman, was among them. When routine business matters had ended, on the afternoon of July 20, a stir began in the Nineteenth Street Baptist Church that soon rose to a crescendo as the assembly learned that Tubman was in their midst. A motion carried that all "courtesies and privileges . . . be extended Mother Harriet Tub-

"Mother" Harriet Ross Tubman (1820?–1913) was among this group of delegates attending the first Annual Conference of the National Federation of Afro-American Women. Courtesy Mrs. Phyllis Terrell Langston and Smith College, Sophia Smith Collection.

man," that folk heroine, legend, and the undisputed "conductor" of the Underground Railroad.

During the evening session, while reciting the history that had brought them to this hour, Mrs. Ruffin informed the meeting that their assembly was a tribute to Frederick Douglass, for the organization of the National Federation of Afro-American Women was the result of a plan that Douglass himself had reviewed and approved sometime before his death. Even though the hour grew late, the announced agenda was followed by the introduction of Harriet Tubman, who electrified the overflowing crowd when she rose to accept its greeting. According to *A History of the Club Movement,* she

> stood alone on the front of the rostrum, the audience, which not only filled every seat, but also much of the standing room in the aisles, rose as one person and greeted her with the waving of handkerchiefs and the clapping of hands. This was kept up for at least a minute, and Mrs. Tubman was much affected by the hearty reception given her.

> When the applause had somewhat subsided, Mrs. Tubman acknowledged the compliment paid her in appropriate words, and at the request of some of the leading officers of the Convention related a little of her war experience. Despite the weight of advancing years, Mrs. Tubman [was] the possessor of a strong and musical voice, which . . . penetrated every portion of the large auditorium in which the Convention was held, and a war melody which she sang was fully as attractively rendered as were any of the other vocal selections of the evening.

On the evening of July 21, the convention delegates were treated to a program of addresses by some of the leading women of the day. Among them were Fannie Jackson Coppin (a noted educator); Josephine Beale Bruce (wife of United States Senator B. K. Bruce); Frances Ellen Watkins Harper (Temperance lecturer and author); and Alice Ruth Moore (a poet and writer who later married Paul Laurence Dunbar). The third morning's session was devoted to the reading of resolutions that

The Colored Woman's Leagues filled a vital need by training kindergarten teachers. This preprimer class was at Tuskegee Institute. Courtesy Library of Congress, Frances Benjamin Johnston Collection.

Josephine Beall Bruce (Mrs. Blanch Kelso), a signer of the Colored Woman's League of Washington, D.C., Articles of Incorporation. Courtesy Moorland-Spingarn Research Center, Howard University.

originated from the reports of committees that were appointed at the Boston meeting. Among them was a resolution to acknowledge Florence Balgarnie's concern for the welfare of Afro-American women; a resolution expressing appreciation for the leadership provided by Dr. and Mrs. Booker T. Washington in promoting "the moral and educational advancement" of black people; and another to send condolences to the family of Harriet Beecher Stowe and to establish her birthday, June 14, as a commemorative day of observance. The final resolution provided that the minutes of the First Annual Meeting of the Federation of Afro-American Women would be printed and sold to defray the expense of the convention.

Representing diverse geographical areas and the national interests of black women, a committee of fourteen had been elected at the beginning of the convention to effect the merger between the Washington, D.C., League, the New Era Club, and the Federation of Afro-American Women's League. The members were Libby Anthony and Fannie Jackson,

Missouri; Florence Barber, Rosa Bowser, and Addie Huntson, Virginia; Selina Butler, Georgia; Coralie Franklin, West Virginia; Anna Jones, Kansas; Julia Jones, Pennsylvania; Victoria Earle Matthews, New York; Josephine St. Pierre Ruffin, Massachusetts; and Emma F. G. Merritt, Mary Church Terrell, and Anna V. Thompkins, District of Columbia. As the last agenda item before adjournment, the convention received the merger committee's report and recommendations, which included the presentation of a new slate of officers. This committee was chaired by Coralie Franklin (later Mrs. George W. Cook), and the report was given by Anna V. Thompkins, who also announced the adoption of a new organizational name, the National Association of Colored Women's Clubs, Inc. After debate and lively discussion, the convention finally adopted the slate of officers as presented, and Mary Church Terrell was elected the first president of the National Association of Colored Women's Clubs, Inc., and Mrs. Washington was elected chairlady of the executive board.

Coralie Franklin (Cook), a professional social worker and a member of the District's Board of Education, was also an elocutionist and an active clubwoman. From *Who's Who in Colored America*.

Mary Church Terrell (1863–1954), the first president of the National Association of Colored Women's Clubs, Inc., 1896. From *A New Negro for a New Century*.

The first headquarters of the National Association of Colored Women's Clubs, Inc., at 1114 O Street, NW, Washington, D.C. From *National Association of Colored Women, Inc., 1896–1952*.

With the merger now completed, the delegates adjourned to return home to work for women's rights, and to await the next annual meeting. In the interim, Anna Cooper and the women of the league busied themselves with recruiting, lecturing, lobbying, and strengthening organizations that would extend their sphere of influence into the next century.

VI.

A Voice from the South

There is to my mind no grander and surer prophecy of the new era and of woman's place in it, than the work already begun in the waning years of the nineteenth century. . . .

There can be no issue more vital and momentous than this of the womanhood of the race. . . . We are the heirs of a past which was not our father's moulding. "Every man the arbiter of his own destiny" was not true for the American Negro of the past; and it is no fault of his that he finds himself to-day the inheritor of manhood and womanhood impoverished and debased by two centuries and more of compression and degradation.

But weakness and malformation, which to-day are attributable to a vicious schoolmaster and a pernicious system, will a century hence be rightly regarded as proofs of innate corruptness and radical incurability. Now the fundamental agency under God in the regeneration, the retraining of the race, as well as the ground work and starting point of its progress upward, must be the BLACK WOMAN.

ANNA J. COOPER, 1892
A Voice from the South

Dr. Anna J. Cooper in her garden. Copyright by Scurlock Studio.

IN 1893 ALBION WINEGAR TOURGEE (1838–1905), jurist, author, and playwright, reviewed Anna J. Cooper's volume of essays, *A Voice from the South: By a Black Woman of the South,* and in that same year Monroe A. Major published Tourgee's critique in his work, *Noted Negro Women—Their Triumphs and Activities.* Tourgee had this to say about Anna Cooper's first literary effort:

> The habit of a lifetime has made the Bystander's pencil almost infallible in its indication of verbal inaccuracy, which is, after all, the very highest test of literary merit. The word which exactly fills the place where it is used—neither too large nor too small for the service assigned, or to the thought it is commissioned to convey—is to literary workmanship what the perfect note is to music. It may be slurred a little—often is—without constituting actual fault, as the rush of some great movement may even hide or excuse a false note now and then, but only precision can give the feeling of finish which attests the genuine literary artist: Rarely has the unsparing pencil passed so lightly over the pages of a book of essays as it did over the pages of this "Voice from the South!" Its perusal would be a new sensation to many a white-souled Christian woman of the "superior race," who, when she had perused its bright pages from cover to cover, would be forced to admit that though she had encountered many a sharp thrust she had not received one awkward or ill-tempered blow.

Concluding that few women writers had shown a "daintier wit," Tourgee enjoyed "the deft but stinging satire, the keen but not ill-tempered wit, [and] the tasteful self-restraint"—characteristics of Cooper's book that were not lost on other literary critics of the day.

A Voice from the South, well received and widely read, was, according to the New York *Independent* (and as Anna herself described it):

An infant crying in the night,
And with no language but a cry.

But the *Independent* conceded that it was "a piercing and clinging cry which it is impossible to hear [and] not to understand—which it is impossible to shake off," and concluded that Anna Cooper wrote "with strong but controlled passion, on a basis of strong facts."

Throughout, Anna Cooper had been consistent in bringing to the fore the two themes that she emphasized and would re-emphasize—her race and black women. The plight of the two were so intricately interwoven that they often seemed as one, and some reviewers considered her book a treatise on the "race problem," or the "Negro problem." Cooper, however, continuously placed black women in juxtaposition with more general themes and issues, and used them as historical analogies to drive home her point. Offering her readers the "feminine side of truth," and "in excellent English," as observed by the *Boston Transcript*, Cooper was stoically unrelenting, uncompromising, and would not retreat from her positions on the important issues. The *Transcript* noted that Cooper also made "an intimate exposition of qualities of her people which whites [were] . . . slow to appreciate," and the *Philadelphia Public Ledger* found that "there [was] sound sense in this author's argument," a rarity, it said, "in controversial literature."

In her own inimitable style, Anna Cooper had found a convincing way to present candidly her side of arguments, often with passion, but without seeming impertinent, and, as observed by the *Chicago Inter-Ocean*, without "the least shade of vindictiveness . . . yet so pointed and honest as to be convincing for its justice." And the *Detroit Plaindealer* believed that:

There has been no book on the race question that has been more cogently and forcibly written by either white or black authors. The book is not only a credit to the genius of the race, but to woman [sic] whose place and sphere in life men have so long dictated.

The *Kingsley* (Iowa) *Times* considered Anna Cooper's to be "one of the most readable books on the race question of the South," and it praised Cooper, "a colored lady with the brains of a Susan B. Anthony, a George Eliot, or Frances [Elizabeth Caroline] Willard," the temperance leader and feminist, who also desired to advance the cause of women and promote reform in many fields. Continuing, the *Kingsley Times* contended that:

The volume is attracting wide attention, owing to its being worthy of careful perusal and because of its originality and great literary strength. It is a neat, cloth bound book, retailing for $1.25, but to anyone interested in this race question it is worth many times its cost. For sale by the author or at all bookstores. The *Times* editor never has seen a stronger picture of the true conditions of affairs in the South than the one coming from this colored lady.

Finally, the newspaper *Public Opinion* found Cooper's book "a fresh attraction" coming "from the eager heart and mind of a 'Black woman of the South,'" and commended the book—"written in a very judicious and elevated way"—to its readers and "to all who wish to keep in touch with the Negro problem."

Thus Anna Cooper had earned her acceptance into the society of scholars and thinkers, and among her peers she was respected as a formidable force. Much sought after as a spokeswoman for her race, Cooper was not hampered or cramped by the fact that she was often a woman alone in a "man's world"; quietly and effectively, and by example, she made a strong case for "woman's touch" and "woman's involvement" in the critical issues of the day.

Before the issue had become either controversial or a popular one to champion or disavow, and even before her attendance at the Second Hampton Negro Conference (1894), Anna Cooper had lectured on the need for industrial and classical education for blacks. In 1892, in a paper entitled "What Are We Worth," she had said:

Industrial training has been hitherto neglected or despised among us, due, I think . . . to two causes: first, a mistaken estimate of labor arising from its association with slavery and from its having been despised by the only class in the South thought worthy of imitation; and secondly, the fact that the Negro's ability to work had never been called in question, while his ability to learn Latin and construe Greek syntax needed to be proved to sneering critics. "Scale the heights!" was the cry. "Go to college, study Latin, preach, teach, orate, wear spectacles and a beaver!"

Stung by such imputations as that of Calhoun that a Negro could prove his ability to master the Greek subjunctive he might indicate his title to manhood, the newly liberated race first shot forward along this line with an energy and success which astonished its most sanguine friends.

This may not have been most wise. It certainly was quite natural; and the result is we find ourselves in almost as ludicrous a plight as the African in the story, who, after a sermon from his missionary pleading for the habiliments of civilization, complacently donned a Gladstone hat leaving the rest of his body in its primitive simplicity of attire. Like him we began at the wrong end! Wealth must pave the way for learning. Intellect, whether of races or individuals, cannot soar to the consummation of those sublime products which immortalize genius, while the general mind is assaulted and burdened with "what shall we eat, what shall we drink, and wherewithal shall we be clothed!"

Even before Booker T. Washington pronounced industrial education as the answer to the South's problems and the black man's ills, Anna Cooper had reasoned that "Work must first create wealth, and wealth leisure, before the untrammeled intellect of the Negro, or any other race, can truly vindicate its capabilities." But unlike Washington, Cooper firmly believed that the seemingly opposing systems of education could coexist beneficially in the struggle for race uplift. Still, Cooper was able to observe that:

Something has been done intellectually. . . . That one black man (W. S. Scarborough) has written a Greek grammar is enough to answer Calhoun's sneer; but it is leisure, the natural outgrowth of work and wealth, which must furnish room, opportunity, possibility for the highest endeavor and most brilliant achievement. Labor must be the solid foundation stone—the *sine qua non* (without which not) of our material value; and the only effective preparation for success in this, as it seems to me, lies in the establishment of industrial and technical schools for teaching our colored youth trades. This necessity is obvious for several reasons. First, a colored child, in most

cases, can secure a trade in no other way. We had master mechanics while the Negro was a chattel, and the ingenuity of brain and hand served to enrich the coffers of his owner. But to-day skilled labor is steadily drifting into the hands of white workmen—mostly foreigners. Here it is cornered. The white engineer holds a tight monopoly both of the labor market and of the science of his craft. Nothing would induce him to take a colored apprentice or even work beside a colored workman. Unless the trades are to fall among the lost arts for us as a people, they must be engrafted on those benevolent institutions for Negro training established throughout the land. The youth must be taught to use his trigonometry in surveying his own and his neighbor's farm; to employ his geology and chemistry in finding out the nature of the soil, the constituents drafted from it by each year's crop and the best way to meet the demand by the use of suitable renewers; to apply his mechanics and physics to the construction and handling of machinery—to the intelligent management of iron works and water works and steam works and electric works. One mind in a family or in a town may show a penchant for art, for literature, for the learned professions, or more bookish lore. You will know it when it is there. No need to probe for it. It is a light that cannot be hid under a bushel!—and I would try to enable that mind to go the full length of its desire. Let it follow its bent and develop its talent as far as possible: and the whole community might well be glad to contribute its labor and money for the sustenance and cultivation of this brain. Just as earth gives its raw materials, its carbon, hydrogen, and oxygen, for the tree which is to elaborate them into foliage, flower and fruit, so the baser elements, bread and money furnished the true brain worker come back to us in the rich thought, the invention, the poem, the painting, the statue. Only let us recognize our assignment and not squander our portion in over fond experiments. . . .

For Anna Cooper, the final decade of the nineteenth century was, to paraphrase Charles Dickens, the best of times and the worst of times, but her message to the black woman of the South would be: *"ce n'est que le premier pas qui coute"* (it is only the first step that is difficult). She conceded that she had had a mother's love and encouragement, and the shelter and training of St. Augustine's College; still she wished to awaken in her less fortunate black sisters of the South the desire to discover their own potentials, interests, life work, and worth.

Contending that "the colored woman [could] no longer be ignored," Anna Cooper wrote in her essay "The Status of Women in America":

> The colored woman of to-day occupies, one may say, a unique position in this country. In a period of itself transitional, her status seems one of the least ascertainable and definitive of all the forces which make for our civilization. She is confronted by both a woman question and a race problem, and is as yet an unknown or an unacknowledged factor in both. While the women of the white race can with calm assurance enter upon the work they feel by nature appointed do do, while their men give loyal support and appreciative countenance to their efforts . . . the colored woman too often finds herself hampered and shamed by a less liberal sentiment and a more conservative attitude on the part of those for whose opinions she cares most. That is not universally true I am glad to admit. There are to be found both intensely conservative white men and exceedingly liberal colored men. But as far as my experience goes the average man of our race is less frequently ready to admit the actual need among the sturdier forces of the world for woman's help or influence. . . .
>
> Fifty years ago woman's activity according to orthodox definitions was on a pretty clearly cut "sphere," including primarily the kitchen and the nursery, and rescued from the barrenness of prison bars by the womanly mania for adorning every discoverable bit of china or canvas with forlorn looking cranes balanced idiotically on one foot. The woman of today finds herself in the presence of responsibilities which ramify through the profoundest and most varied interests of her country and race. . . . No plan for renovating society, no scheme for purifying politics, no reform in church or in state, no moral, social, or economic question, no movement upward or downward in the human plane is lost on her. A man once said when told his house was afire: "Go tell my wife; I never meddle with household affairs." But no woman can possibly put herself or her sex outside any of the interests that affect humanity. All departments in the new era are to be hers, in the sense that her interests are in all and through all, and it is incumbent on her to keep intelligently and sympathetically *en rapport* with all the great movements of her time, that she may know on which side to throw the weight of her influence. She stands now at the gateway of this new era of American civilization. In her hands must be moulded the strength, the wit, the statesmanship, the morality, all the psychic force, the social and economic intercourse of that era. To be alive at such an epoch is a privilege, to be a woman then is sublime. . . .
>
> But to be a woman of the Negro race in America, and to be able to grasp the deep significance of the possibilities of the crisis, is to have a heritage, it seems to me, unique in the ages. In the first place, the race is young and full of the elasticity and hopefulness of youth. It does not look on the masterly triumphs of nineteenth century civilization with that blasé world-weary look which characterizes the old washed out and worn out races which have already, so to speak, seen their best days.
>
> Said a European writer recently: "Except the Slavonic, the Negro is the only original and distinctive genius which has yet to come to growth—and the feeling is to cherish and develop it."
>
> Everything to this race is new and strange and inspiring. There is a quickening of its pulses and a glowing of its self-consciousness. Aha, I can rival that! I can aspire to that! I can honor my name and vindicate my race! Something like this, it strikes me, is the enthusiasm which stirs the genius of a young African in America; and the memory of past oppression and the fact of present attempted repression only serve to gather momentum for its irrepressible powers. Then again, a race in such a stage of growth is peculiarly sensitive to impressions. . . .
>
> What a responsibility then to have the sole management of the primal lights and shadows! Such is the colored woman's office. She must stamp weal or woe on the coming history of this people. May she see her opportunity and vindicate her high prerogative.

Anna Cooper's participation in black organizations promoting a new social and political thought increased her zest for community involvement, and her insatiable appetite for intellectual activity quickened. An active member of the Oberlin Alumni Association and the North Carolina Teach-

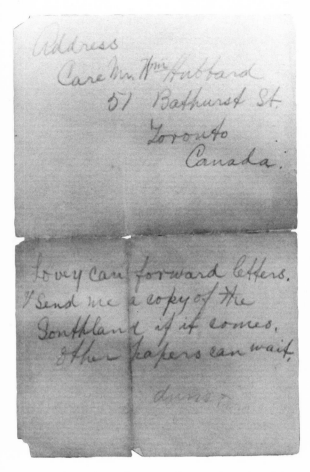

A letter from Anna Cooper to her mother, describing an exchange visit made by some M Street School teachers to Toronto in the 1890s. Courtesy Moorland-Spingarn Research Center, Howard University.

er's Association, which had enabled her to continue ties with her alma maters, Cooper was also a member of the Bethel Literary and Historical Association, the Colored Woman's League of the District of Columbia, the American Negro Academy, the Book Lovers Club, and, later, the Phyllis Wheatley YWCA. But in 1900 Anna Cooper would play a unique role, for a nineteenth-century black woman, at the Pan-African Conference in London.

On November 9, 1881, the date of the first general election following the death of James A. Garfield and the accession of Chester A. Arthur to the presidency, Bishop Daniel A. Payne, historian of the African Methodist Episcopal (A.M.E.) Church, founded the Bethel Literary and Historical Association. One of the society's goals was "to excite interest among teachers of the colored schools by showing how they could spend their summers

abroad . . . visiting the museums of London and Paris. . . ." Through continued study and investigation, Payne believed that teachers could enrich the lives of their young pupils, and through the use of "lantern slides" share with them the beauty of the great cultural storehouses of Europe.

During the 1890s Anna Cooper, Parker Bailey, and Ella D. Barrier (the sister of Fannie Barrier Williams) were three among the District's black teachers who took part in a cultural exchange visit with black Canadian teachers, arranged under the auspices of the Bethel Literary Society. Anna's host in Toronto was William Hubbard, who resided at 51 Bathurst Street. She shared this experience with her mother:

My dear Mother:—I hope you are well & enjoying yoursel[f]. Toronto is a beautiful city right on Lake Ontario. . . . our landlord . . .

took us driving. We saw a boat race, visited the Fair grounds where the Crystal Palace is, passed the parliament building, the University of Ontario & a great many other magnificent buildings & grounds. There are the most beautiful lawns here I ever saw. The grass looks like velvet—so smooth & soft & green & the houses are not generally jammed as they are in Washington, but most of them have extensive grounds & well kept conservatories & flowers. In this it reminds me more of the South where there seems plenty of room for trees & flowers, tho everything here is most artificially arranged. A reception has been given . . . each evening since our arrival—night before last at a public place called Victoria Hall, which was for all the visitors, given by the colored citizens of Toronto. At this there were speeches & music (instrumental & vocal) & recitations; after which refreshments. The only objection I had was that we were out too late—it being after one when we left & all the street cars had stopped running. Last night a few of us, just those stopping here, were entertained till a late hour but most delightfully by Dr. Abbot a very wealthy citizen of this place. He has a son and a daughter about Lovey's age (but not quite so *grown*) who are highly cultivated in music. They play the violin & piano & also sing beautifully. I would have liked so much to have Lovey meet them. Dr. Abbot's baby-boy, a little younger than French Tyson, gave us a little exhibition with Indian clubs before he was sent to bed. All of the children seemed so simple & natural & unaffected that we enjoyed them very much. A Miss Chantz who plays the piano excellently & accompanies all the leading white vocalists was there & played for us delightfully. There was no begging & teasing & saying "I can't" for everyone did her best & seemed happy making others happy. In the back parlor there were some games & conversation & all seemed to have a thoroly good time. . . .

Lovey was the daughter of Rufus Haywood, thus the niece of Anna Cooper. She was educated at Shaw University in Raleigh. According to the 1900 census for the District of Columbia, Lovey lived with her aunt at that time and taught music in Washington's black schools.

The Bethel Library Society's lectures attracted large audiences, and often the meeting place was changed to accommodate the crowds. The broad

The Reverend Alexander Crummell, a Pan-Africanist and founder of the American Negro Academy, was called "both Moses and Prophet" by Anna Cooper. From *The Negro in American History.*

range of discussion topics and the caliber of speakers attest to the social and political thought of the day. During the first year the Honorable John H. Smyth, one of Washington's early black lawyers and later minister to Liberia, delivered a lecture entitled "African Experience." The third speaker, Jesse Lawson, addressed "The Hand of God in America," and the sisters Mary Jane and Channie A. Patterson jointly delivered an essay on "The Trades or the Professions—Which Should Our Young Men Undertake?" Oberlin-trained, both had begun their teaching careers under the tutelage of Fannie Jackson Coppin, in Philadelphia, and were appointed to the District's black schools in 1869.

According to John W. Cromwell's *History of the Bethel Literary and Historical Association* (1896), one of the society's most memorable lectures was Dr. Alexander Crummell's eulogy for the Honorable Henry Highland Garnet, his longtime friend, associate, and colleague. Garnet had been pastor of the Fifteenth Street Presbyterian Church; he died while serving as minister to Liberia. Because of the large attendance, this meeting was held in the Nineteenth Street Baptist Church, where the Honorable John F. Cook, Jr., presided, and Frederick Douglass, Bishop Henry McNeal Turner (A.M.E.), and Professor George W. Cook were among the platform guests to offer tributes and resolutions of condolence.

Of all the organizations founded in the District of Columbia by blacks during the last decades of the nineteenth century, the American Negro Academy was the most politically oriented. Unlike the American Negro Historical Society of Philadelphia, "organized to collect relics and facts pertaining to American Negro progress and development," the academy published "Occasional Papers" that dealt with critical issues.

Anna Cooper was the only woman ever elected a member of the American Negro Academy, founded to provide a forum for "the promotion of literature, science, and art . . . fostering of higher education, the publication of scholarly work and the defense of

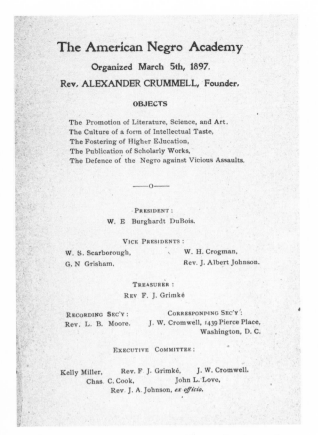

The American Negro Academy
Organized March 5th, 1897.
Rev. ALEXANDER CRUMMELL, Founder.

OBJECTS

The Promotion of Literature, Science, and Art.
The Culture of a form of Intellectual Taste,
The Fostering of Higher Education,
The Publication of Scholarly Works,
The Defence of the Negro against Vicious Assaults.

——o——

PRESIDENT :
W. E Burghardt DuBois.

VICE PRESIDENTS :
W. S. Scarborough,   W. H. Crogman,
G. N Grisham.   Rev. J. Albert Johnson.

TREASURER :
Rev. F. J. Grimké

RECORDING SEC'Y :   CORRESPONDING SEC'Y :
Rev. L. B. Moore.   J. W. Cromwell, 1439 Pierce Place,
                                   Washington, D. C.

EXECUTIVE COMMITTEE :

Kelly Miller,   Rev. F. J. Grimké,   J. W. Cromwell.
         Chas. C. Cook,   John L. Love,
              Rev. J. A. Johnson, *ex officio.*

List of officers of the American Negro Academy during the presidency of Dr. W. E. B. Du Bois. Courtesy Moorland-Spingarn Research Center, Howard University.

the Negro against vicious assault." Dr. Crummell delivered the inaugural address at the Lincoln Congregational Memorial Church on March 5, 1897. Among the organizing members were Francis J. Grimké, pastor of the Fifteenth Street Presbyterian Church; Lewis Baxter Moore, pastor of People's Congregational Church; John Albert Johnson, later a Bishop in the A.M.E. Church; W. E. B. Du Bois, professor of economics and sociology at Atlanta University; William Henry Crogman, professor of classics and president of Atlanta University; William Saunders Scarborough, chairman, Classical Department, Payne Theological Seminary, Wilberforce University; and Kelly Miller, professor of mathematics at Howard University. Jesse E. Moorland; Edward C. Williams; Monroe N. Work; Faduma Orishatukeh from Sierra Leone; J. E. Kwegyir-Aggrey from the Gold Coast, West Africa; Arthur A. Schomburg; Carter G. Woodson; and George W. Cook were also among the select group of forty

The Honorable Henry Highland Garnet, a runaway slave and political activist, who agitated for armed rebellion to end slavery, was president of Avery College and minister to Liberia. From *The Negro in American History.*

109

J. E. Kwegyir-Aggrey, born at Anamabu, Gold
Coast, West Africa, was a professor at Livingstone
College and chief secretary of the executive and gen-
eral committee of the Gold Coast Aborigines' Rights
Protection Society.
From *Aggrey of Africa: A Study in Black and White*.
Courtesy Mr. John R. Kinard.

scholars, poets, clergymen, journalists, academ-
icians, and bibliophiles.

The black "think tank" of its day, the American
Negro Academy only invited and selected the best
minds and scholars into its membership, and they
were needed to deliberate and, through their writings, focus attention on the black community's
mounting concerns. The diverse socio-economic
and political issues considered by the academy are
reflected in the titles of the papers authored by its
members, for as noted by August Meier in *Negro
Thought in America 1880–1915*, "by publishing
scholarly papers, the Academy planned to counter-
act both white prejudice and Negro lack of unity."
Kelly Miller published the first paper, *A Review of
Hoffman's "Race Traits and Tendencies of the American
Negro"*; others were W. E. B. Du Bois's *The Conservation of the Races*, W. S. Scarborough's *The Educated
Negro and His Mission*, Archibald H. Grimké's

Modern Industrialism and the Negro (his poem "Her
13 Black Soldiers" was later cited in a report from
the Justice Department to the United States Senate
as "evil in scope"); Theophilus G. Steward's *The
Message of St. Domingo to the African Race*, and John
L. Love's *The Disfranchisement of the Negro*. While it
is known that Anna Cooper both wrote and lectured
extensively, there is no evidence to suggest that any
of her writings were published under the auspices of
the American Negro Academy; even so, there is no
question but that she was respected by the members
of the academy for her scholarship.

In the summer of 1900, along with Anna H.
Jones of Missouri, Anna Cooper represented her
race and the black women of America at the Pan-
African Conference, in London. The first assemblage of its kind, the conference was held in West-
minster Town Hall from July 23 through 25, and
was scheduled to coincide with the opening of the
"Negro Exhibit at the Paris Exhibition," another
important event that would attract large numbers

OCCASIONAL PAPERS No. 6.

The American Negro Academy.
Rev. ALEXANDER CRUMMELL, Founder.

The Disfranchisement
of the Negro,

By JOHN L. LOVE,

Price 15 cents.

WASHINGTON, D. C.
Published by the Academy,
1899.

The cover of a paper by John L. Love, Anna Cooper's
foster son, 1899. Courtesy Moorland-Spingarn Research Center, Howard University.

110

of people of African descent to Europe. It was for these two reasons then that Anna Cooper went to Europe in 1888, accompanied by Lula and John Love, whose guardian she had become after the death of their parents.

The uniqueness of the role that Anna Cooper and her long-time friend Anna Jones would play at the Pan-African Conference of 1900 (later assemblies were called congresses) has been determined by the fact that both women were invited to address the assembly at a time when women, black or white, were not invited to play dominant roles along with men.

Anna Cooper was among those who presented papers at the first session of the conclave, addressing "The Negro Problem in America" and outlining conditions that the British press called "'pathetic' in an America that described herself as Christian." Anna Jones delivered a paper entitled "The Preservation of Race Individuality." Although Cooper's paper has not been located, documentation of her presence and role at the Pan-African Conference is present in the following letter from H. Sylvester Williams, Esq., to Anna Cooper, dated September 22, 1900:

> I trust you have now safely returned to your home and have profitted greatly by the tour on the European Continent. The Assoc. is progressing slowly but is greatly handicapped for funds. We are now [preparing] to have the papers [and] speeches delivered at the Conference printed for circulation in order to aid our income. Not having yours, the Executives have requested me to write, asking you to send it for us. . . . The incident of the Conference has created quite a furore in the minds of our Eng. friends. One or two have said the occasion & ability displayed have completely transformed their ideas about the Negro. In France mention was made of our Conference & the Appeal. Never before have we as a race had such a recognition. Great as has been the event, greater things are still to come from the children of Ham. . . .
>
> Enclosed is a Copy of the Appeal; let us trust the meeting in Boston in 1902 will be an "eye-opener.". . .
>
> The Appeal is private. One is being sent to President McKinley. Therefore, do not give it undue publicity. . . .

The "Appeal" spoken of by Williams was the "Ad-

Page one of the letter from H. Sylvester Williams, Esq., to Anna J. Cooper, September 22, 1900. Courtesy Moorland-Spingarn Research Center, Howard University.

dress to the Nations" that was also sent to the heads-of-state of Germany, France, Belgium, and Great Britain, calling upon them to permit black rule in the colonies of Africa and the West Indies, "as soon as practicable."

While W. E. B. Du Bois is called the "Father of Pan-Africanism," the idea for convening the first Pan-African Conference, in 1900, was first promulgated by Henry Sylvester Williams and the Haitian Benito Sylvain. The history of the Pan-African movement should include this early beginning, for important work was done at this meeting, which resulted in the drafting of one of the earliest documents by Africans and people of African descent to address the issue of apartheid in South Africa.

According to Owen Charles Mathurin *(Henry Sylvester Williams and the Origins of the Pan-African Movement, 1869–1911)*, the Pan-African Conference of 1900 was called to:

(1) Establish closer communication among people of African descent scattered around the world, as the result of slavery.

(2) To develop plans that would promote more friendly relations between whites and blacks. And,

(3) To start a movement that would result in the recognition of full citizenship rights for all Africans and their descendents living in civilized countries, and "to promote their business interest."

The Pan-African Conference was the outgrowth of the African Association, founded in London on September 24, 1897, by Williams, who, as quoted by Mathurin, "perceived a need for a 'body of Africans in England representing native opinion in national matters affecting the destiny of the African race.'"

The American delegation to the Pan-African

W. E. B. Du Bois (1868–1963), the second president of the American Negro Academy, promoted the doctrine of "the Talented Tenth" to establish a leadership group among Afro-Americans. From *The Negro Problem.*

Bishop Alexander Walters (A.M.E. Zion), persuasive and influential, presided over the National Negro-American Political League and was well known in London for his oratorical ability. From *One Hundred Distinguished Leaders.*

Conference was led by Bishop Alexander Walters (A.M.E. Zion), considered by many to be loyal to Booker T. Washington. Washington himself attended a preconference planning meeting in London on June 12, 1899; earlier, Williams had heard Washington publicly address the "condition and prospects of the colored races in America," and sought his support and endorsement of the conference proposal. Seldom, if ever, is Washington associated with Pan-Africanism, and he himself would deny his unique role as a political figure and power broker, often choosing to adopt a self-effacing posture. Still, the importance of Washington's counsel as a member of the pre-planning committee cannot be overlooked, with the knowledge that Bishop Walters, according to Mathurin, had been preselected to head this important delegation. Too, Washington had strongly urged the participation of his allies, Fannie Barrier Williams and Thomas J. Calloway, at these deliberations.

Anna Cooper, an official American delegate, was among the women attending the Pan-African Conference who were honored with "positions on the platform," and who, Mathurin said, "distinguished themselves." The official report of the conference proceedings cited Anna Cooper as an elected member of the executive committee, and in this capacity she served with the Honorable Henry F. Downing, former United States consul, Sao Paulo de Loanda, Portuguese Africa; Samuel Coleridge-Taylor, the gifted Afro-English composer; John F. Loudin, manager of the Fisk Jubilee Singers; John R. Archer, later mayor of London's borough of Battersea; and Mrs. Jessie Cobden-Unwin, the wife of the publisher, T. Fisher Unwin. It was the executive committee that would issue the official conference report, and "respectfully thank the numerous friends and various organs who . . . contributed to the success of the first assembling of members of the African race from all parts of the globe."

Among the other Afro-American delegates who would vote to establish a permanent organization were John L. Love, Jr., who served on the "Committee on Address," chaired by Dr. Du Bois; Benjamin W. Arnett, Jr., of Illinois, the son of Bishop Arnett; Charles P. Lee, a New York attorney; Fannie Barrier Williams and her sister, Ella D. Barrier; and Ada Harris of Indiana.

Anna Cooper was elected to the committee that would plan the convocation to be held in Boston in 1902, after the conference agreed to meet biennially and convene its next session in America; it also projected a third assembly to be held in Haiti in 1904. This explains, then, what Williams had meant when, in his letter to Anna Cooper, he had written, "let us trust the meeting in Boston in 1902 will be an 'eye-opener,'" for the delegates to the Pan-African Conference of 1900 had adjourned with the expectation that they would meet two years hence and that their organization would continue. There can only be conjecture as to why it did not continue, and why the organization of Pan-African Congresses did not begin until more than a decade later. It should not be interpreted that the Pan-African Conference of 1900 failed because it did not continue, for while it is true that its life was brief, it is also true that it did meet its goals and objectives; namely, it assembled in England as a

Samuel Coleridge-Taylor (1875–1912) was celebrated as a composer on two continents at the turn of the century. He prepared the musical program for the Pan-African Conference. Photograph by Addison Scurlock. Courtesy Robert Scurlock, Scurlock Studios.

united body to address "the treatment of native races under European and American rule . . . in South Africa, West Africa, West Indies [and the] United States of America." Deliberately choosing to meet at the start of a new century, this assembly of men and women of African descent signaled a new beginning and declared their belief that it was now time for black people to speak for themselves, and to develop their talents and energies in an effort to influence public opinion in their favor. To this end, they left the conference satisfied that they had gained both public attention and sympathy. Cited in Mathurin's work, "a contributor to the *Pall Mall Gazette* thought it [the conference] a waste of time." However, the influential editor of the British journal *Review of Reviews* held another view, and in his article, "The Revolt Against the Paleface," W. T. Stead reminded readers that "the Italians had been defeated by Menelik," and noted that this Ethiopian emperor now was an honorary member of the Pan-African Conference, concluding that "the white world was face to face with a determined effort on the part of the colored races to assert their right to live their own lives in their own way without 'the perpetual bullying of the Palefaces.'" Perhaps Stead's assessment was made with the knowledge that this first Pan-African Conference had also drafted a *Memorial* to Queen Victoria that set forth "acts of injustice directed against her Majesty's subjects in South Africa," and that contained the following seven grievances:

(1) The degrading and illegal compound system of native labor in vogue in Kimberly and Rhodesia.

(2) The so-called indenture, i.e. legalized bondage of native men and women and children to white colonists.

(3) The system of compulsory labour in public works.

(4) The "pass" or docket system used for people of colour.

(5) Local by-laws tending to segregate and degrade the natives—such as the curfew; the de-

nial to the natives of the use of foot-paths; and the use of separate public conveyances.

(6) Difficulties in acquiring real property.

(7) Difficulties in obtaining the franchise.

It was while preparing the "Address to the Nations," that Du Bois first penned his prophetic warning and now classical lines, "The problem of the Twentieth Century is the problem of the color line," and later, in *The Souls of Black Folk* (1903), the prophecy was expanded—and in its entirety reads:

> The problem of the Twentieth Century is the problem of the color line, the relation of the darker to the lighter races of men in Asia and Africa, in America and the islands of the sea.

Leaving London, Anna Cooper and Dr. Du Bois both visited the Paris Exposition, and each agreed that one of the more interesting features was a small exhibit housed in a corner of the Social Economy Building that depicted the education and progress of the black race. Consisting of the work of Professor Thomas W. Hunster, the exhibit contained nine scenes, modeled from clay, that began with an emancipated black family with no resources, eking out an existence, and ended with a striking model of the M Street High School, thereby graphically showing the evolution of black Americans from 1865 until 1900. As Anna Cooper would note, the theme of the ninth scene was "the climax of the upward struggles of [her] people and show[ed] the chasm bridged in the second generation along the shadowy path . . . wither none but Omniscience could have foreseen."

Uniquely, Hunster had told the black American's poignant story in a language all who visited the Paris Exposition could understand, and in spite of language barriers, Europeans showed considerable interest in the display, located in the corridor and opposite a sign that read "Exposition Des Nègres d' Amerique." Before it was sent to Paris, the exhibit had opened in the M Street School, and was the source of much community enthusiasm and pride.

The day before the exposition's official opening, an assistant commissioner, General Woodward, was reported to have said:

> The chief attraction of the exhibition will be the educational work that is being done for our Negroes. I think this exhibition will show

Forest Glade, an oil by Thomas W. Hunster, M Street High School art teacher and director of drawing, D.C. Public Schools. The Hunster Gallery at Dunbar High School was named for him. Gift of Mr. William N. Buckner, Jr.

other nations that we know how to solve the Negro problem upon intelligent, civilized lines. Some foreigners think we have nothing for the Negro but the bludgeon and the revolver.

When Anna Cooper returned to Washington, however, she wrote about this exhibit in *The National Capital Searchlight,* concluding that:

The ultimate test of our civilization will be, not how much of material things we have produced and consumed, but what is the status and what the opportunities of the less capable under our regime. Have we given instruction to those who could not procure it for themselves; could the plain and the uninfluential earn and enjoy an honest dollar for an honest day's work; was there a man's chance for the man at the bottom; or have we kept the prizes and emoluments for some and the bludgeon and revolver for others in arbitrary divisions, made with narrow prejudice and shortsightedness, regardless of human strivings and deservings?

Anna Cooper had just begun her duties as principal of the M Street School in the District when, on the other side of the Atlantic on January 16, 1901, H. Bertram Cox, her Majesty's respondent to the Memorial to Queen Victoria, wrote the following letter to "H. S. Williams, Esq., General Secretary, Pan-African Conference:"

Sir: I am directed by My Secretary Chamberlain to state that he has received the Queen's commands to inform you that the Memorial of the Pan-African Conference respecting the situation of the native races in South Africa, has been laid before Her Majesty, and that she was graciously pleased to command him to return an answer to it on behalf of her government.

Mr. Chamberlain accordingly desires to assure the members of the Pan-African Conference that, in settling the lines on which the administration of the conquered territories are to be conducted, Her Majesty's Government will not overlook the interests and welfare of the native races.

A copy of the Memorial has been communicated to the High Commissioners for South Africa. I am, sir, your obedient servant.

Even with her new duties and responsibilities and the demands on her time, Anna Cooper continued lecturing and making her views known, and

The Odd Fellows Hall, Twelfth and U Streets, NW, designed by John A. Lankford. This illustration, reflecting Lankford's ability in design, was exhibited at the Paris Exposition of 1900 to document the progress of the race. Courtesy Library of Congress.

on September 5, 1902, she addressed the Bi-ennial Session of Friends' General Conference at Asbury Park, New Jersey, on the subject of "The Ethics of the Negro Question."

Earlier, the reviewers of Anna Cooper's book, *A Voice from the South,* had favorably commented on her extraordinary good sense and logic as well as her command of excellent English and satirical wit. As Cooper addressed the body of Friends, she did not camouflage her remarks or intersperse her thoughts with trivia as she began to question the morality of "the Negro Question," a subject that learned theologians had been pondering since the arrival of the first black slaves at Jamestown in 1619. Contending that "It [was] no fault of the Negro that he stands in the United States of America today as the passive and silent rebuke to the Nation's Christianity," Anna Cooper then warned her listeners that

A nation cannot long survive the shattering of its own ideals. Its doom is already sounded when it begins to write one law on its walls and lives another in its halls!

WHEELING PLAYGROUND INSTRUCTORS

VII.

The Colored Settlement House and YWCA

Prone in the road he lay,
  Wounded and sore bested;
Priests, Levites, passed that way
  And turned aside the head.
They were not hardened men
  In human service slack;
His need was great; but then
  His face, you see, was BLACK.

ANNA J. COOPER
The Social Settlement—What It
Is, and What It Does, 1913

Anna Cooper's interest in community service programs continued. She is shown here in the first row at far right with a group of Wheeling, West Virginia, playground instructors. Courtesy Moorland-Spingarn Research Center, Howard University.

IN 1901 CHARLES F. WELLER ENTERED UPON DUTY as the executive officer of the Associated Charities of the District of Columbia, and soon he began assessing the needs for social service programs in some of Washington's most neglected neighborhoods. According to Anna Cooper's history of the first Colored Social Settlement in the District, Weller rented a room in an alley and it was made available for use by "colored people of the poorest class, and with the aid of his . . . camera" he began to study and record conditions. Opposition to this phase of his work resulted in a meeting called by the alley dwellers themselves, and this group of black residents arranged to confer with Weller in the offices of the Associated Charities. There they organized the first Colored Social Settlement in Washington, D.C.

The space for this social service center, a small, six-room house on M Street, SW, had been donated by an anonymous young white woman, who was, according to Anna Cooper, "only a salaried clerk in government employ." The rapid growth of the settlement house, which offered services ranging from milk distribution for about sixty babies a day to the operation of a branch library, made it necessary later to erect a large facility at 16 L Street, SW, just about three blocks from its original home. During the summer of 1906, Anna Cooper was appointed supervisor of the Colored Settlement House, and according to Sharon Harley (*The Afro-American Woman Struggles and Images*), "in a city where there were a large number of cultured, resourceful Colored people, Mrs. Cooper [was] one of the most helpful workers for the intelligent advancement of the best interests of less fortunate Colored people."

In May 1907 President Theodore Roosevelt ap-

117

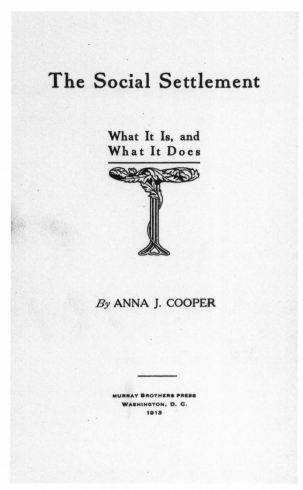

The Social Settlement

What It Is, and What It Does

By ANNA J. COOPER

MURRAY BROTHERS PRESS
WASHINGTON, D. C.
1913

The article in this booklet, *The Social Settlement: What It Is, and What It Does,* by Anna J. Cooper, was first published in the *Oberlin Journal.* Courtesy Mrs. Regia Bronson and Miss Regina Smith.

pointed a fifteen-member "President's Home Commission," one of its members being Professor George W. Cook of Howard University, whose wife, Coralie, was a diligent worker in civic and community affairs. The committees established by the commission illustrate the many concerns that they would investigate. Among them were the Committee on Building Model Houses, the Committee on Improvement of Existing Houses and the Elimination of Unsanitary Alley Houses, the Social Betterment Committee, the Committee on Building Regulations, and the Finance Committee. The work of the commission was financed by a gift of $5,000, which came from a donor outside of Washington, who stipulated that matching funds should be raised among the people of the District. The commissioners solicited $1,800 and public-spirited Washingtonians contributed the rest.

Charles Weller, who had formerly served as superintendent of the Englewood and West Side Districts for the Chicago Bureau of Charities before coming to Washington, was selected to oversee the investigation. The commission hoped to complete its study and report to the President before the expiration of his term in 1909. Entitled "Neglected Neighbors: Stories of Life in the Alley, Tenements and Shanties of the National Capital," the official report was prepared by Weller and his wife, Eugenia Winston Weller, who contributed one chapter. Rosetta E. Coakley Lawson and Lelia L. Amos Pendleton were among the investigators of living conditions of black families trapped in Washington's alley dwellings. Like Rosetta Lawson, Lelia Pendleton had also attended the Preparatory High School and was a civic-minded woman who, for thirteen years headed Anacostia's Alpha Charity Club. A trained teacher who had had to leave the District's schools when she married, Mrs. Pendleton wrote two books for black children: *A Narrative of the Negro* (1912) and *An Alphabet for Negro Children* (1915).

In her report on the participation of black women in pioneering social welfare efforts, Dr. Inabel Burns Lindsey observed "that the majority of them had to earn a livelihood through some vocation other than social services," and that "welfare services were generally undertaken on a voluntary basis." The work of the first Colored Settlement House was to be no exception, and its broad program engaged a large cadre of volunteers from all across the city. Organizations, church groups, high school youths, and individuals volunteered and did everything from bathing babies to fund-raising. In its first published report, the Colored Social Settlement listed all who gave time, talents, and resources. (A listing appears in the Appendix.) According to Anna Cooper, this settlement house was "distinct from the Associated Charities and [was] not supported by the latter although in cordial and constant co-operation with it." It did not gain fiscal support through the United Charities Drive in the District until 1934. Thus, from its founding and until it became a Community Chest agency, the total operation of this volunteer agency was an entirely black effort.

Charles Weller offered the following definition of

118

a "social settlement," and it was with this thought and spirit in mind that the first Colored Social Settlement House program was organized and developed:

> A social settlement is not "a charity," although friends may contribute to its support. It does not offer alms, but opportunities. It is not a means of patronage or condescension—instead it is a "level bridge" between different people . . . a common meeting ground. It is not "a mission" or a church; it does not seek, by preaching or other distinctively religious methods, to convert people to any creed, although it humbly strives to work out in practical ways the commandment, "love thy neighbor as thyself."

Anna Cooper described the first programs as an effort to find immediate solutions to day-to-day

Lelia Amos Pendleton founded the Alpha Charity Club in 1898. From *A Narrative of the Negro*.

The Colored Social Settlement House received support from community groups like the Washington Trio at the Washington Conservatory of Music, which aided with fund-raising. From *Self-Educator for a Rising Race*.

Social Settlement members and volunteers worked to improve family and child care services. From *Self-Educator for a Rising Race.*

problems, many of which had resulted from the necessity of making adjustments from a rural to an urban lifestyle. The settlement house and its programs were there to help make the transition and adjustments easier, and the activities were supported entirely by community contributions and volunteer help for the program year 1904–1905. A typical week's schedule included daily (except Sunday) nursery day care for the infants of neighborhood families where mothers were required to work away from home a full day. Supported mainly through the efforts of Mrs. H. W. Gilfillan, a white patron-

The "Belles of the Ball" basketball team from Normal School No. 2. The Colored Social Settlement and the Colored Public Schools cosponsored programs like these for young women. From *Self-Educator for a Rising Race.*

120

ess, mothers were only charged the cost of the infant's feeding. A small "bank" that was open daily encouraged thrift through a saving-stamp program, and Monday through Saturday a free kindergarten was open from 9:00 a.m. until noon. Mrs. Anna Murray directed this program, and she was assisted by Miss Lily Moore. On Mondays a boys' club was conducted by the residents themselves.

Mrs. E. M. Thomas conducted a sewing class for older girls on Tuesdays, and interestingly a "self-conducted" reading club for boys met on this same day. The Misses Dillard and Welsh held sewing classes for the younger girls on Wednesdays, while a boys' military club was conducted by cadets from the Armstrong Manual Training School. A Thursday afternoon singing class was the project of students from Normal School No. 2, and from 4:30 until 6:00 p.m. the residents conducted a mothers' sewing club. A Friday boys' club was led by J. C. VanLoo and James E. Walker, who also conducted a Sunday School program for boys.

Students enrolled in the Normal School gained practicum for their training and service in the day nursery and kindergarten programs, as they learned to bath and feed the infants along with their duties as instructional staff. High school young men became "Big Brothers" and provided positive male images for those youngsters without fathers. At the Social Settlement House, mothers without hope found understanding and encouragement; abandoned children found love and new homes; and a unique program called the "Back Yard Garden and Beautification Project" supplemented the family table and improved the appearance of the neighborhood. When basic human needs were met, the Colored Conference Class (the name adopted by the organizing group of residents) began to plan a "Summer Outing Camp" and recreational programs that included an excursion down the Potomac River on a steamer.

Among those who visited and endorsed the Settlement House in southwest Washington, D.C., was Mary White Ovington, herself a settlement house program manager in Brooklyn, New York, and a special investigator of city conditions among Negroes. In her opinion, "You could not anywhere find a settlement carried on upon finer, more practical, more sympathetic lines." Another observer, Catherine Siebert, a reporter for the *Columbus* (Ohio) *Press Post,* wrote "In my days of various

study and investigation nothing has half so much impressed me as the modest Settlement conducted in the very poorest section of Washington." In November 1905 H. B. F. Macfarland—then president, Board of Commissioners of the District of Columbia—wrote the following assessment of the Colored Social Settlement House:

> From personal observation I am able to commend most heartily the Social Settlement at 118 M Street, S.W., Washington, D.C. . . . No better work of its kind is done anywhere. It has peculiar value and significance, because it is being done by and for the colored people and has the promise through its efficiency and success of inspiring other effort in the same direction. As one of the pioneer colored social settlements it deserves the sympathy and support of philanthropists, and ought to stir many hearts to do the same thing for colored people elsewhere.

Anna Cooper was among those who had labored for the success of the first social service agency for the District's black residents. Benefiting from the best academic training at the time, trustees and staff rendered professional and skilled service. Along with Anna Cooper, members of the trustees were Roscoe Conkling Bruce, H.E. Williams, Mrs. Elizabeth Brown-Ufford, Mrs. Clara Burrill-Bruce, George William Cook, the Reverend Francis J. Grimké, Mrs. G. D. Hawkins, the Reverend W. J. Howard, Dr. Thomas Jesse Jones, Miss Emma F. G. Merritt, Samuel Middleton, Mrs. L. D. Moore, Dr. E. L. Parks, Mrs. Mary Church Terrell, Major James E. Walker, E. C. Williams, and Garnet C. Wilkinson. Staff members included William L. Washington, head worker-director of playgrounds; Mrs. Blanche Washington, matron; and Mrs. Lula Love Lawson, extension secretary. Anna Cooper was supervisor.

The following account of the work and history of the first Colored Settlement House was written by Anna Cooper, and was found among the small collection of her papers at Howard University. Probably written in the early 1930s, the undated but signed fragment of typescript disclosed that

> The Colored Social Settlement here described was commandeered by the Federal Government during World War I. The sum of $2,500 was placed at interest in the Washington Loan & Trust Company, 9th and F Sts. N.W., Wash-

Picture of Proposed Building for the Day Nursery

$500.00 To Be Given Away

Enrol your name at once as captain to enter Membership Campaign of the Day Nursery, 1135 New Jersey Ave., N. W., Washington, D. C. We are asking 25,000 men and women with $1.00 and a heart to make this New Year's offering in January for the proposed new building and wipe out the indebtedness of $1,000.00 owing by the Nursery and to provide the running expenses of 1920.

Wanted 100 Captains to enter New Member Contest at Once

The 14 Leading Captains will receive $500, as follows: First award will be $100 for highest amount over $100; Second, $75 highest amount over $75; Third, $50 for highest amount over $50. The next eleven highest persons on list will receive $35 each.

CONTEST OPEN TO ALL ALIKE who agree to work in accordance with the rules of the contest. If you have already paid $1.00 within the past six months to the Day Nursery send $1.00 with this coupon. If you have not paid $1.00 within six months, send $2.00 with this coupon to Rev. Dr. Francis J. Grimke, Treasurer, 1135 New Jersey Ave., N. W., as evidence of good faith and your name will be entered as captain, and you will be given credentials and instructions.

COUPON
To be filled in, signed and sent with money to Rev. Francis J. Grimke. Treasurer of the Alley Improvement Association, 1135 New Jersey Ave. N.W. Washington, D. C. Enclosed find .... Please enter my name as captain for the New Year's Campaign for the Day Nursery. I agree to comply with the conditions of the contest in making reports, etc.
NAME.................................
DATE.................... ADDRESS.................................

The Reverend Francis J. Grimké was treasurer of the "Membership Campaign of the Day Nursery," which was to be located at 1135 New Jersey Avenue, NW. From the *Washington Bee.* Courtesy Library of Congress.

ington, D.C. Mr. H. W. Williams, Weather Bureau, Treasurer. Later, after Mr. Williams' resignation and final demise, a full meeting of all living members of the Trustee Board, called by Anna J. Cooper, was held at Phyllis Wheatley Y.W.C.A. Dr. Francis J. Grimké, President, Rev. William Washington, Secretary. Garnet C. Wilkinson was elected Treasurer and instructed to take necessary measures to fulfill the unanimous decision of the Trustees to donate the money with its accrued interest to the Community Chest in the name of the First Colored Social Settlement of Washington, D.C.

Also concerning the Colored Social Settlement, in a letter addressed to an old and dear friend on New Year's Day, 1934, Anna Cooper in part wrote:

Anna Cooper's account and financial history of the Colored Social Settlement, which later became the Southwest Settlement House. Courtesy Mrs. Regia Bronson and Miss Regina Smith.

The Colored Social Settlement here described was commandeered by the Federal Government during World War I. The sum of $2,500 was placed at interest in the Washington Loan & Trust Company, 9th and F Sts., N. W., Washington, D. C., Mr. H. E. Williams, Weather Bureau, Treasurer. Later, after Mr. Williams' resignation and final demise, a full meeting of all living members of the Trustee Board, called by Anna J. Cooper, was held at Phyllis Wheatley Y.W.C.A. Dr. Francis J. Grimke, President, Rev. William Washington, Secretary. Garnet C. Wilkinson was elected Treasurer and instructed to take necessary measures to fulfil the unanimous decision of the Trustees to donate the money with its accrued interest to the Community Chest in the name of the First Colored Social Settlement of Washington, D. C.

Anna Cooper

My dear Doctor Grimké,

You know before I write it my prayers & hearts desire for your health, happiness & long life in this & many succeeding newyears.

You have received ere this a copy of Elwood Street's communication concerning the Social Settlement Fund of $3,078.08 entrusted to the Trustees of Community Chest to be by them invested as a perpetual foundation bearing interest to be expended for the social betterment of Colored people thro agencies recognized by the Chest. I rejoice in this happy termination of a rather protracted struggle to bring about what seems a most just & reasonable recognition of the life history of the first Colored Social Settlement & I want to thank you for your consistent cooperation & support in that struggle. It is morally certain that without this persistent & insistent effort on our part, no such satisfactory result would have ever been accomplished. . . .

By the spring of 1905 the idea of the work of the Young Women's Christian Association was beginning to catch on in Washington, where Mrs. Rosetta Lawson had attended a meeting conducted by a representative of the Chicago YWCA. In March of that year, she sent a note to her daughter Josephine, then a student at Oberlin College, saying "I want you to join the Y.W.C.A." A few days later the following notice was sent to the members of the Book Lovers Club:

The Booklovers earnestly request your presence at a meeting to be held at Berean Baptist Church, April 5, 1905, at 7:30 P.M., to consider the advisability of organizing a Young Women's Christian Association.

Mrs. Rosetta E. Lawson,
 President.

Mrs. L. J. Moss,
 Secretary.

That evening the meeting focused attention on the continuing and increased need "for better lodging places for girls and women seeking work in Washington." Following a lively discussion, those in attendance agreed to meet on May 5, 1905, and formally organized what would become the first YWCA to be founded in the District of Columbia. Incorporated under the laws of the District on June 30, 1905, the Y established a temporary office and a shelter for women in rented rooms in the old Miner Institution Building (not to be confused

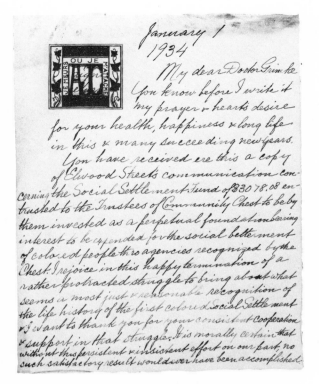

The letter concerning the Social Settlement from Anna J. Cooper to the Reverend Mr. Grimké, January 1, 1934. Courtesy Moorland-Spingarn Research Center, Howard University.

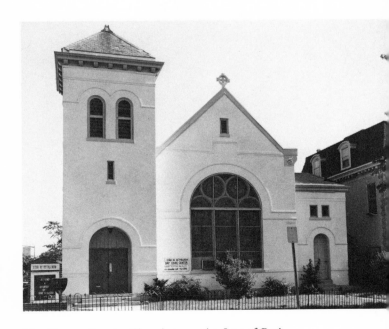

The Berean Baptist Church (now the Star of Bethlehem Church) at Eleventh and V Streets, NW, site of the organizational meeting of the first YWCA in the District of Columbia.

The Miner Institution Building, at Fourth and One-Half Street and Maryland Avenue, SW, was the first site of the Colored YWCA in Washington. From *A History of the Phyllis Wheatley Y.W.C.A.* Courtesy Moorland-Spingarn Research Center, Howard University.

with the Miner School Building) at Fourth and One-Half Street and Maryland Avenue, SW.

First called the Colored Young Women's Christian Association, the incorporators were Mrs. Bettie Francis, Mrs. Coralie F. Cook, Miss Lucinda Cook, Mrs. Mamie E. Hilyer; Mrs. Rosetta E. Lawson, Mrs. D. F. Rivers, Mrs. Josephine B. Bruce, Mrs. Henry E. Baker, Mrs. L. J .Moss, Miss Marion P. Shadd, and Mrs. Ida Gibbs Hunt. The members of the first Board of Managers were: Mrs. Bettie Francis, Miss Mildred E. Gibbs, Mrs. Annie E. Crom-

well, Miss Ella D. Barrier, Dr. Amanda S. Gray (she was a pharmacist), Miss Erminie F. Shimm, Mrs. Fannie Ware Taylor, and Miss Marion P. Shadd. The executive committee was chaired by Mrs. Lawson, and the following is a list of the new organization's permanent committees:

Miss Anna E. Thompson
Membership Committee
Miss Fannie M. Clair
Hope and Help Committee
Mrs. Sarah C. Fernandis
Social Settlement Committee
Mrs. Martha E. Tucker
Entertainment Committee
Mrs. Mary C. Terrell
Education Committee
Miss Emma F. G. Merritt
Building Fund Committee
Mrs. Louisa R. Cabiniss
Employment Committee
Miss Silence R. Rivers
Library Committee
Miss Mary L. Beason
Auditing Committee
Mrs. Annie E. Waddleton
Devotional Committee
Mrs. Oceanna Brooks
Mothers Committee
Mrs. Lelia L. Pendleton
Printing and Press Committee
Miss Roberta Quander
Flower and Fruit Committee

Other members of the executive committee were Mary L. Merriwether, Lucy E. Moorland, Luella C. G. Craig, Jane Tyson, Carrie E. Pierre, Laura Queen, Ida G. Richardson, and Anna Cooper's foster daughter, Lula Love.

Anna Cooper and Bettie Francis became life members of the Colored Young Women's Christian Association, and the membership had grown to 193 members by the end of the first year. Programs developed slowly at first, but by its third year of operation the Y occupied the entire Miner Institution Building. By the end of its fifth year, the association had to look for new quarters, when the school system acquired the Miner Building. Meantime, Emma Merritt had begun negotiating for the purchase of a ten-room house in LeDroit Park, 429 T Street, NW, which stood on a lot 50 by 100 feet, and was in a quiet residential neighborhood with tree-lined streets in the vicinity of Howard Univer-

Emma F. G. Merritt (1860–1933), a noted educator, public school administrator, and social activist, founded the Teacher's Benefit and Annuity Association. Courtesy Association for the Study of Afro-American Life and History.

sity. The purchase price was $4,300, and in two years the building was paid for. In its new location the Colored YWCA program expanded to include classes in sewing, cooking, Bible study, missionary work, music, and Negro history.

By 1910 Anna Cooper had returned to Washington and the M Street School after four years of self-imposed exile, and from that time served as chairman of the girls' programs at the Y. Earlier, she had given up her home at 1706 Seventeenth Street, NW, for her mother had died in 1899, and John and Lula Love, whom she had raised, were now on their own. With no immediate family responsibilities, she now lived in the home of her longtime friend, Emma Merritt, on Tenth Street, NW, and both women were deeply involved with and devoted to the work of the Y.

During World War I, the activities of the Y accelerated as the women tried to keep pace with the demands. Additional cots were brought into their overcrowded building in an effort to accommodate the growing numbers of young black wom-

en who were arriving in the city seeking wartime jobs. There were also the young girls with idle time, whose mothers had joined the ranks of the war workers.

The Colored Young Women's Christian Association celebrated its first decade of community service on a sad note, for Bettie Francis was forced to retire. By all accounts, Mrs. Francis and Miss Merritt were acknowledged to be the driving force behind the successful development of the YWCA. Now, the death of her husband, Dr. John R. Francis, and her own failing health made it necessary for Mrs. Francis to leave her post; she was also leaving the city. Under her able leadership the Y had not only developed the traditional kinds of programs that have long been associated with that organization, but it had also become an articulate and outspoken advocate for full citizenship rights for Negroes. The women of the Y had sent an official protest to President William H. Taft (1909–1913) against the hanging of a woman named Mattie Lomax. In 1913 they voiced their opposition to the opening of the "5¢ Sunday Movie"; and also lobbied successfully for the appointment of matrons at public beaches to "look after the welfare of colored boys

The first permanent home of the Colored YWCA, at 429 T Street, NW. From the Fifth and Sixth Annual Report of the Phyllis Wheatley Y.W.C.A. Courtesy Moorland-Spingarn Research Center, Howard University.

and girls." Also, the women began making plans to "affiliate with the mother organization," which had made no overture to its "Colored" sisters in the nation's capital.

Mrs. Frances Boyce was Mrs. Francis's successor, and in 1917 she took the case of the Colored YWCA to the War Work Council. After several meetings, Eva D. Bowles, administrator of all war work among colored women, cited the Washington group as a national model that women in other communities around the country might emulate. Begrudgingly, in January 1918, Mrs. Cordella Winn was assigned to come to Washington to investigate the administration and programs of the Colored Y. Impressed with what she saw, Mrs. Winn remained for six months and made positive suggestions for the continuation of the work, also preparing a strong justification for the women to receive $200,000 from funds that had been contributed by Americans of every persuasion to the War Work Council. This money was to be used to finance the construction of a "demonstration building in Washington for colored work," for Mrs. Winn had been unable to negotiate an amicable affiliation between the Central and the Colored Y's. Mrs. Boyce and her women had been willing to affiliate with the Central Y in April 1918, but that group declared its inability to accept the "burden" of additional financial responsibility. Yet for more than a decade, the black Y had successfully financed its own programs through strong community support and participation. It had responded to immediate needs, engaged in long-range planning for future programs, and had demonstrated an ability to manage the funds intelligently. Still, white women were unwilling to affiliate as equals with black women who shared the same interests and concerns. There were some who believed that the real crux of the matter stemmed from the fact that the Colored Young Women's Christian Association had predated the founding of the Central Y in the District of Columbia. The policy of the Governing Board of Managers of the National YWCA was entrenched with "Jimcrowism," and the local white women—who professed to give "Christian" service—could see neither the incongruity nor the inhumanity of their prejudicial attitudes.

To meet growing needs, Anna Cooper had founded the Y's first chapter of the Camp Fire Girls as early as 1912, and Fannie M. Clair, wife of the

Eva D. Bowles, administrator of the War Work Council programs among "Colored" women during World War I. From *The Work of Colored Women.* Courtesy Mrs. Regia Bronson and Miss Regina Smith.

pastor of the Asbury Methodist Church, had expanded her Hope and Help Committee to include travelers' aid services, for the soldiers from nearby camps were coming into the city in ever-increasing numbers. A legion of fifty members, who included George W. Cook and young men from the Twelfth Street YMCA (now named for its founder, Anthony Bowen, a former slave) and students from Howard University, the Traveler's Aid Committee rendered immeasurable service at Washington's Union Station, where trains were met every hour on the hour. Because of the presence in Washington of southern sentiments, which had persisted since the Civil War, Negro office-seekers, war workers, soldiers, and others who came into the city in large numbers had to be directed to "Colored" lodgings, eating houses, and places of safe entertainment. Soon after the war ended, when Major James E. Walker returned home to lead his 372nd regiment triumphantly past the White House and the Treasury Department Building and onto New York Avenue, the city erupted. The story of the nation's shame was reported by James Weldon Johnson, field officer for the National Association for the Advancement of Colored People (NAACP), who had been sent to Washington to report on the "Red Summer of 1919." He told of black citizens being forcibly dragged from public street cars and beaten, while others were mobbed on the White House lawn, where they had sought refuge. Even though the National Guard was called upon to help restore order, their efforts proved futile until the third day of rioting when it was learned that now blacks had armed themselves and were prepared and determined to strike back. During this period—the first of the "long hot summers"—women of the Y began to respond to emergency situations and drafted an official statement of protest that was sent to the President and members of Congress.

In 1892 Anna Cooper had prophetically written:

The woman of to-day finds herself in the presence of responsibilities which ramify through the profoundest and most varied interests of her country and race. [She counseled that] not one of the issues of this plodding, toiling, sinning, repenting, falling, aspiring humanity can afford to shut her out, or can deny the reality of her influence.

By 1920 the interests and activities of black women had extended beyond home, neighborhood, immediate community, and even city, as they addressed every immediate and basic issue. Their sphere of influence was significant, and they became an integral part of the wartime work force and industry, very vocal on the issues of disparity in wages and working conditions. While footsore from lobbying, these women demonstrated that they had lost none of their mettle for the struggle as they buttonholed members of the District Committees on Capitol Hill, wrote letters to out-of-town friends urging that they also write to their congressmen, lectured—winning friends where they could—and testified before boards, committees, and commissions. In the meantime, the women's plans to build a permanent YWCA continued.

Immediate exigencies during and immediately after World War I had caused unavoidable delays in the building of the Colored Women's Y and since construction funds allocated by the War Work Council had not been expended and the building begun, Eva Bowles sought the assistance of Emmett J. Scott, assistant secretary of war, to save the funds. A convincing case was made for a continuing

need, the project was carried over as a "wartime measure," and on December 19, 1920, the Phyllis Wheatley YWCA was dedicated

TO THE GLORY OF GOD
IN SERVICE FOR OUR YOUNG WOMEN
THIS BUILDING IS DEDICATED
IN THE YEAR OF OUR LORD
MCMXX.

In March of that year Emma Merritt had launched a building fund campaign that would net an additional $18,000, and thus make it possible to complete construction. The building would contain offices, a gymnasium, showers, a cafeteria, forty-three single rooms, and one double room. A single note of elegance: "The panel over the fireplace in the Social Hall representing a 'Harvest Procession' [was] reproduced from a photograph of a chimney piece discovered in the demolished theater at Gand, Belgium, and had been taken from the ancient Chateau de Gielenkerich; it dated back to 1559."

Now the YWCA would have a paid staff, and Mrs. Martha Allan McAdoo was appointed general secretary, a position she had held in Chicago. When the new building was ready for service, on April 5, 1921, all departments were fully operational and among the staff that reported to continue the Y's program were Mary F. Thompson, Lettie Nolen Calloway, Florence G. Brooks, Harriet E. Kin, Florence Franklin, and Sadie A. Harper.

The success it achieved during its first eight months of operation in the new building at 901 Rhode Island Avenue, NW (where the programs continue today), is recorded in the 1921 report for the Colored Young Women's Christian Association. By this time, the membership had increased to 3,115, with 1,950 black girls and young women enrolled in classes and conferences. In addition, Anna Cooper had enrolled 618 girls in the Camp Fire and Girl Reserves programs, and 500 girls were actively engaged in "industrial" programs. Also, 345 persons were assisted with housing and 63 additional clients were helped with housing needs through the Y's room registry service; 37,830 meals were served (Dr. Carter G. Woodson, founder of Negro History Week, who lived near by, was a regular dinner guest); 12 emergency cases were handled; 37 young women found employ-

Girl Reserves took part in organized activities, including exercise programs such as this. From *The Work of Colored Women.* Courtesy Mrs. Regia Bronson and Miss Regina Smith.

The architectural rendering for the new Phyllis Wheatley YWCA, named for the African-born slave poet. Dedicated in 1920, the building is located at 901 Rhode Island Avenue, NW. From *The Work of Colored Women.* Courtesy Mrs. Regia Bronson and Miss Regina Smith.

ment; and 15 community organizations and agencies used the building's meetingroom facilities.

The experiment had worked! At the end of their first year in the new building, Mrs. Winn—who had first come from New York with some doubts— enthusiastically testified that "The business management of the Association is well done [and] the women are proving they can carry the big responsibility." In addition to the management and supervision of the new main building, and the many activities, programs, and projects that emanated from that site, the women continued to render service from the Gibbs House, at 429 T Street, NW, where emergency care was given to transients unable to pay the modest dormitory rates at the Phyllis Wheatley Y. This house was named for

Mildred E. Gibbs, a life member and teacher who, for many years, had rendered invaluable service to the organization. It was in this building, too, that Anna Cooper, along with Mary Mason and Edna Gray, organized six groups of Camp Fire Girls. Mrs. Cooper was appointed guardian of the troop. Extending this much-needed program into the community, girls' clubs were also formed in the "Colored" elementary, junior and senior high schools, the Metropolitan A.M.E., St. Paul A.M.E. Chapel, Zion Baptist, Union Wesley A.M.E. Zion, and Trinity Baptist Churches, and all were under the auspices of the Phyllis Wheatley Y. With the able support of Edith Fleetwood

Bettie G. Cox Francis (wife of Dr. John R. Francis), an effective leader in the Black Clubwomen's Movement, advocated women's involvement in community affairs. From *A New Negro for a New Century.*

Sponsored by black women volunteers, the "Blue Triangle Girls" program offered social development to young black women. From *The Work of Colored Women.* Courtesy Mrs. Regia Bronson and Miss Regina Smith.

(daughter of Christian A. Fleetwood), Portia Daniels, Anita Turpeau, and Dr. Dorothy Boulding (Ferebee), a founder of the Southeast Neighborhood House, the work of organizing girls extended into the communities of Alexandria, Virginia; Ivy City, D.C. (now in Far Northeast Washington); and into the Southeast Neighborhood House. With an initial grant of $2,000 from the War Work Council, the women also operated a community recreation center at 1634 Fourteenth Street, NW.

In March 1923 the Articles of Incorporation of the Colored Young Women's Christian Association were amended to change the organization's name to the Phyllis Wheatley Young Women's Christian Association. On April 1 of that year, Frances Boyce received the deed to the new four-story red brick building at 901 Rhode Island Avenue, NW, from Emily Bailey Speer, president of the Board of Directors of the National YWCA, in New York. We are reminded of Bettie Francis's closing remarks when she, on the occasion of the twentieth anniversary of the Phyllis Wheatley Y, addressed the ladies and said, "We have built, with God's help, better than we knew."

130

VIII.

The Third Step: Doctorate from the Sorbonne

I may say honestly and truthfully that my one aim is and has always been, so far as I may, to hold a torch for the children of a group too long exploited and too frequently disparaged in its struggling for the light.

ANNA JULIA COOPER
December 29, 1925

IN 1906 ANNA COOPER HAD DECIDED TO MOVE TO Jefferson City, Missouri, where she taught at Lincoln University. During the summer months between 1907 and 1910, she renewed her contact with Oberlin College and began to give serious thought to the pursuit of a doctorate. Applying to Oberlin's president, she learned that the college was unable to offer academic study at that level. Contenting herself then with a course of study simply for the joy of it (a luxury never before indulged), she found the diversion of belles-lettres "stimulating."

Returning in the fall of 1910 to the M Street School and the city of Washington, the scene of past educational triumphs and personal humiliation, Anna Cooper faced significant changes and adjustments in her professional and personal life. The past four years had been spent teaching and discharging administrative duties on the college level, and now she was teaching Latin in the school she had once headed as principal.

She had given up the Seventeenth Street home and the independent social life it had afforded her, in 1906, and now she shared the home of her friend, Emma Merritt. Although it was to a very different professional and home situation that Anna Cooper returned, it was not long before she had reordered her priorities and accepted new and varied challenges.

Anna Cooper's first opportunity to travel abroad had come in the winter of 1896, when she visited the birthplace of her husband—the island of Nassau in the British West Indies. Later, after addressing the Pan-African Conference in London, in 1900, Anna and her foster daughter, Lula Love, toured Europe. They visited the Paris Exposition and went

Dr. Anna Julia Cooper. Photograph by Addison Scurlock, about 1923. Courtesy Robert Scurlock, Scurlock Studios.

131

Lula Love (Lawson), Anna Cooper's foster daughter, graduated from the M Street School in 1890 and earned a Normal School certificate from Howard University in 1892. She worked for the Southwest Settlement House and taught Physical Education in the District. From *A New Negro for a New Century*.

to Oberammergau to see the Passion Play, which each decade brought tourists by the thousands to the Bavarian village near Munich. Then on to Italy, where the two women enjoyed the opera and the beauty of Milan. Journeying southward, they stopped at the museums of Florence and saw the Bay of Naples. Enroute home they visited Rome, Pisa, and the ruins of Pompeii.

Anna Cooper returned to France during the summer of 1911, and became a student at La Guilde Internationale in Paris. She returned again during the summers of 1912 and 1913 to study French literature, history, and phonetics. She was pleased to earn "certificates" for each of these courses, with honorable mention, from Paul Privat Desohanel, whom she described as "the most brilliant and fascinating teacher of history. . . ." Now in her mid-fifties, Anna Cooper's life took on new meaning and purpose.

She enrolled as a doctoral student at Columbia University in New York City on July 3, 1914, having been accepted on the basis of courses taken

in Paris over the preceding summers. With work for the "long dreamed of Ph.D" begun, by the summer of 1917 Anna Cooper had earned thirty-two credits, and Columbia certified her proficiency in French, Latin, and Greek. She had also completed all course work in the French language, including Old French and French literature. The university was satisfied with Anna's demonstrated ability to undertake research leading to the preparation of a college edition of *Pèlerinage de Charlemagne*, the eleventh-century epic of the king of the Franks (A.D. 768–814) and "emperor of the Romans" (800–814). Having successfully met all requirements of the Romance Language Department, Anna Cooper was not able to undertake further work without difficulties and more personal sacrifices, for while she was contemplating a way to meet Columbia's one-year residency requirement, a new challenge presented itself. Once again the dream had to be deferred. In 1939, when Anna Cooper wrote an account of this period of her life, she began:

> At dawn on Christmas Day, in 1915, I walked into the Haywood Cottage in Raleigh where lay five sleeping children whose mother had lately been called to Heaven. Not all were asleep, the baby of six months was awake at this early hour, immediately began to coo [and] held out both arms as if she knew something was happening.

Becoming the guardian of five children and unable to leave her teaching post from September until June without losing her job, Anna Cooper's dilemma was how not to "utterly abandon" several important irons she had in the fire.

The adopted son of Andrew and Jane Haywood, John R. Haywood, recently widowed, was left with five children after the death of his wife, Margaret ("Maggie") Hinton Haywood. Ranging in age from six months to twelve years, the three girls and two boys were Regia, John, Andrew, Marion, and the baby, Annie Cooper Haywood, who would be called "little" Annie. At about the age of fifty-five, then, Anna Cooper was called upon to make a decision that would necessitate further adjustments in her lifestyle and resources. Relocating the family, she assumed responsibility for the upbringing and education of her great-nephews and great-nieces. She began searching for a new house, which she

later described as a place that "wou'd be a home to house their Southern exuberance—a place with room enough all around. . . ." Such a home was found in Washington's community of LeDroit Park, which, said Cooper, "in the historic past had been forbidden ground for colored people except as servants." The home had once been the residence of Congressman Benjamin Le Fevre, a Democrat first elected to the Forty-sixth Congress from Shelby County, Ohio. Now retired from political life, Le Fevre was called "General," for after the Civil War he was brevetted brigadier general. Anna Cooper described Le Fevre as "a unique combination of the perfect gentleman with a Christ-like attitude toward little children 'regardless of race, color, creed or national origin.' "

How Le Fevre became the owner of the LeDroit Park home is not known. The 1900 census for Washington City listed him among the residents of 201 T Street, NW, then living with his sister, Mary, and her husband, William M. Goodlove, cited as head of the household. Other occupants of

Anna Cooper's home at 201 T Street, NW, Washington, D.C. From *Decennial Catalogue of the Frelinghuysen University.* Courtesy Mrs. Regia Bronson and Miss Regina Smith.

the home included the Goodloves' son, Charles, and his wife, Mary, and Le Fevre's brother, Milton. Benjamin Le Fevre continued as a member of this household until 1909.

Recorded on January 28, 1916, the deed of sale stipulated that Le Fevre, "in consideration of the sum of Ten ($10) Dollars" agreed to sell Anna Cooper "in fee simple" the LeDroit Park property for $5,000. With a down payment of only ten dollars, Anna Cooper acquired a five-bedroom house on a lot measuring 156 by 30 feet, which would be "subject to a lien for deferred purchase money in the sum of Five Thousand Dollars." Le Fevre permitted Anna Cooper herself to dictate the conditions of repayment in accordance with "her needs and desires." Not occupied when first seen by Anna, the house required extensive work to make it

133

Anna Cooper's restored balustrade with a gazebo on the east end. From *Decennial Catalogue of Frelinghuysen University.* Courtesy Mrs. Regia Bronson and Miss Regina Smith.

ready for the five motherless children she affectionately called her "North Carolina Colony." In a booklet entitled *The Third Step (Autobiographical),* Anna wrote a description of the house at that time:

> The place had been used as a chicken yard by its white tenants and I immediately set about landscaping, threw an octagon sun room across the square cornered porch, changed the wooden pillars to graceful Italian columns and installed a concrete balustrade all round, none of which brought me any nearer the residential requirements at Columbia University.

At an age when families usually begin to enjoy relief from mortgage payments and the expense and problems of parenting, Anna Cooper acquired a mortgage and a family of five children, while continuing to teach at the high school. In the meanwhile, to "keep her hand in" her studies, she assigned herself "Home Work" and later began the arduous task of translating an Old French epic into modern French, with the assistance of the rare German edition of Charlemagne by Koschwitz. With the approval of her doctoral adviser at Columbia University, Anna Cooper began by working on the glossary for *Le Pèlerinage de Charlemagne.* The completed translation and first edition, with an introduction by the Abbé Klein of the Catholic Institute

The deed of sale from Benjamin Le Fevre to Anna Cooper, recorded January 25, 1916. Courtesy District of Columbia Recorder of Deeds.

of Paris, would be published in Paris in 1925. The following critique of this work, by a French author, was preserved by Cooper in *The Third Step,* and will help the reader to appreciate the significance of this work:

> Whatever the faults or the merits of the Pèlerinage de Charlemagne, it was not easy hitherto to discover them. The edition published in London in 1836 by Fr. Michel has become extremely rare, and in France the editions of Koschwitz are quite as hard to find. The first of these, which appeared in 1870 and which is very incomplete, is the only one that we find in any of the libraries of Paris: at la Nationale, at l'Institut and la Sorbonne. Mazarine, Sante-Genevieve, l'Ecole des Chartres

CHARLEMAGNE, par Albert Dürer.

LE PÈLERINAGE
DE CHARLEMAGNE

PUBLIÉ AVEC UN GLOSSAIRE

PAR

ANNA J. COOPER
Graduée d'Oberlin College, Ohio
Docteur
de l'Université de Paris.

Introduction de l'Abbé Félix KLEIN
Professeur honoraire
à l'Institut Catholique de Paris

PARIS
A. LAHURE, IMPRIMEUR-ÉDITEUR
9, RUE DE FLEURUS, 9
1925

Anna Cooper dedicated *Le Pèlerinage de Charlemagne* to "three great teachers . . . Jas. H. Fairchild, Chas. H. Churchill and Henry Churchill King," all of Oberlin College. Courtesy Mrs. Regia Bronson and Miss Regina Smith.

have none at all. Nowhere can a consultant find a complete copy of the manuscript that disappeared from London. Mme. Cooper in her preface says modestly that the present volume without pretense to erudition will render service perhaps to American students. It will be no less appreciated by French students and by their masters (profs'), happy to be able, *grace à elle,* to peruse directly a work which *does not fail to hold its own place in the history of our literature.*

This work did find its way into American college libraries, and in 1933 was used by Northwestern

NORTHWESTERN UNIVERSITY
COLLEGE OF LIBERAL ARTS
EVANSTON, ILLINOIS

ROMANCE LANGUAGES

November 17, 1933

Mrs. Anna J. Cooper,
201 T Street, N. W.,
Washington, D. C.,

My dear Mrs. Cooper:

Professor William C. Holbrook and I, both of Northwestern University, are preparing, for early publication with D. Appleton-Century Co., an anthology of medieval French literature in modernized versions, and should be very grateful to you for permission to reprint certain excerpts from your translation of *Le Pèlerinage de Charlemagne* (Paris, Lahure, 1925).

The passages which we should like to use are as follows: p. 2, pp. 25-31 passim, 37-43 passim. Unfortunately I have not the text at hand at the moment, but if there is any question about the extent of the material we wish to use, I should be glad to give you the exact lines.

Apparently the book is not copyrighted in the U. S., but we have hesitated to use even the brief passages indicated without your authorization. Needless to say, we shall make full acknowledgement of the source upon which we have drawn.

We are indebted to Professor Jameson, of Oberlin, for obtaining your present address.

Very truly yours,

Thomas R. Palfrey

A letter from Thomas Palfrey to Anna Cooper, November 17, 1933. Courtesy Moorland-Spingarn Research Center, Howard University.

135

General affidavit of 1920 by the Reverend A. B.
Hunter on behalf of Mrs. Jane Haywood, widow of
Andrew Haywood. Courtesy National Archives and
Record Service.

University professors Thomas R. Palfrey and William C. Holbrook in the preparation of an anthology of medieval literature "in modernized versions," for publication by D. Appleton-Century Company. Requesting permission to reprint certain excerpts from her translation, Palfrey wrote to Anna Cooper, "Apparently the book is not copyrighted in the U.S., but we have hesitated to use even the brief passages indicated without your authorization. Needless to say, we shall make full acknowledgement of the source upon which we have drawn."

While adjusting to the new experience of parenthood, Anna Cooper began to consider the plausibility of transferring the credits earned at Columbia University to the University of Paris, all the time learning the intricacies of household budgeting while also taking on even more family responsibility. In *The Third Step*, published about 1950, Anna Cooper treats the reader to brief but engaging glimpses of her thoughts and life during this period. By her own account, Anna "was conscious of just how far [her] income from teaching would stretch, with butter at 75¢ per lb. [and] still

soaring," and she confides that "raising this family with youthful exuberance was not easy during the years of World War I, with sugar severely rationed at any price and fuel oil obtainable only on affidavit in person at regional centers." Anna reminisced that when appearing before the Children's Court to assume guardianship of the Haywood children, the judge observed, "My, but you are a brave woman!" and she recalled thinking at the time, "only stubborn, perhaps, or foolhardy, according to the point of view." Among her friends and colleagues there were some who had tried to dissuade her from assuming this enormous responsibility. Perhaps Anna had done so with some feeling of nostalgia, recalling when others had opened the door of opportunity for her. Of her decision, she wrote, "I had taken them [the children] under my wing with the hope and determination of nurturing their growth into useful and creditable citizens." And after all, these children were her kin, the grandchildren of her brother Andrew, himself ill and away from home in a veterans' hospital. When his wife, Jane, became confused and bewildered because of Andrew's absence, Anna would bring her to Washington, where it was hoped that once reunited with her son and grandchildren she would be restored to good health.

Anna Cooper was obviously touched by the life of this unlettered black woman, who, according to St. Augustine's College's principal, the Reverend A. B. Hunter, had worked as a cook and engaged in other work for a salary of four dollars per week. In a story that Anna Cooper described as concerning "a Mid-Victorian Negro Marriage," and entitled "The Tie That Used to Bind," the scenario more than coincidentally parallels a story that began to unfold in the Spanish-American War records for Andrew J. Haywood, Major, Company "C," of the 3rd North Carolina Infantry. Although Cooper called her characters Andrew and Caroline McPherson Anderson, they are at once recognizable as Andrew and Jane McCraken Haywood.

Andrew Jackson Haywood first applied for pension benefits in 1899; he had been examined by physicians, and comrades who served with him testified to certify the disability that he claimed. He died without receiving the benefits, but Congress passed an act on July 16, 1918, making Jane Haywood eligible for widow's benefits. When Jane died, Anna Cooper insisted that the government,

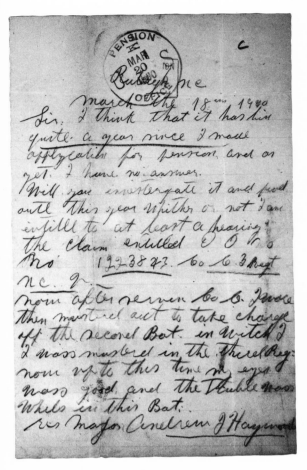

A letter from Andrew Haywood to the commissioner of the Pension Bureau, March 18, 1900. Courtesy National Archives and Record Service.

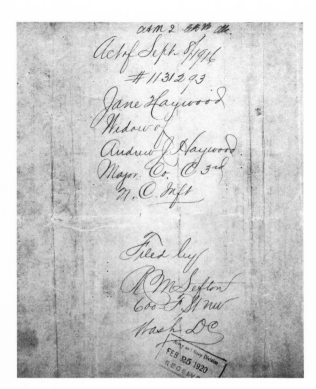

The endorsement for Jane Haywood's application for widow's benefits, filed in accordance with the congressional act of 1918. Courtesy National Archives and Record Service.

having denied Andrew a twenty-dollar-a-month pension for a service-connected disability for nearly nineteen years, place a suitable marker on his wife's grave and pay for it from the pension fund. For, as Anna Cooper observed, during all those years when the government had failed to assist Andrew and Jane, she had helped to care for them both, and had alone born the expense of Andrew's burial. Ironically, it was the claim for a veteran's disability pension that produced the name of Andrew Haywood's (and possibly the other family members') master. According to the expert testimony of Dr. H. O. Hyatt, of Kingston, North Carolina, "He [Andrew] was once the slave of Dr. Fab. Haywood [Fabius J. Haywood, Sr.] of Raleigh, N.C." From these records we also learn that Andrew had been blind in his right eye since childhood. The blindness had resulted from an injury, sustained when he was a young slave, that went unattended, and for

this reason he was denied the pecuniary benefits he had sought. The government produced another witness who refuted the claim. "Dr. Hood . . . a colored man of superior intelligence [whose] credibility [was] rated . . . good," testified that Andrew had worn corrective eyeglasses prior to military service. Although Andrew Haywood contested the opinion of the physician he said did not know him, and had never examined or treated him, the Pension Bureau's special examiner denied the claim on April 5, 1901. But until his death in 1918, Andrew persisted in making claim, contending that he was "fatally injured in his eyes with total loss of sight in [the] right eye and serious damage to the left eye from glare of sun in constant drilling on the beach at Fort Macon during the months of June, July and August, 1898."

While attending to matters relating to Andrew and then to his wife, Anna Cooper continued to provide for the grandchildren, who, in turn, were sent to boarding schools, thereby making it possible for her to continue her studies. By the mid–1920s Regia was attending St. Augustine's College while John Wesley attended Tuskegee Institute; Andrew and Marion attended Catholic schools at Rockcastle, Virginia (St. Emma's for boys and St. Frances de Sales for girls). In time, "little" Annie would also attend St. Frances. Anna Cooper, called "Sis" Annie by the children, would reunite the family at home at Christmas and other vacation times. It was at just such a time that she made the final decision concerning the completion of her doctoral work. As Anna said, "a fortuitous bout with the flu," the Christmas of 1923, presented her with the golden opportunity. She explained it this way:

> 'Twas the night before Christmas. After a hectic day of last minute shopping and preparations, late at night I was busy sorting out gifts and filling the children's stockings, when suddenly, things began to swim before me and grow black. I left the stockings to the oldest girl and staggered off to bed. The next day and many after I was not able to raise my head above the pillow and when I did get back to school I realized I was not at my best and decided to ask for a year's sick leave. This ostensibly was granted but the string to which it was attached turned out later to have elastic claws. . . . [I]t transpired that the substitutes' compensation for every day of my absence was larger than my own per diem pay.

The summer after the attack of influenza, Anna Cooper was on her way to France and the "Third Step" of her educational aspirations. When the Abbé Klein learned of her plan to transfer to the University of Paris, he offered the following prayer: "Que Dieu vous protège et benisse vos courageux desseins" (May God protect you and bless your courageous plans).

By the summer of 1924 Anna Cooper had been in Paris several times, but new regulations and requirements had to be satisfied before permission could be gained for her to use certain documents needed to support her program of studies. Too, Anna needed a new passport (a picture with *two* eyes, please!—she was partial to a profile portrait)—and the endorsement of the American Embassy to study official documents at the French Archives and to investigate special dossiers at the Bibliothèque Militaire. Finally, registration at the College des Etrangères was completed, necessary conferences were arranged with faculty advisers, and the government revenue stamp on the application for "'les épreuves du Docteur d'Université devant la Faculté ês Lettres'" was acquired.

When the time came to select the subject of her doctoral thesis, Anna's decision was influenced by positions taken by French President Poincaré on the question of racial equality. She was impressed by this Frenchman, who had instigated the building of a monument at Dakar (Senegal, West Africa) "A la Gloire de l'Armeé Noire" (to the glory of the Army of the Blacks). Much excited by the philosophy of Liberté! Egalité! Fraternité!—a sentiment dating from before the French Revolution and officially adopted by the government in 1793—Anna Cooper first decided to study "L'Attitude de la France a l'Egard de l'Egalité des Races" (The Attitude of France Regarding the Equality of the Races), but her advisers thought the topic too broad and "too vague!" She then restricted the discussion to the era of the French Revolution, and the dissertation subject "L'Attitude de la France dans la question de l'Esclavage entre 1789 et 1848" ("The Attitude of France on the Question of Slavery between 1789 and 1848") was approved.

Preparing for the defense of her dissertation, Anna Cooper eagerly devoured "the writings and speeches of and about La Societé des Amis des Noirs," and by her account "read avidly . . . the contribut[ors] to current thought as Franz Boaz—Jean Finot—[and] Gobineau." At each turn of the pages she found "her heart pounding and her mind racing ahead" to learn more, more! She was especially impressed with the writings of Alphonse Marie Louis de Lamartine (1790-1869), French author and orator, whose "drame à clef" about Toussaint L'Ouverture, "presented by Lemaitre at Paris [on] April 15, 1850," ended with the thrilling words:

> Je signai la liberté des Noirs, l'Abolition de l'Esclavage et la promesse d'indemnité aux colons. Ma vie n'eut elle eu que cette heure, je ne regretterais pas d'avoir vecu.
>
> (I have signed the emancipation of the blacks, the abolition of slavery and the promise of indemnity to the planters. If my life had had only this hour, I should not regret having lived.)

Anna Cooper had left the United States without the request for the year's leave of absence having been satisfactorily acted upon by her supervisor.

4 rue Rollin Ve
15 janvier 1934

Monsieur:

Je voudrais retenir l'assistance d'un collaborateur qui a l'entrée aux archives nationales dont j'ai besoin en préparant ma thèse: "l'attitude de la France à l'égard de l'égalité des races," que je désire présenter à la Faculté des Lettres de la Sorbonne. Je cherche: 1) Histoire de la Société des Amis des Noirs, formée 1788 pour achever l'abolition de l'esclavage. Les discours dans l'Assemblée Constituante sur ce sujet. Les travaux de l'Abbé Grégoire. 2) La loi actuelle du droit de cité à l'égard des coloniaux. 3) Les lois à l'égard des immigrés du Japon, d'Afrique, d'Inde, etc.

Permettez-moi de dire, Monsieur, que j'ai les plus agréables souvenirs de votre cours précieux à la Guilde Internationale il y a dix ans, et j'estime votre certificat signé parmi mes plus chers trésors.

Je sais que vous avez sans le chercher les matières que je veux, et que vous pourriez m'indiquer sans que vous vous dérangiez, les livres et les manuscrits dont j'ai besoin.

J'espère que vous voulez bien m'accorder le privilège d'être encore une fois sous votre habile direction. Veuillez agréer, Monsieur, mes plus respectueux sentiments.

Anna J. Cooper.

Forced to return to her teaching post, Anna Cooper wrote this letter in 1924 to seek research assistance in Paris for needed reference material. Courtesy Moorland-Spingarn Research Center, Howard University.

This, as Cooper would later recall, was "before the Be-Kind-to-Teachers Era" when educational institutions and systems began to grant sabbatical leave for further academic study. Rather, the prevailing attitude seemed to have been that such study might more appropriately be pursued during scheduled recesses or summer vacations. Either believing that her request for sick leave had been granted (she was still recovering from the flu and paying a substitute's fee), or would be granted, Anna had left for Paris to recover her health and obtain the much-sought-after degree. With only fifty days of the residence requirement fulfilled, it came as a surprise to her, then, when a trusted friend cabled disquieting news: "Rumored dropped if not returned within 60 days." As incredible as it may seem, Anna Cooper, not wishing to be let go from the school's faculty (M Street had now become Dunbar High), with the inherent risk of the loss of retirement benefits and annuity, returned to her classroom "5 minutes before 9 on the morning of the 60th day of my absence." Greeted by the cheers and applause of her students, she resigned herself to working every available hour in an alcove assigned for her use at the Library of Congress (blacks were not admitted then into the main reading room and facilities set aside for white scholars). By Thanksgiving vacation, 1924, Cooper's dissertation was ready for typing, and this time Anna requested an excused absence for an "emergency," as provided for under "Board Rule 45," that she might return to Paris and prepare for the *soutenance,* or oral examination, before the panel of scholarly judges. Unfortunately for Cooper, the request went no further than her supervisor, who felt that the ten-day Easter recess was adequate to meet the situation that Anna had described as "an emergency." Again, Anna Cooper returned to the Library of Congress, until March 1925, when in desperation and in a mood of defiance she returned to Paris. Of this episode she later wrote, "if they drop me this time it shall be for doing as I darn please. If I perish, I perish!"

The *soutenance,* an open inquiry requiring a discussion of two preliminary or supplemental questions related to the overall topic of the dissertation, was held on March 23, 1925. With only one week to prepare for this intense, three-hour oral examination, Cooper began to consider the questions her professors had selected for discussion: "Legislative Measures Concerning Slavery in the United States

139

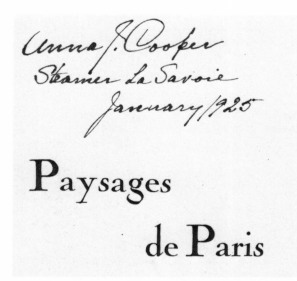

Paysages de Paris

A souvenir kept by Anna Cooper as a memento of her passage to Paris on the steamer *La Savoie* in January 1925. Courtesy Mrs. Regia Bronson and Miss Regina Smith.

between 1787 and 1850" and "Equality of Races and the Democratic Movement." (Later, Anna Cooper would translate the questions, and the discussion that accompanied each, for her course in American history at Frelinghuysen University.)

On the way to the Salle de Richelieu, on the morning of March 23, 1925, Anna Cooper felt a sense of pride and accomplishment as she passed a sign on the University of Paris quadrangle that announced, "Thèse pour le Doctorat 23 Mars a 9 heures . . . Mlle. Cooper." Dressed in her academic gown with the crimson and gold master's hood of Oberlin College, Anna was escorted at the appointed hour into the Salle du Doctorat and to the front of the gallery with the audience seated behind her. The three judges entered through a door to the rear of the platform, and the signal was sounded for the formal academic inquiry to begin. Anna Cooper rose to her feet to await the beginning of an experience that she later described as "significant and informative." For Anna believed

> a soutenance "sustaining," supporting, defending if need be, an original intellectual effort that has already been passed on by competent judges as worthy a place in the treasure house of thought, affords for the public a unique opportunity to listen in on this measuring of one's thought by the yardstick of great thinkers, both giving and receiving inspiration and stimulus from the contact.

No ostentatious display was made when, with great dignity and at the end of the *soutenance,* one of the judges delivered the verdict: "vous etes Docteur" (you are a doctor). In that instant, the dream became a reality!

Anna Julia Cooper, the former slave girl who had thirsted for knowledge and an education, stood four-square to be judged worthy of the title and honor bestowed upon her by the Sorbonne. She returned to Dunbar High School and to the District of Columbia, the first woman of the city to accomplish this academic feat, a feat all the more noteworthy because Dr. Cooper was then about sixty-five years of age. News of her attainment had been reported in the Paris edition of the *Chicago Tribune,* and in the *Oberlin Alumni,* the *Crisis* and *Opportunity* magazines, and on April 12, 1925, the *Washington Post* reported "Dunbar Teacher Wins French De-

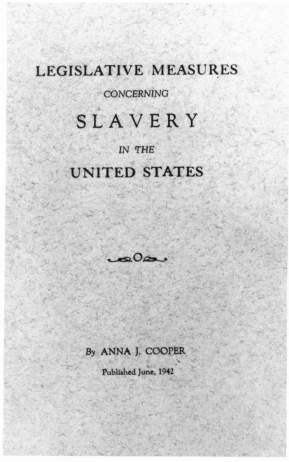

Some years later, Anna Cooper published her dissertation questions and discussion for Frelinghuysen students. Courtesy W. E. B. Du Bois Collection, University of Massachusetts.

An engraving of the church at the Sorbonne. Founded in 1257 as a theological college that was suppressed in 1792, the Sorbonne became the seat of the faculties of arts and letters of the University of Paris. Gift of Mr. and Mrs. Benjamin T. Layton.

gree." It noted that "The diploma entitling Mrs. Cooper to her degree [would] be awarded by the District commissioners, to whom it [would] be forwarded by the University of Paris." The *Post* went on to observe that "Mrs. Cooper [was] the fourth negro woman to receive the [Ph.D] degree in America, and the third at the Dunbar High School." The *Post* was partially in error, however, for all four of the black women, the first of their race to earn doctorate degrees, were associated with the M Street-Dunbar High School. As mentioned earlier, they were Drs. Georgiana Rose Simpson, Eva Beatrice Dykes, Sadie Tanner Mossell Alexander, and now Dr. Anna Julia Cooper.

There was no official recognition of Anna Cooper's accomplishment until December 29, 1925, when the degree was awarded at Howard University's Rankin Chapel in a ceremony sponsored by the Alpha Kappa Alpha Sorority's Xi Omega Chapter. A report of this tribute appeared in the January

A letter from the Cunard Steam Ship Company to Anna Cooper, inviting her return passage to America on their line. Courtesy Moorland-Spingarn Research Center, Howard University.

DUNBAR HIGH TEACHER WINS FRENCH DEGREE

DUNBAR HIGH TEACHER WINS FRENCH DEGREE

Mrs. Anna J. Cooper, teacher of Latin, at Dunbar High school, has just returned from Paris, France, where she was awarded the degree of doctor of philosophy at the Sorbonne, on March 23. Her diploma entitling Mrs. Cooper to her degree will be awarded by the District commissioners, to whom it will be forwarded by the University of Paris. Mrs. Cooper is the fourth negro woman to receive the degree in America, and the third at the Dunbar High school.

A *Washington Post* article reporting on Anna Cooper's accomplishment at the Sorbonne, 1925. Courtesy Moorland-Spingarn Research Center, Howard University.

Souvenir
Xi Omega Chapter
Alpha Kappa Alpha Sorority

December 29, 1925
Washington, D. C.

Anna Julia Cooper
University of Paris

The souvenir program of the recognition ceremony honoring Dr. Anna J. Cooper on December 29, 1925. Courtesy Mrs. Regia Bronson and Miss Regina Smith.

14, 1926, issue of the *Dunbar Observer*. Present among the platform guests were the sorority's basileus, Harriet B. Allen, Mrs. Coralie Franklin Cook, Mayme A. Holden of New York, and Howard University's Professor Wesley Howard, who conducted the Alpha Kappa Alpha Glee Club. The principal speaker was Dr. Alain LeRoy Locke (America's first black Rhodes scholar, 1907–1910), who believed that Dr. Cooper's "significant achievement would have beneficial effect upon the youth of the race."

Anna Cooper's degree was awarded by Dr. William Tindall (1844-1932), a longtime servant of the city, who represented the District commissioners. Retrospectively, Tindall seems to have been a good choice, for it has been said of him, "he dared to tell the whole truth . . . he sought no publicity [and] he had no desire to stir up controversy for his own self-aggrandizement. He wrote the story as he saw the battle." According to the *Dunbar Observer*, the ceremony was attended by "officials of the public schools of Washington as well as of Howard University," and after the warm words of praise, Dr. Cooper responded:

. . . I take at your hands . . . this diploma, not as a symbol of cold intellectual success in my achievement at the Sorbonne, but with the warm pulsing heart throbs of a people's satisfaction in my humble efforts to serve them.

When Anna Cooper had disclosed her plan to matriculate at the Sorbonne to the Abbé Klein, he had prayed that God would bless her "courageous designs." Indeed, it had taken courage for Anna to

UNIVERSITÉ DE PARIS

Nous, Doyen & Professeurs de la Faculté des Lettres,

Vu l'article 15 du décret du 21 juillet 1897;

Vu la délibération, en date du 28 mars 1898, du Conseil de l'Université de Paris & l'arrété ministériel du 1er avril 1898 approuvant cette délibération;

Après avoir constaté que Madame *Cooper* née *Haywood Anna*, née à *Raleigh North Carolina (Etats-Unis)* le *10 Octobre* 1863,

a rempli toutes les conditions exigées par les règlements, l'avons admis à présenter & soutenir une thèse sur *l'attitude de la France à l'égard de l'esclavage*

pendant la Révolution

Et interrogé sur les questions suivantes, choisies par lui & agréées par nous : 1° *Les mesures législatives concernant l'esclavage aux Etats-Unis de 1787 à 1850;*

2° *Les idées égalitaires et le mouvement démocratique.*

Et, attendu qu'il a subi ces épreuves avec succès, l'avons déclaré digne du titre de Docteur de l'Université de Paris.

Paris, le *23 mars* 1925

Le Doyen,   Les Membres du Jury,

Nous, Président du Conseil de l'Université de Paris, vu la déclaration ci-dessus, conférons à

M _____ *le titre de Docteur de l'Université de Paris & lui délivrons le présent diplôme.*

Paris, en Sorbonne, le _____ 19 __

5412

Signature de l'Impétrant :

faithfully pursue an idea that had first begun to germinate in 1902, when, by chance, the Abbé Klein had visited the M Street School, until the dream—that often seemed illusionary—was realized on March 23, 1925. The morning after the *soutenance,* Anna joined her friend for breakfast and the Abbé confided, "Je priais pour vous" (I was praying for you). Unable to be with the crowd of well wishers the following December, the Abbé wrote to Anna explaining that only the celebration of the fortieth anniversary of his ordination and first Mass prevented his coming; yet he had included her among the friends remembered in his souvenir book and always in his prayers.

Not long after Anna Cooper had experienced the joy and personal satisfaction of achieving her educational goals, her courage, tenacity, and determination would again be put to the test. While she had worked to earn the coveted degree, the M Street High School had become the Paul Laurence Dunbar High School. With Dr. Garnet C. Wilkinson at the helm, it had opened on October 2, 1916. Wilkinson's history is an interesting one in relation to

Anna J. Cooper was awarded the title of "Docteur de l'Université de Paris," on March 23, 1925. Courtesy Mrs. Regia Bronson and Miss Regina Smith.

Anna Cooper, for he was a graduate of the M Street High School (1898) and Oberlin College (1902), and he had returned to M Street where he had begun his teaching career during the administration of Dr. Cooper. Wilkinson had risen through the ranks; before the principalship at Dunbar he had served as principal of the Armstrong Technical and Manual High School, and now he was the First Assistant Superintendent of the District's Colored public schools.

The proposal to build the new "Colored High School" had been advanced as early as February 27, 1908, when the newly created Schoolhouse Commission (established by an act of Congress, June 20, 1906) made its report and recommendations during the first session of the Sixtieth Congress. Addressed to Vice-President Charles W. Fairbanks, as president of the United States Senate, the report was signed by A. T. Stuart, school superintendent;

143

Dr. Garnet C. Wilkinson (1879–1969) became the assistant superintendent of the District's Colored Schools in 1921. From the *Dunbar High School Yearbook,* 1923. Courtesy Mrs. Ella Howard Pearis.

James Knox Taylor, supervising architect, United States Treasury; and Jay J. Morrow, engineer commissioner of the District of Columbia. Cited in Section 11 of Public Law No. 254, the membership and authority of the commission had been approved by the Fifty-ninth Congress. It was created for the purpose of submitting to Congress at its session beginning in December 1906:

> A general plan for the consolidation of the public schools in the District of Columbia and the abandonment and sale of such school buildings and sites as may by them be deemed necessary and desirable for the best good of the public school service.

The commission was also to develop "a general plan for the character, size, and location of school buildings in accordance with which the educational and business interests of the public school system may be subserved." In the District appropriation act for 1907, Congress had included $1,500 for the sup-

port of the commission, an amount that was taken from the school system's operating funds.

The Schoolhouse Commission made eighteen major recommendations to Congress, and the ninth was to convert "the present Colored High School (M Street) into an elementary school and construction of a new colored high school with provisions therein for commercial instruction." The commission concluded that:

> The present M Street High School for the colored pupils in academic and scientific subjects is too small for the purpose and is not well adapted for high school instruction. The Commission recommends that this building be converted into an elementary school, which can be done at small expense, that a large site be purchased in the vicinity, and that a high school be erected to accommodate 1,200 pupils. In this high school provision should also be made for commercial courses of at least three years' duration.

Just a few years earlier, the Supreme Court had ruled that federal intervention in matters relating to the operation of state and local schools was undesirable, but this did not deter Congress from involving itself in the affairs of the District's public schools. Many wondered at the propriety of its actions, when it investigated courses of study and classroom methodology; approved legislation giving itself far-reaching powers and authority in the day-to-day administration of the schools; created a commission that by-passed the school superintendent and Board of Education and reported directly to the Senate on matters concerning new school construction and the existing conditions of the school system's physical plant; and funded the commission it had created directly from the District's allocation for public school instruction. Congress went even further: it established personnel policies and procedures related to the firing and retention of classroom teachers and school officers; set the term of office for the school superintendent; established the positions of assistant superintendents of schools, thereby involving itself in structuring the central administration. Last but not least, Congress determined both the size and racial composition of the District's first Board of Education (earlier bodies were called School Trustees). In 1900, during the first session of the Fifty-sixth Congress, Report No. 711 accompanied Senate Resolution No. 140, and it established the mechanism for

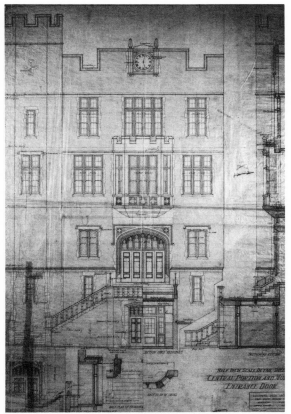

This elevation drawing of the M Street High School was approved by Edward Clark, Architect, U.S. Capitol. Courtesy District of Columbia Department of General Services.

selecting members of the Board of Education (see *Statutes Enacted by Congress That Governed the District's Public Schools,* GPO, 1929). The report provided "That there shall be a department of public schools in the District of Columbia," and then determined that "the President of the United States [was thereby] authorized to appoint by and with the advice of the Senate" those who would be invited to serve on this body. Further, the Organic School Law of 1906 provided for the enlargement of the board, and established that its membership would include three blacks and three women.

The worst fears expressed by the District's early residents in 1802, when they first petitioned the national government for self-determination, had

Elevation drawing of the "Central Portion and North Entrance Door" of the Dunbar High School, by Snowden Ashford, municipal architect, October 15, 1914. Courtesy District of Columbia Department of General Services.

Completed in 1916, the Paul Laurence Dunbar High School was razed in 1976. From the *Dunbar High School Yearbook,* 1923. Courtesy Mrs. Ella Howard Pearis.

been realized. And Congress excused its conduct by claiming its right to "exclusive jurisdiction" over the affairs of the District under the provisions of the Organic Act of 1791, the act that gave it authority to create the Federal District from land acquired from Maryland and Virginia.

Anna Cooper is credited with naming the new Paul Laurence Dunbar High School, an impressive-looking building with fifty-two instructional rooms. In *Capital Losses,* James Goode described the building (razed in 1976) as "Tudor Collegiate" in style, with two "crenelated towers." Lyrics for Dunbar's alma mater were written by Anna Cooper, and set to the music of Mary L. Europe, a former

pupil and now a colleague. Dunbar, like its proud predecessors, provided quality education that motivated and encouraged the students, and instilled in them a strong sense of racial pride and self-worth. It was this academic preparedness, together with nurtured innate abilities, that resulted in the achievements of Charles Richard Drew, the developer of blood plasma; the success of William Henry Hastie, the first black federal judge; and the accomplishments and contributions of Nannie Helen Burroughs, Georgiana Rose Simpson, Eva Beatrice Dykes, James and Mary Europe, Ruth E. Weatherless, Julia Evangeline Brooks, Mary Gibson Hundley, Willis M. Menard, Jean Toomer, and many, many others.

Found among Anna Cooper's papers, the first draft of Dunbar's alma mater (penned on the back of an envelope) was written in 1915, and Cooper assigned to "Fairest Dunbar" the task of becoming

Mary L. Europe

The Dunbar High School Alma Mater, lyrics by Anna
Cooper and music by Mary Europe, about 1916. From
the *Dunbar High School Yearbook*, 1923. Courtesy Mrs.
Ella Howard Pearis.

a "light to beacon dark souls' wandering feet." The
final lyrics were finished in time for the dedication
of the school, scheduled by the District commissioners for January 17, 1916. Building on the work
of her predecessors, Anna Cooper had wished to
inspire succeeding generations when she wrote:

> God bless thee, Dear Dunbar, thy radiant star,
> Like the sun of morning, illumining far,
> Shall strengthen and hearten and quicken with
>   life
> Minds fettered in darkness, hearts deadened by
>   strife.
> Thy sons and thy daughters, firing torch from
>   thy flame,
> Go forth with their banners aloft in thy name.
> We pledge, Alma Mater, with hearts and
>   hands and breath,
> Eternal devotion, come honor or death.
> With faith in thy mission, in self, in the All
> And loyally serving humanity's call
> For justice, God's justice, ev'n handed, open
>   eyed,

> For love universal—no creature denied.
> Thy precept in action—self-poise, self-
>   control—
> Nerve answering to will, steady onward to
>   goal;
> "Truth, brotherhood, temperance," thy stan-
>   dards unfurled,
> Come pledge loyal service—DUNBAR for the
>   world.

As written in *Black Women in Nineteenth-Century
American Life*: "achievements of the talented and
well-placed few were not enough, Anna Julia Cooper looked to the elevation of the many."

As the decade of the 1920s began to wane, Anna
Cooper drew closer to retirement age. Having
reached all of her academic goals, she still possessed
a strong will, a clear mind, and the mettle to wage
yet another battle and endure yet another struggle.
Now Anna had become involved in a dispute pro-

147

Dr. Charles R. Drew (1904–1950) is shown in the front row, second from right, with the 1922 Dunbar High School championship basketball team. During World War II, Drew perfected a technique for making blood plasma. Photograph by Addison Scurlock. Courtesy Robert Scurlock, Scurlock Studios.

voked by her claim that she had received an unfair professional rating, and, if left unchecked, the rating would place her long-worked-for retirement benefits and annuity in jeopardy. Those involved in the dispute included Nelson E. Weatherless, school superintendent Frank W. Ballou, G. David Houston, Marion P. Shadd, and Dr. Garnet C. Wilkinson—all members of the school system's Board of Examiners. Weatherless served in a dual capacity as a member of this special certification review body and also as its official secretary. Anna Cooper's very long letter of May 24, 1925, to Dr. Garnet C. Wilkinson is presented here in its entirety, in order that the reader may better understand all of the issues:

Dear Mr. Wilkinson:

Once again I shall try (without offense I hope) to write you as a man rather than as an official.

The year 1927–1928 will mark my fortieth as a teacher in the High School of the District of Columbia, barring an interim of four years as college professor at Lincoln University. One year later (1928-9) I shall be retired automatically from the system by the age limit rule. I have therefore only about three years more of public school service before me, even if I am not excluded before that time by some unforeseen disability. My ratings by officials immediately concerned have been uniformly "excellent" and "excellent superior." There has never been, to my knowledge, any question of my efficiency as a teacher or of my spirit of willing cooperation in all the deepest concerns of our school population. Much of my aims, ideals and principles of action is personally well known to you and many of my achievements have been consciously aided, inspired and abetted by you. I believe I have had many evidences of the sincere esteem and appreciation with which my service is regarded by the humble laity whom I serve, and yet it must be admitted that official recognition still seems tardily and grudgingly accorded and pecuniary emolument, so eagerly sought by most persons, is stubbornly withheld while every opportunity is seized in some quarters to excuse this material injury by detraction and misrepresentation.

Now I should utter no word of complaint for all this were it not my firm conviction that nothing vitiates the morale of any educational system more completely than a sense of unfairness in the distribution of rewards. Once let the conviction take root that merit does not count, that service, however long and faithful and efficient can be outstripped any day by sheer pull of flimflam, and no administration would be secure. The strength of the head rests on those loyal hearts that respond to a sense of justice and fairplay and on that support that goes out spontaneously always to unselfish devotion.

It may be that you can without jeopardising your own interests prevent the perpetuation of those studied attempts at persecution and humiliation which have been so patent in my case. I do not ask you to say or do one thing to embarrass yourself. But as it seems to me now and as it has seemed all along to a few very thotful friends of mine, it could only strengthen your hold on the community and give real significance to your position in the eyes of the country, if you would take a firm stand for justice and fair play in the bestowal of those favors that involve the taxpayers' burdens. You, if any one, can say that neither N. E. Weatherless nor Marion P. Shadd can convince one who had ever been a student under Anna J. Cooper that she does not know her subject. Surely the testimony of Oberlin and Columbia and La Sorbonne should not be allowed to be discredited by any Factitious "board of Examiners" in the Washington Public School.

A report from Mr. Hine dated May 11 . . . *in re* my appeal before the Committee on Complaints contains this paragraph: "The Committee is impressed with Mrs. Cooper's atainments [sic] as a scholar and student and takes pride in the recognition which her work has lately received. But a 'passing mark' on the written examination is required for pro-

Nelson E. Weatherless, four-time winner of the Kelly Miller Gold Medal in mathematics, became head of the M Street Science Department in 1906. From *Who's Who in Colored America*.

motion and as Mrs. Cooper at the hearing held before the Complaints and Appeals Committee did not claim that she should have been given a passing mark on the written examination it is therefore impossible for her appeal to be granted."

The whole ground of my complaint and appeal to the Board was from the first that several candidates were given the promotion over my head whose educational claims were admittedly below mine, altho their written examination papers by the first set of judges had been marked below the required passing mark, as had my own presumably. I have never raised a question of those markings. I think I could show if I were allowed to see my papers that I gave a fairly good account of myself, I have never in my life failed in a written test and I have taken on an average I am sure one at least for every year of my teaching experience. The quantity of work required in these Washington

G. David Houston taught at Tuskegee Institute before heading the M Street School's Business Practice Department (1919–1926). In 1926 he was appointed principal of Armstrong High School. From *Dunbar High School Yearbook,* 1923. Courtesy Mrs. Ella Howard Pearis.

examinations is purely arbitrary and the questions themselves designed rather to "stump" the candidate than to test his ability to teach the subject. In this case the questions had been carelessly mimeographed or typed and were full of errors that had to be unravelled in order to give any sort of intelligent answer. The translation was wholly sight work and as I recall it the first question had five or six subheads for comments, mythological, historical, or interpretative, on certain lines of a poem that must first be scanned to mark the rhythm, show the caesura and classify the meter. There may have been ten or could have been fifty questions after this—I never knew. I think I answered something like two or three after the first, which had consumed most of the forenoon. Then since as you know there is no hostelry near the Franklin where a colored person can procure a glass of milk, I had to walk all the way to the "Y" 9th and R. I.

Ave. for lunch. Caught a cab coming back but was not so fortunate going. When I returned the others were already under way, but I put in the time remaining as best I could, on the afternoon work consisting of principles and methods, conduct of department, etc. etc. I mention these trifling details to show why I employed a lawyer to plead for the "merging" of the written and "oral" marks in giving the final standing. The law of Congress provides that "Teachers shall be promoted for superior work from Group A of Class 6 only after *oral and written examinations* by the Board of Examiners upon recommendation of their respective principals thro and with the approval of the Superintendent of Schools and with the additional recommendation of the Colored Assistant Superintendent for the Colored Schools," and provided further that "No teacher shall be eligible to Group B who has not attained the maximun of Group A." Fixing entire weight of eligibility exclusively on the written test papers is in the opinion of my lawyer wholly extra-legal. Indeed the law nowhere says that the written examination shall even be passed or any defined standard shall be met therein. The teacher is promoted for "superior work" only after *oral and written examinations."* Now the word oral as interpreted in practice by the Superintendent of Schools sums up the whole arc of personal efficiency in the work of the schools and should if anything be made the *sine qua non* of a "superior" teacher's claim for promotion. Yet strangely enough I was excluded from consideration under this head until the Board of Education at the instance that my lawyer ordered first that the Oral be given me and later that the ratings be affixed to the several items. It was on this so-called oral test that my complaint rested and still rests. The law was clearly violated in promoting to group B a teacher who had not reached her maximum in Group A; it was violated only by implication in promoting those whose test papers in a written examination were rated below 210. Again all the more was it violated in my case in altogether disallowing the "oral examination," just as legally necessary as the other, and insisting on an arbitrary standard of 210 on the written examination before any other claims could be considered. Now altho the Board at the instance of my attorney granted my plea for a rating on the oral involving the most important items of personal fitness, educational qualifications and general efficiency as a teacher, these items largely demonstrable by documentary evidence that would be incontestable in any educational center of the civilized world were systematically discredited and given a mark below passing in each particular. My complaint then is solely against these ratings, a copy of which is enclosed herewith. It will be noted that the items discredited are questions of fact open to mathematical proof. One item only (B under III) is given full credit and here personal judgment is fairly permissible and a "zero" mark could not have been gainsaid. One successful candidate had been in the system less than five years, had no degree whatever when taking the examination, took it then as a kindergartner and failed according to the first ratings received from competent judges of her test papers. The statement of my lawyer that was contradicted in a way to disrupt the proceedings and forestall his ever reappearing before the Board was literally true. It is well known that several were promoted in spite of the fact that they did not receive a passing mark on their written examination from the first judges who rated them that the longevity law which is very explicit was not always enforced. In "Education Preparation" and Educational Courses taken, in both of which I am rated below passing by the Chief Examiner, I think I can say without self-conceit or egotism that there is no one in the system producing a more extensive record by actual count and measurement. If Miss Shadd can say that my scholarship is not up to standard I have a right to inquire what is the standard and who the judge. This is just why I appeal from Miss Shadd to you, not only as First Assistant Superintendent in charge of colored schools but as one better qualified, in every way to pass judgment on the academic question involved. I expressed to the committee my dissatisfaction at your absence from the hearing as likewise my opposition to the presence there of the already discredited N. E. Weatherless who presumed to criticise the previous action of the Board of Education in allowing any consideration whatever of the "Oral Examination" and had the hardihood to employ the expression "Speaking as a lawyer" when the committee knew the circumstances under which my own lawyer had been unjustly disbarred from appearing there.

The Superintendent's circular had estimated

Marion P. Shadd, a noted educator, began her administrative climb in 1887 when appointed principal of the Lincoln Elementary School. Courtesy Association for the Study of Afro-American Life and History.

300 points for written, 300 for oral and 400 Personal characteristics and Teaching Ability. My 700 superior points as elements of actual teaching service were discredited for the first 300, a purely arbitrary element of written examination.

I wish distinctly and unequivocally to disclaim any disrespectful remarks concerning either the Superintendent of Schools or any member of the Board of Education made by *David A. Pine* who was employed to present my appeal to the Board. He may not have been tactful; he certainly was not successful in representing my own attitude of mind regarding the question at issue. But the Administration cannot be willing to play the role of persecuting a faithful servant who has from the beginning been innocent of any intention to offend.

And may I not at least hope, Mr. Wilkinson, that you with your usual judicial mind

This bust of Paul Laurence Dunbar was sculpted by May Howard Jackson, whose husband, William T. S. Jackson, succeeded Anna Cooper as the M Street School's principal in 1906. Courtesy Virginia State University.

will see this somewhat from my point of view and that your natural love of justice and fairness will not rest till due consideration is given where it deserves.

Very respectfully yours,

The winter of Anna Cooper's discontent languished on into spring without resolve, and it now seems that she did not receive the superior rating and the accompanying salary increase in contention. The decision reached by Weatherless and the members of the Board of Examiners, in retrospect, seems to have been one that was inappropriate, and at the same time fraught with inherent risks. It certainly raises in question the probability of a fair and impartial decision being rendered, in the matter of assigning points and scoring candidates seeking merit promotions. We can only wonder at the wisdom of the practice of having teachers and administrators sitting as the Board of Examiners; thereby, rating their peers. In the instance of Anna Cooper, the decision, considering the conclusive evidence to the contrary, seems to have been both vindictive and spiteful.

To understand fully the issues disclosed in Anna Cooper's letter to Wilkinson, the reader must also know the complexities of the District's public school system and its continued relationship with Congress. An institution in which black teachers were then clearly in the minority, the school system promoted a rivalry for economic success and professional and social recognition. The schools employed only about half the teachers who were being trained in the black normal and teacher training institution, and, as observed by Dr. Leona C. Gable (unpublished manuscript, *Anna J. Cooper: From Slavery to the Sorbonne and Beyond*), the times were remarkably "notorious for political favoritism and patronage in appointment." Beyond the appointment of the Recorder of Deeds and the three delegated seats on the Board of Education, black Washingtonians could not aspire to political offices, thus, while not condoned, it should be understood that people who themselves were powerless and kept outside of the political arena often made power plays in institutions like the school system. In the District's schools, where "grass roots" politics would become a fait accompli, no significant changes had been made by 1925, and, as observed by historian Cassandra Smith, "the entire school system [had] the feel of a treacherous, cut-throat, dog-eat-dog atmosphere. . . . Congress regarded [it] as its own spoils system."

The practice of re-examining and re-evaluating teachers yearly to satisfy eligibility for appointments and promotions, begun by Superintendent William Chancellor (called William the "Chancellor" by Anna Cooper) in 1906, placed teachers and their job security in a very precarious position. In this regard, while the Board of Education had tried to design and devise rules that would protect teachers' jobs "during good behavior," the will of Chancellor prevailed down to the time when Anna Cooper began to consider retirement from the system that she had served for nearly four decades.

Much had happened since Anna Cooper had first arrived at the M Street School to assume her first teaching position in the District, and in spite of the "frays" she could leave the Dunbar High School confident that "minds fettered in darkness" had been given an opportunity to learn, and "hearts deadened by strife" now quickened to the stimuli of humanity. In summing up this period of her life, Anna Cooper wrote:

I am as sensitive to handicaps as those who are always whining about them & the whips & stings of prejudice, whether of color or sex, find me neither too calloused to suffer, nor too ignorant to know what is due me. . . . We women are generally left to do our . . . battling alone except for empty compliments now & then. Even so, one may make the mistake of looking at . . . handicaps thro the wrong end of the telescope & imagining that oppression goes only with color. When I encounter brutality I need not always charge it to my race. It may be—& generally is—chargeable to the imperfections in the civilization environing me for which as a teacher & trained thinker I take my share of the responsibility. . . .

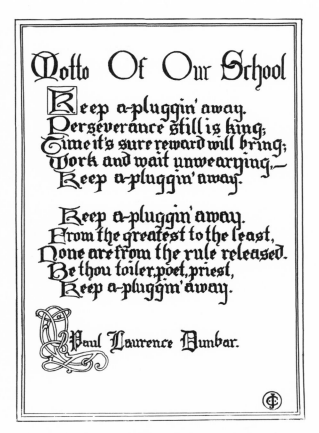

The Dunbar High School motto, a poem selected from the writings of Paul Laurence Dunbar, for whom the school was named. From the *Dunbar High School Yearbook,* 1923. Courtesy Mrs. Ella Howard Pearis.

154

IX.

The Frelinghuysen Years

Perhaps others will think first of the Defense in French before a jury of French Doctors at the Sorbonne of my [thesis] on the attitude of France on Slavery. . . . My own preference is the building of a beautiful home at the Capital on unsubsidized earnings to be dedicated in the name of my slave Mother to the education of colored working people. I am called President of Frelinghuysen University, started . . . 27 yrs ago . . . [a] group of Schools for Adult Education.

ANNA J. COOPER, 1932 [?]
"Individual Occupational History"

Anna Cooper, the new president of Frelinghuysen University. Courtesy Moorland-Spingarn Research Center, Howard University.

ANNA COOPER HAS WRITTEN THAT "THE FRELING-huysen idea [was] an innovation of American education," and she pleaded that it not be judged by its size or the rating others might assign it; rather that it be assessed on its merits and "by the soundness and sanity of its departure and the nation's undeniable need for such [a] departure." Anna Cooper, of course, was not the only one to express faith in the soundness of the Frelinghuysen concept, for at its inception the idea, promulgated by Jesse Lawson in 1906, was reviewed by a committee of Princeton University's faculty. But before exploring this educational concept, advanced in the first decade of this century, what of the man and his comrades who fostered the idea?

Jesse Lawson, one of Jesse and Charlotte Price Lawson's several children, was born at Nanjemoy, Charles County, Maryland, on May 8, 1856. Although his family was free, Lawson never forgot the unsettling sight of slave coffles that traveled the nearby roads, enroute to neighboring fields or the intricate network of inland waterways where they labored from dawn to dusk (the slave's expression was "from can see to can't see"). The scene of these morning and evening processions left an indelible image on Lawson's young mind; one that even benevolent treatment by a kind benefactor could not expunge.

Only a few sheets of an autobiographical account, begun by Lawson about 1927, are extant—yet it is known that after the death of the father the family's fortunes waned. According to Lawson, he and a sister, Josephine, were separated from their family and raised by a white family then living in Georgetown, D.C. Educated in New Jersey grammar schools, where the family relocated, Lawson

Jesse Lawson, about 1904. "Nihil tetigit quod non ornavit" (He touched nothing without embellishing it)—Anna J. Cooper. From *How to Solve the Race Problem*. Courtesy Mr. James J. Lawson.

The gavel of Jesse Lawson.
Courtesy Mr. James J. Lawson.

later returned to Washington and attended Howard University. There, he came under the influence of John Mercer Langston, founder of the school's Law Department and acting president in the absence of General Oliver O. Howard. Although he was assured of a good position with a New Jersey firm, Lawson, after graduation in 1881, was determined to make good without the assistance of his benefactor. An activist on Howard's campus in the 1880s and 1890s, with the help of his wife, Rosetta Coakley Lawson, whom he married in 1884, Jesse Lawson devoted himself to the cause of uplifting blacks through education.

According to the *Howard University Directory of Graduates* (1965), Lawson completed the university's Preparatory School in 1877; a bachelor of laws degree was earned in 1881, and in 1886 he was awarded a master of arts degree. From 1901 until 1905, Lawson attended a course of lectures in sociology, held under the auspices of the American Academy of Political and Social Science at the University of Pennsylvania. Lawson's effort to gain higher education is exemplary, for at that time three of his four children were in college; two boys earned degrees in medicine and theology from Howard University and his only daughter earned a degree in pedogogy from Oberlin College.

According to the *Annual Catalogue of the Frelinghuysen University, 1926-1927,* "on or about April 27, 1906, at a meeting held at the residence of Professor and Mrs. Jesse Lawson . . . it was decided by those present to organize a branch of the Bible Educational Association at the Nation's Capital." Those in attendance were the Reverend Samuel L. Miller; Mifflin Wister Gibbs, United States consul to Madagascar (a position later held by his son-in-law, William H. Hunt); Judson W. Lyons, Register of the United States Treasury; the Reverend Walter H. Brooks; the Reverend Sterling N. Brown, pastor, Lincoln Temple Congregational Church; the Reverend Daniel E. Wiseman, pastor, Church of Our Redeemer Lutheran; Kelly Miller, dean of Howard University's College of Arts and Science; and Jesse and Rosetta Lawson. At this meeting, Dean Kelly Miller was named president of the Bible Educational Association of the District of Columbia, and Lawson was named president of the Inter-Denominational Bible College, which, on February 22, 1917, would be named Frelinghuysen University. Then the group of schools was "dedi-

Rosetta E. Coakley Lawson. Courtesy Mrs. Georgia R. Lawson.

third of Washington's black population was church-going—a decided departure from their former lifestyle in smaller, rural communities. This break with tradition was attributed to problems associated with urban living; many of these blacks had come from the South, where education beyond the sixth grade was not possible. Working to give their children new educational advantages and opportunities, many among the working class had had no hope of furthering their own education. So the original incorporators of Frelinghuysen University decided to take educational, as well as socially and morally uplifting, programs to the people. Home

The home of Jesse and Rosetta Lawson, the site of the founding of the Frelinghuysen University, as it looks today.

cated to the life and character of the late Senator Frederick Theodore Frelinghuysen," who from 1881 to 1885 had served as President Chester A. Arthur's secretary of state. According to Lawson, Frelinghuysen "had been of great service to the cause of the Colored people, while a member of the U.S. Senate [and] in the reconstruction days following the close of the Civil War." Along with Senator Charles Sumner of Massachusetts, Frelinghuysen had seen to it that "Colored Americans were written into the statutes of the United States."

As originally conceived, Frelinghuysen University was not a campus with a network of buildings; rather, it was a combined effort to provide social services, religious training, and educational programs for the people who needed them the most. For before Charles Weller published *Neglected Neighbors*, the school's organizers had conducted their own investigation, and they had found "fully twenty thousand people . . . living in the courts and alleys of this city," who, far "removed from the public's gaze," were surrounded by "evil influences." According to the data collected, only one-

The Honorable Judson W. Lyons, register of the United States Treasury and an organizer of Frelinghuysen University. From *How to Solve the Race Problem*. Courtesy Mr. James J. Lawson.

Lillian G. Dabney, in her excellent doctoral dissertation, *The History of Schools for Negroes in the District of Columbia, 1807-1947,* wrote, "the courses offered ranged from practical arts through high school and college work included both undergraduate and graduate courses." The development of the concept is evident from the following advertisement that was published in the *Washington Bee,* on November 15, 1919:

FRELINGHUYSEN UNIVERSITY

The sessions of the college of liberal Arts, the Academy, the Commercial College and the School of Theology...will be held at Lincoln Temple, Eleventh and R Streets, northwest, Mondays, Wednesdays and Fridays, from 7 to 9:30 p.m., until further notice.

The sessions of the John M. Langston School of Law will be held at the Offices of Prof. Zeph P. Moore, Pythian Building, Twelfth and U Streets, northwest, every Tuesday, Thursday and Saturday evening, at 7 o'clock. . . .

The school of Pharmacy and the School of Useful Arts will be held at the apartment of Dr. and Mrs. W. H. Jackson, Cameron

Senator Frederick Theodore Frelinghuysen of New Jersey. Courtesy National Archives and Records Service.

schools and educational centers were established in several sections (usually the poorest) of the city, and ". . . a campaign was inaugurated for the education and social salvation of the unreached." According to Jesse Lawson, "As the people gathered at these centers, from time to time, for instruction in spiritual awakening and social service, there was a yearning for more and better education by persons who had had no opportunity for intellectual training in their earlier days." Soon it was recognized that a structured program of formal training was needed. A Chautauqua Conference was held "by the Seaside, at Point Pleasant, New Jersey," during the summer of 1908. It was attended by Woodrow Wilson, then president of Princeton University. Also in attendance were the Reverend Russell E. Conwell, president of Temple University, Philadelphia; and Dr. Rendall, president of Lincoln University, Chester, Pennsylvania. The conferees heard lectures on the character and scope of higher education. It was there that the promoters of Frelinghuysen University began to develop plans to take on the higher branches of education, while also establishing a system of practical educational schools.

Woodrow Wilson

Frelinghuysen University seal. Courtesy Mrs. Regia Bronson and Miss Regina Smith.

The campus of Princeton, where the founders of Frelinghuysen met with Wilson, then president of the university, and six Princeton educators in 1908. Courtesy The Woodrow Wilson House, National Trust for Historic Preservation.

An early home of Frelinghuysen University, at 1800
Vermont Avenue, NW, Washington, D.C.

Apartment House, Vermont Avenue at T
Street, northwest, every evening. . . .

The School of Fine Arts, Department of
Photography, will be held at the studio of
Daniel Freeman, 1833 Fourteenth Street,
northwest, every day.

The College of Embalming and Sanitary Science will be held at the establishment of Dr.
Robert G. McGuire, 925 Florida avenue,
northwest, every day.

For further information consult Prof. Jesse
Lawson, president, office—Frelinghuysen University, 2011 Vermont avenue. Phone North
5864. Enter now.

While the curriculum had expanded, Frelinghuysen University still operated as a galaxy of sat-
ellite "home schools" with educational centers at
several locations, and continued its effort to carry an
inter-disciplinary program to the "unreached." By
the school year 1920–1921, Frelinghuysen had
published a catalogue of its programs and courses.
The offerings were as varied as the School of Useful
Arts, Nurses Training, the College of Liberal Arts,
University Extension, and the John M. Langston

School of Law (this last would later become an issue
when, under Anna Cooper, the school applied for
accreditation). Certainly this was an ambitious un-
dertaking, but then these were not colleges in the
traditional academic sense as we have come to know
them.

By the school year 1926–1927, the courses of
study and the organization of the instructional program at Frelinghuysen had undergone revision,
consolidation, and refinement. Course work ranged
from an Academy offering a thorough high school
education to a business high school offering short-
hand and the touch system of typing, bookkeeping,
filing, business mathematics, business law, elementary banking procedures, and business English.
Courses or departments at the junior college and
college level included the Schools of Liberal Arts,
Sociology, Applied Science, Fine Arts, Applied
Christianity, Theology, Law, and Pharmacy. And
in that year Frelinghuysen University was incorporated under the laws of the District of Columbia.

Some incorporators of Frelinghuysen also became
the university's first officers and members of the
board of directors; among them were Jesse Lawson,
the Reverend William H. Jernigan; attorney Edmund Hill, Jr.; Bishop Edward W. D. Jones of the
A.M.E. Zion Church; and Sylvester L. McLaurin,
president of the Colored Bar Association. Also,
some members of the board served as faculty and
supported the institution's educational program
through volunteered services. Others from Washington's black community gave of their time and
expertise; among them were attorneys Louis R.
Mehlinger and Augustus W. Gray (later incorporators of the Robert H. Terrell Law School); Mary
Church Terrell—who taught belles-lettres and a
course in French literature; and the Reverend
George O. Bullock (the father of Mrs. Walter E.
Washington, wife of the District's first black
mayor), a special guest lecturer on the subject of
recruiting and training blacks for the field of foreign missions.

During the early years of organizational growth
and development, under the helm of Jesse Lawson,
Frelinghuysen University was located at 1800 Vermont Avenue, NW, and 601 M Street, NW, after
its embryonic days in the Lawson home. The M
Street site was called "The Main Building, 'Greater
Frelinghuysen University,'" and had formerly
served as a white Methodist Old Folk's Home. Ac-

160

cording to Lawson, "this site was purchased at great sacrifice by the University authorities and was done in the cause of education for the benefit of the masses of colored people, not only at the Nation's Capital but throughout the country." He described the M Street location as a very desirable one that was "... both the central and highest point in Washington.... the University [was] thus advantageously situated." Lawson believed that Washington, D.C., was destined to become a great and promising educational center, and Frelinghuysen was to become "a beacon light in that center." His great optimistic spirit was captured in the university's motto, *Sic Itur Ad Astra* (Such is the way to the stars—or to immortality).

Nineteen twenty-seven was the last year of Jesse Lawson's life. Although ill, his spirits were buoyed

Frelinghuysen's incorporators began to purchase this former Methodist Old Folks Home, at 601 M Street, NW, Washington, D.C., about 1927. Courtesy Moorland-Spingarn Research Center, Howard University.

and the sense of hope he felt must have been shared with those who were inspired by this charismatic man and his belief in the work and destiny of Frelinghuysen. John A. Lankford's design and architectural rendering for a permanent building (published in the university's catalogue of 1926–1927) is indicative of this hope for the future. A visionary who cared deeply, Lawson was confident that members of his race could advance and compete in a free and open society—once they had gained the opportunity and benefits attainable through educational,

The proposed Frelinghuysen University, an architectural rendering by John A. Lankford, published in 1927. Courtesy Moorland-Spingarn Research Center, Howard University.

social, and moral development. Convinced that education was the key to success, Lawson contended that both the church and the public schools had failed the Negro, and he believed that the educational system of that day

> was lacking in social culture that should extend into the homelife of Colored Americans. . . . that the church was not reaching the great masses of the people for the reason that it, too, failed to go out [to] them instead of waiting for them to come [into the] church, and that there was in reality "A VACANT CHAIR IN OUR EDUCATIONAL SYSTEM". . . that [he] the founder of [the Frelinghuysen] educational plan [had] first overlooked, but now recognize[d].

The occupancy of a new building and the unveiling of its revised educational program suggested

a promising future for Frelinghuysen University. The preceding year its student enrollment had reached 117, and in the 1926–1927 academic year Lawson optimistically projected that through the payment of tuition and a successful fund-raising campaign the university would gain the $300,000 needed to liquidate the mortgage on the M Street site, maintain the building and grounds, pay for machinery and equipment, and pay teachers' salaries. But Lawson died on November 8, 1927, just two months after the announcement of this unendowed and extraordinary undertaking. Kelly Miller was among those who felt his loss and eulogized him, and of Jesse Lawson, Anna Cooper wrote:

> A life consecrated to service and purposely concentrated on the promotion of interracial harmony has just ended. No man white or black has wrought more valiantly, constantly, and untiringly, according to his lights and opportunities to further the cause of Negro recognition and Negro advancement than Doctor Jesse Lawson; and no one has more directly and more effectively than he strived to bring

about a sane, humane and mutually respectable reagard from both sides [of] the American color line.

It is the fashion these days to sneer and scoff at uplift methods and measures and particularly to decry efforts toward conciliation and peace. America has its Cole Bleases and its Tillmans of all colors and persuasions. And if one does not square his elbows and run off at the mouth in a constant stream of abusive language, these fire eaters are ready to excoriate him . . . [as] a traitor to the Big Cause. Jesse Lawson was not one of these; and yet one of the ablest, most exhaustive and unanswerable speeches ever delivered in the United States Senate in defense of the Negro race was prepared and written, verbatim et literatim [word for word], right in his modest home on Vermont Avenue.

Let us beware of the wild hysteria of our time; let us look deeper than the spectacular stunts and be ready to give honor to the life which in humble obscurity has pushed forward the cup bearing our most precious home interests as to one who has danced nude before the Prince of Europe.

The speech referred to in Dr. Cooper's published "Appreciation of Jesse Lawson" was one he had drafted at the request of Senator Seldeon P. Spencer, and it became Senate Bill S-291, *a bill to Create A Race Commission.* Introduced in the last session of the Sixty-eighth Congress, it was recommended for passage by President Calvin Coolidge in his first message to Congress. Those who had known Lawson since his student activist days at Howard University were not at all surprised by the depth of his commitment or by the breadth of his intellect. Regarding Lawson's arduous and unheralded work in the field of race relations, Anna Cooper wrote: "I know of no man whose work & every effort can claim a more direct & consistent bearing on this most important American problem, nor one who has gone farther in influencing the

Meeting at the John Wesley A.M.E. Zion Church in September 1918, the Colored American Forward Movement of Frelinghuysen University resolved that "Congress authorize the President . . . with the advice and consent of the Senate [to appoint] a permanent Commission on the Racial Question in the United States." From the *Washington Bee.* Courtesy Library of Congress.

FORWARD. MOVEMENT.

Frelinghuysen University Celebrates. Eminent Speakers.

The meeting under the auspices of the Colored American Forward Movement of the Frelinghuysen University, held at the John Wesley A. M. E. Zion Church, September 22, in celebration of the fifty-seventh anniversary of the issuance of the first emancipation proclamation by Abraham Lincoln, September 22, 1862, was well attended. The addresses delivered by Senator Sherman of Illinois, Lieut. Thomas H. R. Clarke and Judge Terrell were well received.

The following resolutions were unanimously adopted:

Whereas the best interests of the country demand that all classes of American citizens should feel secure in the full enjoyment of their rights as guaranteed by the law of the land, and since the security of these rights is largely dependent upon a harmonious relation between the different elements of the American people, a thorough understanding between them and a hearty cooperation of all; and

Whereas the frequent outbreak of violence in almost every section of our country has caused alarm and great unrest among the colored people of the United States, the chief source of labor in the agricultural districts of the South, and constituting, as they do, nearly one-eighth of the entire population of the country; therefore, be it

Resolved (1) that the Colored American Forward Movement of the United States and persons associated with them do hereby humbly petition the Congress of the United States of America, now assembled in the city of Washington, to enact a statute authorizing the appointment by the President of the United States, by and with the advice and consent, of the Senate, a permanent Commission on the Racial Question in the United States;

(2) That said commission shall consist of nine (9) persons, as follows: Three white men from the South, three white men from the North and three colored men, whose duty it shall be to investigate, study and report on the causes of racial friction and conflicts and to suggest remedies therefor, and to offer means whereby greater racial harmony may be secured.

lawmakers of the land to take a deep & sympathetic interest in its just & righteous solution."

Like Jesse Lawson, Anna Cooper believed that the opportunity for education was a gift to be bestowed on all—the mighty and the lowly. And, according to Cooper, she had been "elected to succeed [Lawson] in 1929, but, inasmuch as [her] term of service at Dunbar High School did not expire until the end of that fiscal year," she did not accept the challenge until June 15, 1930, when she was inaugurated the second president of Frelinghuysen University. The installation service was held on Baccalaureate Sunday, at the Metropolitan A.M.E. Church in the District of Columbia.

Several educational institutions sent representatives to Dr. Cooper's installation ceremony; among them were Ernest Hatch Wilkins of Oberlin College; Cyrus Adler of the Dropsie College of Hebrew and Cognate Learning, in Philadelphia; J. R. E. Lee of Florida A&M College for Negroes, in Tallahassee, Florida; William Stuart Nelson, assistant to Dr. Mordecai W. Johnson, the first black president of Howard University; Edgar H. Goold, St. Augustine's College; and William John Clark, Virginia Union University, in Richmond. Dr. Edward Porter Davis, dean of the College of Liberal Arts at Howard University represented the University of Chicago, and Mary Church Terrell represented the president of Oberlin College.

Dr. Cooper's first official function as the newly installed president of Frelinghuysen University was to preside at graduation exercises, also held at the Metropolitan A.M.E. Church on the Thursday evening following her inauguration. The commencement address, delivered by the Reverend William H. Thomas (Metropolitan's pastor), was followed by remarks from Rosetta Lawson (Jesse Lawson's widow) and J. Q. Adams, director of physical education at Armstrong High School. The graduates were Elliott Floyd Scott, the Samuel G. Miller School of Theology; Louis Rogers Scree and J. Faison, College of Embalming and Sanitary Science (then headed by W. Ernest Jarvis); George Abraham Allen; William Columbia Wilson; John Douglass Dye; John Wesley Charleston; Howard Brandon Wiggins; William Henry Bailey; Raymond Powers; William David Parker; Ernest S. Hartgrove; and Charles Henry Cook, all members of the class of the John M. Langston School of Law.

At the time of Jesse Lawson's death, it had

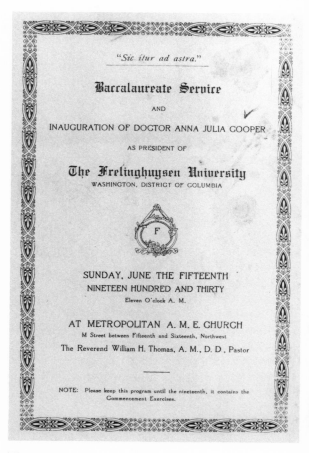

The program of the baccalaureate service and inauguration of Dr. Anna Julia Cooper as president of Frelinghuysen University. Courtesy Moorland-Spingarn Research Center, Howard University.

seemed that the Frelinghuysen University program would finally be launched, but the school had floundered for nearly two and a half years. By the time Anna Cooper became president, the institution had again changed locations and was occupying the Wilder Building at 217 Eye Street, NW. We can only conclude that the fundraising proposed by Lawson was unsuccessful, or that, in the absence of his leadership, efforts expended earlier had severely waned. Anna Cooper herself, upon accepting the mantle of leadership of this enterprise, expressed concern that the black community itself was not supportive. In a letter to the Reverend Francis J. Grimké, she wrote, "I have made no intensive drive for funds and do not intend to ask for money till it is clearly demonstrated that there is enough devotion to the cause of education among ourselves to sustain a work for our own working people." Yet Cooper did not expect that those furthest down the economic ladder, and with the greatest need, should or would be able to finance the Frelinghuysen concept of education; rather she had hoped that those who had had educational advantages and opportunities and now had the resources, would invest in the future of their heretofore "neglected neighbors."

During the intervening years Frelinghuysen University had lost the M Street site and acquired a new and modest mortgage of $12,000 on the Wilder Building. Anna Cooper, however, discovered that the school was barely subsisting on a "hand-to-mouth" budget, and was totally dependent upon student tuitions for operating funds. It had no endowment, no cash in reserve for exigencies, and no sound fiscal policy. She reported her findings at her first formal meeting with the school's board of directors, in October 1930—and by June of the next year Frelinghuysen's accounts were in order. In March 1931, Anna Cooper sent out the first of several letters of appeal for funds to each former student of Frelinghuysen. She wrote:

> To all who believe in this worthy ideal and this immensely worthwhile undertaking, I appeal to [you] to make this twenty-fifth anniversary the year for settling forever the location of a Home for this institution by clearing from debt and future embarrassment the building at 217 Eye Street, Northwest, to be known henceforth as the Jesse Lawson Building of Frelinghuysen University.

Apparently the goals of the appeal were not met, and the school received a notice to vacate the Wilder Building by June 11, 1931.

Since the university had no funds to relocate, Dr. Cooper offered the use of her residence to house the educational program, retaining only the three upstairs bedrooms, the family dining room, kitchen and pantry for her personal use. Anna Cooper was too much of a pragmatist to consider Dr. James R. Wilder's proposal to allow the school to remain on his property in exchange for the personal note of Frelinghuysen's president. Acceptance of that offer would have encumbered her own property, and, as Anna Cooper would note later, at her age such an offer presented "too heavy a responsibility and made too complicated a problem."

Some of the trustees, like John Lankford, with a long history of association with Frelinghuysen during the Lawson era, opposed the offer to relocate the

The Metropolitan A.M.E. Church (the national church of the A.M.E. denomination in Washington, D.C.), the site of Dr. Anna J. Cooper's inauguration as president of Frelinghuysen University. Courtesy Library of Congress.

school in Anna Cooper's home. However, the final decision to do so was reached by a committee of the trustees who were empowered to obtain a new site for the institution. Lankford, it should be recalled had designed a building that both he and Lawson had believed would become the permanent home of Frelinghuysen University. Although the dream did not come to fruition, he, perhaps, more than others among the trustees, simply could not accept this move that would return the school to its primal state. Still, after an affirmative vote by a majority of its trustees, Frelinghuysen did resume operations at 201 T Street, NW, in October 1931. It did so under the provisions of a five-year lease, signed by Rosetta Lawson, Dr. Simeon L. Carson (founder of Carson's Hospital), and Campbell Johnson (later a trustee of Howard University and a colonel in the United States Army) for the trustees, and Anna

Dr. James R. Wilder, a successful physician, owned the Wilder Building. From *How to Solve the Race Problem*. Courtesy Mr. James J. Lawson.

Cooper. Later, Anna Cooper wrote that it had never been her intent to rent the home; rather she had planned all along to bequeath the property to Frelinghuysen. But before doing so, she had wanted some assurance that the school—given all of its exigencies and just then emerging from a period of "interregnum"—could succeed.

The major point of contention between Anna Cooper and a small group of dissidents among the trustees was her expressed wish to establish and annex to Frelinghuysen the Hannah Stanley Opportunity School—an independent corporation that would remain under her control and management. In her judgment, Cooper, because she accepted no salary and gained no pecuniary benefits from the arrangement, believed she had the right to protect "that . . . small accretion my labor has contributed to the common weal," and she held that it should "not be allowed to take the usual course from shirtsleeves to shirtsleeves nor, through ignorance and mismanagement be gobbled up by sharks and shysters before a generation shall have passed." Perhaps some trustees associated with the early development

of the Frelinghuysen concept had felt threatened by Cooper's attitude and pronouncements, but the school had lost other properties. Clearly stating that she had "no wish to pose as a heroine or magnify the sacrifice [she had made] in thus devoting the earnings of a life spent in teaching to a continuation of the benefits of teaching for the people [she had] served," Anna Cooper wished to entrust her property "to . . . men and women whose character . . . guarantee that it will remain a monument to the social efficiency of Colored Americans and . . . a silent vindicator of their culture, their moral strength and their altruistic initiative." Too, Cooper claimed "the only private and personal right and privilege to honor my mother by giving her name to this monument . . . dedicated to the educational and social advancement of her race."

The property was then valued at $20,000, with only a balance of $3,400 remaining that was due the Teacher's Benefit and Annuity Association (an amount she repaid from private earnings and her retirement annuity). Anna Cooper was "anxiously using my best endeavors to wipe out the last vestiges of debt in order that the trustees of Hannah Stanley Opportunity School may be entirely free from embarrassment in [the event] of my death." In support of her unyielding position, Cooper contended that "the University is advantaged . . . by [gaining] permanency and a basis for financial stability which will defeat . . . the most serious . . . objection to its recognition [by] . . . its critics . . . namely, that having no abiding place, [they, the trustees] were shifting as the sands . . . without assurance [of] . . . survival in the struggle for existence."

Later, and as a bequest, Anna Cooper did will her property to Frelinghuysen University and to the care of seven trustees, including herself. The others were Samuel D. Matthews, W. H. C. Browne, Louise K. Pickett, G. Smith Wormley, Charles F. M. Browne, Lula Love Lawson, and Ethelyn G. Johnson. A self-perpetuating board, this group was to inherit Cooper's property, which then included an undeveloped lot in Upper Marlboro, Maryland, and the home she had built in Raleigh, North Carolina, should Frelinghuysen University fail. These plans were disclosed to the Reverend Dr. Grimké in a letter Cooper wrote to him on March 19, 1932, making known her wishes for the final disposition of her property. To assure that it would be kept and used in the way that represented her ideals, she restated her plan "to devote it to the education of colored people." To this end Cooper selected seven additional trustees, covenanting them to "carry out the terms of my last will and testament." (Not located at the time of her death many years later. A subsequent will had been drawn up that made no mention of the school, then defunct.) Those selected to serve with and succeed her were Mrs. Joseph B. Allen, Dr. Marie B. Lucas (her personal physician), Dr. Simeon L. Carson, Dr. Henry L. Bailey (an old friend and colleague from her M Street High School days), Mrs. Smallwood-Pickett, and Judge W. C. Hueston. This special group of trustees was incorporated under a separate charter to hold the title and right to her legacy, the Hannah Stanley Opportunity School. (Without a word of explanation, Cooper had dropped the surname Haywood from her mother's name.) According to Anna Cooper, she added "an iron-clad pro-

The seal of the Hannah Stanley Opportunity School, named in memory of Anna Cooper's mother, Hannah Stanley Haywood. The omission of the surname *Haywood* was not explained. Courtesy Mrs. Regia Bronson and Miss Regina Smith.

viso" in 1933, making it impossible for future members "to dissolve either The Hannah Stanley Opportunity School or the bequest." This codicil provided that:

> [N]o man or body of men shall have the right to mortgage or sell or in any sense to alienate the property known as 201 T Street, Northwest, devised to the trustees of the Hannah Stanley Opportunity School of Frelinghuysen University and devoted *in perpetuo* to [the] Education of Colored Adults.

Anna Cooper's devotion to Frelinghuysen University would place her, once again, at loggerheads with the D.C. Board of Education, for the school had lost its authority to confer degrees—without which it could neither attract the needed operating funds nor a sizable student body. The problem resulted from legislation enacted by the Seventieth Congress (Public Law No. 949), and approved on March 2, 1929. Under this act to amend subchapter I of chapter 18 of the Code of Laws for the District of Columbia Board of Education, the board gained the authority to license all educational insti-

Judge W. C. Hueston. Courtesy Moorland-Spingarn Research Center, Howard University.

167

The Frelinghuysen Group of Schools

for employed colored persons

Founded 1906 by Dr. Jesse and Mrs. Rosetta E. Lawson

School of Religion

School of Law

Academy

Opportunity

201 T Street, Northwest, Washington, D.C.

FACULTY

President—Anna J. Cooper, A.B., A.M., Oberlin; Ph.D., Sorbonne, University of Paris.

Vice-President—Mrs. James F. Lawson, B.A., Howard University.

Secretary—Rev. Julius S. Carroll, B.A., Morgan; B.D., Drew Theological Seminary; D.D., Morgan.

Treasurer—Charles F. M. Browne, A.B., LL.B., Howard University.

Mrs. Hyman Y. Chase, A.B., M.A., Howard University.

Mrs. M. Phipps Clark, A.B., M.A., Howard University.

Rev. R. A. Fairley, A.B., Johnson C. Smith; S.T.B., Lincoln University.

Mrs. E. E. Just, A.B., Ohio State University; M.A., Boston University.

Rev. John W. Lavall, B.Th., Howard University.

Rev. H. T. Medford, A.B., Livingstone College; B.D., Hood Theological Seminary.

Evening classes ten hours a week daily except Saturday and Sunday. Law from 5 to 7. Religion, 7 to 9. Academic, Secondary and Collegiate, 8 to 10. No degrees are offered, but certified credit is given for standard work completed. The Opportunity School is for unclassified persons whose employment will not permit adjustment in regular classes, and who are given individual instruction at such hours as may be convenient.

Tuition in all departments is $5.00 per month for the term of eight months, October 1 to June 1. Summer work for Opportunity School in Academic subjects only.

The Aim: To enable men and women who cannot make their leisure time fit into the schedule of a grade A College or University to pursue under competent instructors the higher and broader education in such lines as seem suited to their several capacities and aspirations.

The faculty list of the Frelinghuysen Group of Schools, about 1940. From *Decennial Catalogue of Frelinghuysen University*. Courtesy Mrs. Regia Bronson and Miss Regina Smith.

tutions that operated in the District—whether or not they were incorporated there.

Before granting a license, the board was empowered to require satisfactory evidence that the majority of the directors and trustees were "persons of good repute and qualified to conduct an institution of learning"; that degrees would only be awarded for work that was commensurate in quality and quantity with that usually required by reputable educational institutions offering the same degrees; that candidates for the degrees possess that usual high school diploma or qualifications; and that the applying institutions have a number and type of courses proportionate to those of established accredited schools; a faculty of reasonable number and qualifications, and "suitable classroom laboratory, and library equipment."

Incorporated and chartered by Jesse Lawson in the District of Columbia in 1927, Frelinghuysen

University must have met the licensing requirements at that time, since the school had conferred degrees for a brief period until June 1930, when Anna Cooper became its president.

Frelinghuysen University withstood still another setback when, in 1931, former instructors of the John M. Langston School of Law withdrew their support and organized the Robert H. Terrell Law School. Incorporated in the District of Columbia on August 12, 1931, this school (also no longer extant) was founded by attorneys Augustus W. Gray, George A. Parker, and Louis R. Mehlinger. All graduates of Howard University, they had earned their degrees in 1903, 1919, and 1921, respectively.

In 1937 Anna Cooper, now clearly beyond retirement age, sought the assistance of Congressman Harold D. Cooley of North Carolina when seeking a position with the Education Division of the Works Progress Administration (WPA), a program of President Franklin D. Roosevelt's administration. Finding that fund-raising programs in the community, along with student tuitions, did not bring in the sorely needed revenue, Cooper had sought to earn additional funds in order to keep the doors of Frelinghuysen open. To support her effort to become gainfully employed once again, Congressman Cooley sent a letter of recommendation to Dr. L. R. Alderman, the WPA's director of education, on Anna Cooper's behalf. In part, he wrote:

> Her work [as president of Frelinghuysen University] has been very highly endorsed by prominent citizens, both white and colored, in Washington and in North Carolina. I have in my files letters in her behalf from some very prominent citizens of Raleigh, [and] in each . . . she is represented to me as a woman of unquestionable character and of splendid ability. She is highly educated and I am satisfied that she will be found energetic, thoroughly reliable and in every way well qualified to perform satisfactorily the duties of the position for which she has applied.

Although Anna Cooper was in good health and still presented a youthful appearance that belied her now more than seventy-five years, the fact that she did not get the position sought must be attributed to her age. Yet she had felt it her duty to seek employment in order to help make Frelinghuysen financially solvent. She was willing to shoulder this

A class at Frelinghuysen University, about 1940.
From *Decennial Catalogue of Frelinghuysen University*.
Courtesy Mrs. Regia Bronson and Miss Regina Smith.

additional responsibility while also trying to meet the requirement for licensing and accreditation.

Under a provision of the 1929 law (familiarly called the "Diploma Mill Law"), the Frelinghuysen trustees appealed in 1936 to the D.C. Board of Education for recognition of the John M. Langston Law School as a separate entity. When the appeal was denied on the grounds of an absence of students and an inadequate law library, the trustees filed a suit (Equity No. 64,287) in the D.C. Court of the United States for the District of Columbia. However, the relief sought was also denied, the court holding that the Board of Education (the defendants) had acted "within the power conferred upon them by the [Congressional] Act of March 2, 1929." This irreversible decision of the court was to be the Waterloo of an already declining institution,

The library of Frelinghuysen University was also used as a classroom. From *Decennial Catalogue of Frelinghuysen University*. Courtesy Mrs. Regia Bronson and Miss Regina Smith.

FRELINGHUYSEN UNIV
COMMENCEMENT 1935

Dr. Cooper leads the procession of Frelinghuysen University graduates on the portico of her home. From *Decennial Catalogue of Frelinghuysen University.* Courtesy Mrs. Regia Bronson and Miss Regina Smith.

which had neither the physical plant nor the fiscal resources to meet the new licensing requirements for institutions of higher learning. According to the *Washington Daily News* (May 1, 1937), the Frelinghuysen court case was one of placing "a cart before the horse."

When all else had failed, Anna Cooper made what might best be described as a last-ditch effort, appealing directly to the school superintendent, Frank W. Ballou, on October 27, 1936:

> Without your endorsement I cannot carry on. I am unwilling to preside at a farce, and I refuse to take the pitiful earnings of an already disadvantaged people for a service that is not at par throughout the [educational] community. If you refuse to recognize my work as of standard worth, you proclaim your want of confidence either in my educational judgments

or in my civic honesty. . . . While several have received diplomas [during] . . . my incumbency, only one could have been eligible for a degree under our rules.

Now approaching her eightieth birthday, Anna Cooper decided that "a decade is long enough for one to head the fight for recognition," and in 1940 she became the registrar of the Frelinghuysen Group of Schools for Colored Working People—a name the trustees must have adopted when they were unable to obtain licensing and award degrees. Then the presidency of Frelinghuysen passed to the Reverend Adolphus A. Birch, who also headed the trustee board. By this time, with only a handful of students in the school, both positions had become largely ceremonial and were continued in a rather pathetic effort to carry on.

Because she still recognized the need to care for

Anna Cooper in the parlor of 201 T Street, NW, then the Registrar's Office of Frelinghuysen University. Photograph by Addison Scurlock. Courtesy Robert Scurlock, Scurlock Studios.

The Reverend Adolphus A. Birch, rector of St. George's Protestant Episcopal Church in LeDroit Park, Frelinghuysen University's third president and Anna Cooper's successor. From *Second Decennial Catalogue of Frelinghuysen University.* Courtesy Mrs. Regia Bronson and Miss Regina Smith.

those working people who did not have the opportunity to attend other institutions of higher education, Anna Cooper looked forward to the day when her great-niece and namesake, Annie Cooper Haywood, would succeed her. The educational opportunities for Washington's black population were dwindling. In *Washington Past and Present* (1932), John Clagett Proctor wrote that the city had seven full-time universities and only one of these—Howard University—admitted black students. According to Cooper (*Second Decennial Catalogue of Frelinghuysen University,* 1950?), of the eighty-eight part-time or special instructional institutions or educational centers in the District, none would admit Negroes. But Anna's dream was not to be realized, and in a letter dated January 1, 1934 (her annual New Year's Greeting), she confided to her old and trusted friend, Grimké, "I regret to have to tell you that . . . Annie has left school and married giving up all hope of a college career. A great and sore disappointment to me for I was building great hopes on her becoming a teacher to succeed me in

the work I am now doing." At age twenty-four, in December 1939, Annie Cooper Haywood Beckwith died. Her death, more than anything else that the stoic Cooper had experienced, brought to a close this chapter of her story. Even though she would live another quarter of a century and remain alert for many of those years, the hope that had unfailingly recharged her energy and rekindled her spirit was gone.

Anna Julia Cooper lived until February 27, 1964, in her "beautiful home at the Capital," and she lived the credo that she had espoused—*education for service.* As an educator she had given freely of her talents, knowledge, and limited resources, and was rewarded when students learned. She neither sought nor expected personal recognition, and was courageous in the face of adversity and opposition to her point of view. Perhaps no finer testimony and tribute to the life and work of Anna Cooper has been written than the expression of appreciation that follows:

> 345 N. 8th Street
> Salina, Kansas
> September 14, 1949

Dr. Anna J. Cooper: My beloved teacher who guided me into the complexities of Euclid and the intricacies of the language of Homer and induced 5 fellow teachers to deny themselves a portion, a generous portion of their not too liberal salary—*bread cast upon water*—to start me on my collegiate mission. . . . I am making my primal installment . . . donated to F. U. [Frelinghuysen University] foundation in memory of the above mentioned teacher's voluntary sacrifice. . . .

> As ever,
>
> WILLIAM H. BAWLEY

Anna Cooper herself wrote finis to this chapter, when in retrospect she contemplated her "second decade of work for F.[relinghuysen] U.[niversity]." In the *Second Decennial Catalogue,* she wrote. "there is always a veiled suspicion of dotage to becloud memoirs of a nonagenarian, [so] I have made this story of my . . . work . . . a simple catalog of events . . . easily verifiable from printed programs." And "with grateful memory," she publicly acknowledged the friendship and unfaltering assistance of Emma Merritt, Dr. Georgiana Simpson, Henry L. Bailey, Agnes Regan (National Catholic School of Social Service), and Samuel D. Matthews,

Annie Cooper Haywood Beckwith (1915–1939), the great-niece and namesake of Anna Cooper. Courtesy Mrs. Regia Bronson and Miss Regina Smith.

"all gone to a much higher reward than any poor encomiums of mine could possibly bestow." She wanted "the world to know . . . the understanding cooperation . . . unstintingly and unselfishly" given, which had made it possible for the work to go on in an effort to solve the educational and social problems of her world.

For herself, Anna Julia Cooper asked very little. She prefaced a very simple request regarding the preservaton of her personal papers and mementos with the following—an introspective and insightful assessment of her personal philosophy and her own work.

"AND NOW IN CONCLUSION:

Fully conscious of the fact that no will or testament drawn by the most astute lawyer is immune from attack and upset by those who want to break it (and I am no lawyer) nevertheless I believe I am within my legal rights and wholly on reasonable grounds when I ask that my will be respected regarding this house that I have builded, much of it literally with my own hands and brain; and while less gruesome than Shakespeare's "Cursed be he who moves my bones," just as effective I hope may be my blessing on those who will now and hereafter work in intelligent public spirited harmony to perpetuate . . . this simple unpretentious effort toward community goodwill and cooperating service. I have built it, paid for it, improved and beautified it, met every obligation, paid all the taxes, Federal and District, even cashing in . . . Savings Bonds to meet [the] tax on income already spent in this service. Contributions from others . . . were religiously deposited to Endowment. . . . proceeds from my own writings went to the same fund. Tuition from students was distributed equally among teachers, deficiencies supplied from my own pocket.

. . . My entire earnings have been spent in this service. I have received no favors and taken no handouts. . . .

It is a kind Providence which enables my mental faculties to continue into the 91st year. . . . I cannot take it with me and . . . it is presumptuous to expect this small accumulation of a lifetime to go on serving in its own small way. The one disappointment, the only failure that can come, is not the absence of eulogistic sanction and public adulation, but a lack, if proven, of the ability to appreciate and utilize advantages here made possible and of the character and insight to know and judge true worth in spiritual values.

No flowers please.

Anna Cooper wished simply to be remembered as "Somebody's old Teacher on Vacation now!' Resting a while, getting ready for the next opening of a Higher School."

X.

Epilogue: A Retrospective

*In the language of our beloved Cicero: Nothing
dumb can delight me. I ask no medal in bronze or
gold. There is nothing in life really worth striving
for but the esteem of just men that follows a sincere
effort to serve to the best of one's powers in the
advancement of one's generation.*

ANNA J. COOPER
December 29, 1925

IN HOWARD UNIVERSITY'S RANKIN CHAPEL ON
the occasion of the recognition ceremony of the Xi
Omega Chapter, Alpha Kappa Alpha Sorority,
when Anna Cooper officially received the coveted
Ph.D, she said, "no deeper joy can come to anyone,
no richer reward than the pure pleasure of this
moment from the expressions of appreciation of this
assembly on the part of the community in which
the best service of my life has been spent." About
1950, when Cooper published the *Second Decennial
Catalogue*—her last report to the Frelinghuysen
University trustees—she closed her public life with
the request for "one small recognition" in return for
her many years of devoted service. She wrote, I
desire the sunroom planned and constructed by me
be kept without change as the repository of my
personal mementos, books, letters, pictures . . . an
honor, it seems to me which should be begrudged
to no one."

On her one-hundredth birthday, August 10,
1958, Anna Cooper was interviewed by a *Washington Post* reporter. Seated in her parlor surrounded by
papers, while speaking of her plans for the future
and the book she must write, she proudly "fussed
over" the two congratulatory messages received
from President and Mrs. Dwight D. Eisenhower.
Although her hearing was impaired and her vision
faulty, she spoke, according to the *Post*, in a voice
that was "clear and full," that took "on a surprising
vitality." And on this day, Anna Cooper summed
up the philosophy upon which she had built her
life, observing that "It isn't what we say about
ourselves, it's what our life stands for." At 5 o'clock
that afternoon, family, friends, and alumni and
trustees of the Frelinghuysen University began
to arrive at Cooper's home to honor her in the
sunroom.

In the pages that follow, we invite the reader
into Anna Cooper's sunroom, to browse a spell
among her personal mementos, books, letters, and
pictures.

Anna Julia Haywood Cooper, on the porch of her
home, 1930s. Photograph by Addison Scurlock.
Courtesy Robert Scurlock, Scurlock Studios.

Wendell Phillips, the abolitionist. Plaster, n.d., from Anna Cooper's sunroom. Courtesy Mrs. Regia Bronson and Miss Regina Smith.

This metal sculpture in the classical style, *A Woman with a Globe,* is symbolic of Anna Cooper's faith in the intellectual capability of women. Courtesy Mrs. Regia Bronson and Miss Regina Smith.

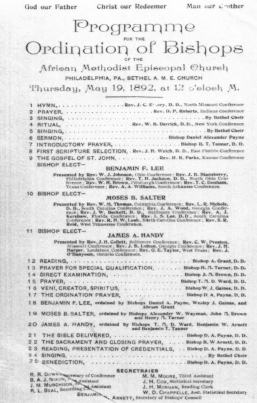

Program for the ordination of Benjamin F. Lee, Moses B. Salter, and James A. Handy, of the African Methodist Episcopal Church, in 1892. Courtesy Moorland-Spingarn Research Center, Howard University.

Prayers in the Senate

PRAYERS

OFFERED IN THE SENATE OF THE UNITED STATES

IN THE WINTER SESSION OF 1904

BY

EDWARD E. HALE
CHAPLAIN

BOSTON
LITTLE, BROWN, AND COMPANY
1904

Dear Mrs. Cooper:—
Will you accept
this and keep it
in memory of our
pleasant visit to
your School.

Sincerely

Edward E Hale

Feb. 16. 1905:—
Washington

Found in Anna Cooper's sunroom, this reproduction of the famous Venus de Milo might have been purchased when Anna and Lula Love toured Europe in 1900. Courtesy Mrs. Regia Bronson and Miss Regina Smith.

Inscribed to Anna Cooper, this volume of Senate prayers by Chaplain Edward E. Hale was a memento of his visit to the M Street School in 1905. Courtesy Mrs. Regia Bronson and Miss Regina Smith.

Andrew Jackson and John Wesley Haywood, two of the five great-nephews and great-nieces Anna Cooper brought to live with her in 1915. Courtesy Mrs. Regia Bronson and Miss Regina Smith.

Lula Love, foster daughter of Anna Cooper, married Dr. James Francis Lawson, the son of Jesse and Rosetta Lawson. Courtesy Mrs. Regia Bronson, Miss Regina Smith, and Mrs. Anna Rosetta Lawson Prescott.

Old State House, a painting by Jacob Marling, also shows the home of Fabius J. Haywood, Sr. The canvas dates from between 1818 and 1831. From *North Carolina's Capital, Raleigh*.

The works of Victor Hugo from Anna Cooper's library. Courtesy Mrs. Regia Bronson and Miss Regina Smith.

St. Simon of Cyrene, by Frank J. Dillon. The Reverend George A. Christopher Cooper Memorial Window, a gift to St. Augustine's College Chapel from Anna J. Cooper. Courtesy St. Augustine's College.

Presented to Anna Cooper with the accompanying note from J. George Stewart, Architect of the Capitol, this American flag was flown over the Capitol building on August 10, 1958, her 100th birthday. Courtesy Mrs. Regia Bronson and Miss Regina Smith.

Stained glass window by Frank J. Dillon, in the parlor of Anna Cooper's T Street home. Courtesy Mrs. Regia Bronson and Miss Regina Smith.

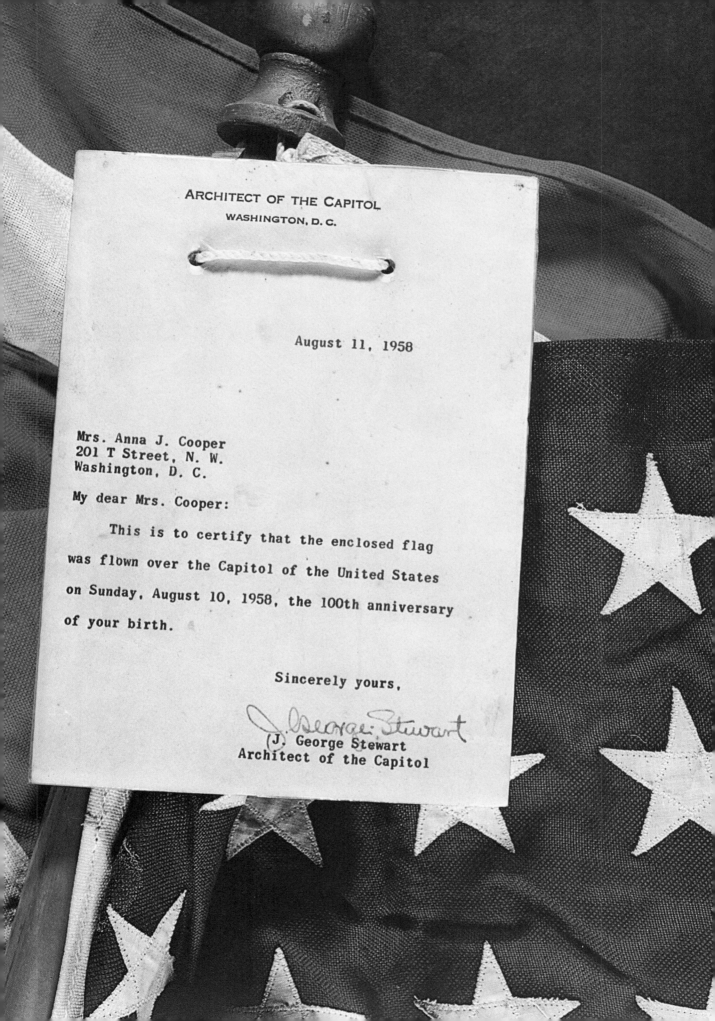

ARCHITECT OF THE CAPITOL
WASHINGTON, D. C.

August 11, 1958

Mrs. Anna J. Cooper
201 T Street, N. W.
Washington, D. C.

My dear Mrs. Cooper:

This is to certify that the enclosed flag
was flown over the Capitol of the United States
on Sunday, August 10, 1958, the 100th anniversary
of your birth.

Sincerely yours,

J. George Stewart
Architect of the Capitol

The Sunroom, by Frank J. Dillon, about 1948. A birthday gift to Anna Cooper from the artist. Courtesy Mrs. Regia Bronson and Miss Regina Smith.

This fireplace, designed by Anna Cooper, is still in her T Street home. Each ceramic tile represents a book of Shakespeare. Courtesy Mrs. Regia Bronson and Miss Regina Smith.

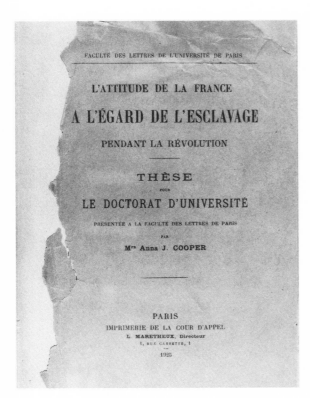

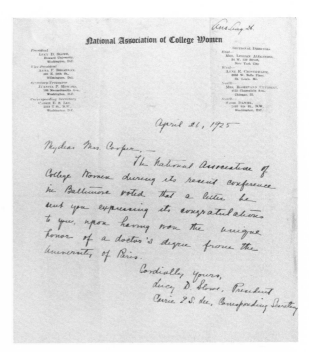

The cover of Anna Cooper's doctoral thesis, 1925. Courtesy Mrs. Regia Bronson and Miss Regina Smith.

A congratulatory letter to Anna Cooper from Lucy D. Slowe, president of the National Association of College Women, for "having won the unique honor of a doctor's degree," 1925. Courtesy Moorland-Spingarn Research Center, Howard University.

An Oberlin College reunion, class of 1884. Anna Cooper is in the front row, second from right, holding the class pennant. Mary Church Terrell is third from left, front row. Courtesy Mrs. Phyllis Terrell Langston.

A letter to W. E. B. Du Bois from Anna Cooper, December 31, 1929, urging him to answer *The Tragic Era*—a book that seriously maligned the character and contributions of black people. Later, Du Bois wrote *Black Reconstruction*. Courtesy University of Massachusetts, W. E. B. Du Bois Collection.

Simon of Cyrene, a poem by Anna J. Cooper. She wrote that "St. Simon was not pictured in my mind as a slave . . . but as one elect thruout the Ages to play his part in the Drama when Asia betrayed and Europe crucified." Courtesy Mrs. Regia Bronson and Miss Regina Smith.

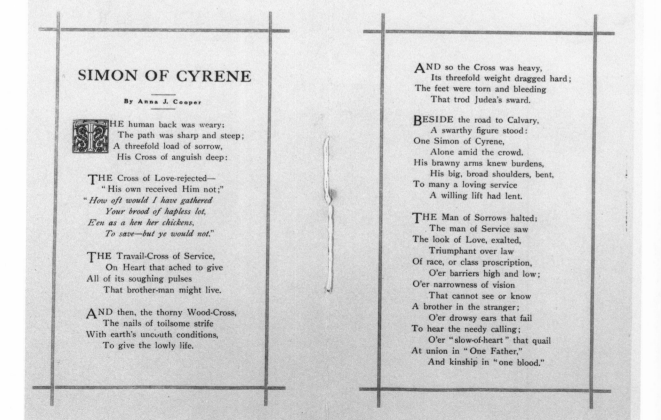

SIMON OF CYRENE

By Anna J. Cooper

THE human back was weary;
  The path was sharp and steep;
A threefold load of sorrow,
  His Cross of anguish deep:

THE Cross of Love-rejected—
  "His own received Him not;"
"How oft would I have gathered
  Your brood of hapless lot,
E'en as a hen her chickens,
  To save—but ye would not."

THE Travail-Cross of Service,
  On Heart that ached to give
All of its soughing pulses
  That brother-man might live.

AND then, the thorny Wood-Cross,
  The nails of toilsome strife
With earth's uncouth conditions,
  To give the lowly life.

AND so the Cross was heavy,
  Its threefold weight dragged hard;
The feet were torn and bleeding
  That trod Judea's sward.

BESIDE the road to Calvary,
  A swarthy figure stood:
One Simon of Cyrene,
  Alone amid the crowd.
His brawny arms knew burdens,
  His big, broad shoulders, bent,
To many a loving service
  A willing lift had lent.

THE Man of Sorrows halted;
  The man of Service saw
The look of Love, exalted,
  Triumphant over law
Of race, or class proscription,
  O'er barriers high and low;
O'er narrowness of vision
  That cannot see or know
A brother in the stranger;
  O'er drowsy ears that fail
To hear the needy calling;
  O'er "slow-of-heart" that quail
At union in "One Father,"
  And kinship in "one blood."

180

I have read with interest the strictures of Professor Davis on the Negro College Student & likewise the three or four answers from students in a subsequent issue of Crisis. I am impressed particularly with the true teacher-spirit of Mr. Davis' faultfinding & the high detachment of his aim & purpose in writing. His criticism while severe is not carping or slanderous neither is it the flippant sort that seizes an opportunity to rush to print for the vain glory of making talk thro the news papers; rather is it the honest findings & chastening of an intelligent father who wishes to correct an imperfect son — constructive, as all criticism should be, with an eye single to the ideal, not a relative standard. The answers too so far are not the tiresome attack & counter attack that get us nowhere beyond the over brilliant sparring exhibition of hit & thrust: they suggest causes & further criticisms — one, the need of ripe scholarship among teachers themselves, specifically the frivolous fledgelings just out of college & serving an indeterminate sentence to teach on their way to something hoped for; a second the dry-as-dust abstractions & mental gymnastics embalmed in an outworn college curriculum that have no discoverable connection with the practical life interests of the student & never made to grip his attention & disclose where he, the individual John Jones, can catch on, etc. &c.

If you will allow, I should like to add one other point of view in the same spirit of meeting our

sent their sons all the way to Rhodes to get the touch of Apollonius. An instructor who is himself keen about the enigma of the Universe, or even about the enigma of Mississippi & Texas, will find his flaming torch as "catching" from a chair in Greek & Latin as he would with a stereotyped or borrowed syllabus in Civics or a "book plan" on the Reconstruction period.

The trouble I suspect is that those who furnish the coin & "suggest" the promotions in Negro Education are not themselves a-wearying & a-worrying to see any Renaissance or primal naissance of real thinking in Negro Schools, & yet God knows they need it.

Anna J. Cooper

Qui sert bien son pays   N'a pas besoin d'aieux

WASHINGTON, D.C.

September 19/30

My dear Doctor DuBois:

I thot this suggestion might be of some use to teachers who read Crisis.

Very truly

Anna J. Cooper.

The first and last manuscript pages of Anna Cooper's article, "The Humor of Teaching," for publication in the *Crisis* (1930). It was accompanied by this note to Du Bois. Courtesy University of Massachusetts, W. E. B. Du Bois Collection.

ANNA J. COOPER, PRESIDENT
ALPHONZO J. HARRIS, CHR. BOARD TRUSTEES

JAMES A. DAVIS, SECRETARY
ERNEST JARVIS, TREASURER
W. E. LINDSAY, REGISTRAR

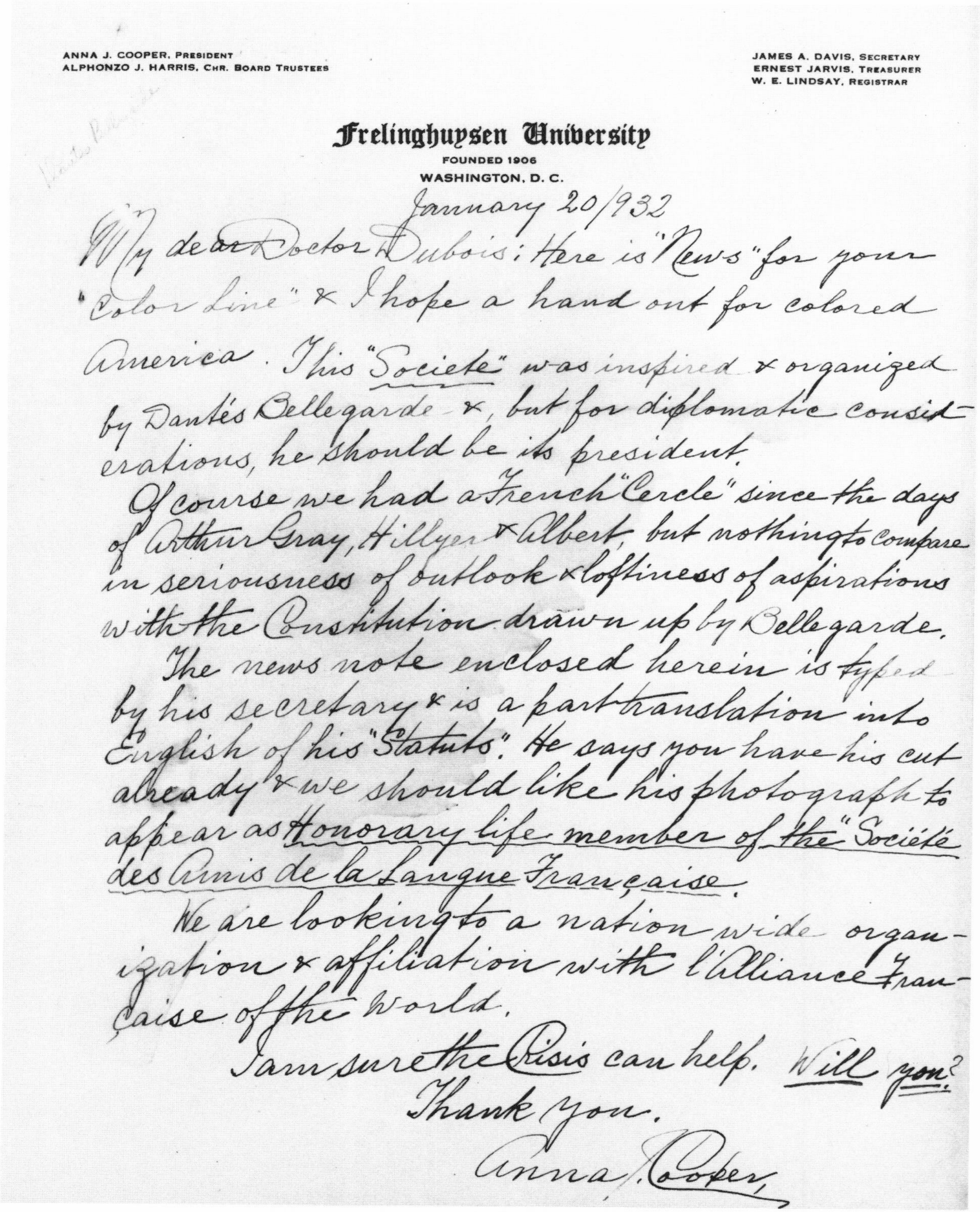

Frelinghuysen University
FOUNDED 1906
WASHINGTON, D. C.

January 20/932

My dear Doctor Dubois: Here is "News" for your "Color Line" & I hope a hand out for colored America. This "Societe" was inspired & organized by Dantés Bellegarde & but for diplomatic considerations, he should be its president.

Of course we had a French "Cercle" since the days of Arthur Gray, Hillyer & Albert, but nothing to compare in seriousness of outlook & loftiness of aspirations with the Constitution drawn up by Bellegarde.

The news note enclosed herein is typed by his secretary & is a part translation into English of his "Statuts". He says you have his cut already & we should like his photograph to appear as Honorary life member of the "Société des Amis de la Langue Française".

We are looking to a nation wide organization & affiliation with l'Alliance Française of the World.

I am sure the Crisis can help. Will you?

Thank you.

Anna J. Cooper.

As president of the "Societé des Amis de la Langue Francaise," Anna Cooper continued her interest in the French language and literature. She urged Du Bois to note the goals of the society in his *Crisis* column, "Color Line." Courtesy University of Massachusetts, W. E. B. Du Bois Collection.

HOUSE OF REPRESENTATIVES
WASHINGTON

Nov. 16 1932.

Dr. Anna J. Cooper,
President,
Frelinghuysen University,
201 T Street, N. W.,
Washington, D. C.,

My dear Dr. Cooper:-

I beg to acknowledge receipt of your letter of
the 9th on behalf of yourself and Frelinghuysen
University and to thank you for your kind words
of congratulation and confidence.

Sincerely yours,

Oscar De Priest, M. C.

The first black elected to the United States Congress in the twentieth century, Oscar De Priest was among Anna Cooper's correspondents. Courtesy Moorland-Spingarn Research Center, Howard University.

SAINT AUGUSTINE'S COLLEGE
RALEIGH, N. C.

August 28, 1936

My dear Dr. Cooper:

I am writing a history of St. Augustine's
College, and I have been told by many persons
that no such work could be complete without a
contribution from you. I should like to have a
personal interview with you, in addition to any
written contribution in the way of personal
memoirs and historical facts you would be kind
enough to put in writing.

Especially acceptable from you would be
personal memories of Dr. J. Brinton Smith, Dr.
Smedes, Dr. Sutton, Prof. Cooper, and the early
teachers.

I am planning to come to Washington September 2 or 3. Please let me know by an early
reply if I may call on you about that time.

Sincerely yours,

Cecil D. Halliburton
Professor of Sociology

Dr. Anna J. Cooper
Second and T Streets NW
Washington, D.C.

When preparing a history of St. Augustine's College, Professor Cecil D. Halliburton wished to interview Anna Cooper to collect her reminiscences. Courtesy Moorland-Spingarn Research Center, Howard University.

Obituary

ANNIE COOPER HAYWOOD BECKWITH. Twenty-four years ago on Christmas day at dawn, I walked into the Haywood Cottage in Raleigh where lay five sleeping children whose mother had lately been called to Heaven. Not all were asleep, the baby of six months was awake at this early hour, immediately began to coo, held out both arms as if she knew something was happening.

Christmas morning of this week I knelt beside a hospital bed where that same baby, now grown to womanhood herself a mother, lay battling for breath against the dread pneumonia while the vicar besought God's blessing in the touching service of the church. The end came Tuesday morning a little past 10 o'clock. The gentle spirit rested in peace leaving the world a little lonelier for some of us, yet brighter, too, for her having walked with us awhile.

Annie Cooper Haywood, youngest of five children, of John R. Haywood and Margaret Hinton deceased, was born at Raleigh, April 22, 1915, baptized in St. Luke's Church, Washington, D. C., on Esther day, 1916, her sponsors being the Rev. Francis I. Grimke, Miss Ernest F. G. Merritt and Mrs. Joseph B. Allen. She was confirmed by Bishop Freeman with a class from St. George's Chapel, at the Cathedral on May 23, 1933.

She was graduated from Dunbar High School June 20, 1933 and entered Howard University the following fall. October 12, 1932, she married Charles Sterling Beckwith. One daughter, Madeline Beckwith blessed their union. A sweet intelligent child now in kindergarten. The funeral from her late residence, 201 T Street, Northwest, at St. George's Chapel, Second and U Streets, at high noon on Friday, December 29. A communion service for the family at 10 a.m. in the chapel.

Interment in Lincoln Memorial Cemetery, Washington, D. C.

May she rest in peace.
ANNA J. COOPER.

Anna Cooper wrote this obituary for Annie Cooper Haywood Beckwith, her great-niece, who died in 1939. She expresses both her sense of loneliness and her joy "for . . . having walked with [her] awhile." Courtesy Mrs. Regia Bronson and Miss Regina Smith.

CHRISTMAS BELLS

A One Act Play for Children

by

ANNA J. COOPER

DRAMATIS PERSONAE

HANNAH, aged eleven, "the little Mother," who has the care of her two sisters, while the Mother works by the day, away from home. The Father is a soldier, across the sea.

NANNETTE, aged eight

ANNIKINS, aged four

THE THREE KINGS,—
Gaspard, a European,
Melchior, an Asiatic,
Balthazar, an African.

Chorus of Angels

Chorus of Shepherds

Sunshine Club of the Community Service. Soldiers. Red Cross Nurses.

1906   1941

FOUNDERS DAY

LOYAL SONS AND DAUGHTERS OF FRELINGHUYSEN UNIVERSITY

Invite their friends and the public generally
to meet in honor of its Founders

Dr. and Mrs. JESSE LAWSON

Thursday, April 10
At 8:15 P. M.

201 T Street, N. W., Washington, D. C.

"Every citizen of the United States who has felt in his own life or heard through the experience of others the earnest devoted efforts of Jesse Lawson for the advancement of his race and the educational improvement especially of the under privileged, every lover of progress, peace and goodwill among men should honor Jesse Lawson and determine to carry forward the ideal for which he worked, suffered and died."

Christmas Bells, a one-act play for children, was written by Anna Cooper to raise funds for Frelinghuysen University. Annie Beckwith's daughter, Madeline, starred in it. Courtesy Moorland-Spingarn Research Center, Howard University.

This loving cup, a memento from Anna Cooper's home, was presented to her by the Frelinghuysen University trustees on May 29, 1941. Courtesy Mrs. Regia Bronson and Miss Regina Smith.

Program for the Frelinghuysen University Founders Day, April 10, 1941. The new president, the Reverend Adolphus A. Birch, presided on this occasion. Courtesy Moorland-Spingarn Research Center, Howard University.

Anna Cooper delivered her "Farewell Address" as Frelinghuysen University's president at the school's Lincoln-Douglass Day observance in 1942. Courtesy Mrs. Regia Bronson and Miss Regina Smith.

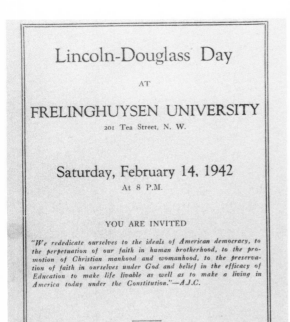

This is a reminder of Anna Cooper's early days at the first Colored YWCA. Courtesy Mrs. Regia Bronson and Miss Regina Smith.

Aunt Charlotte

Swing low, sweet Chariot, swing lower—
Way down for the humblest and poorest;
From the pearly white gate where thou soarest
To the hole of the pit where I cower.
In bondage my mother conceived me,
In bondage my first breath I uttered,
Eight babies in bondage I've suckled,
And prayed the prayer bond-women muttered.

Swing low, sweet Chariot, swing lower!
My God has not left me unfriended;
Gnarled hands, broken hearts are soon mended.
The toil and the ache now are o'er,
My robe shall be radiant with morning,
My feet shod to tread pathways golden,
My little ones once more adorning
Their fond mother's breast as of olden.

Swing low, sweet Chariot, swing lightly!
You find me all ready and outside;
A glad heart alone by the roadside;
The Promise marked daily and nightly.
I know He will come to stand by me.
His Hand firmly holding, I hie me
On board, welcome Chariot, swing gently,
Come quickly to carry me home.

A. J. C.

Anna Cooper wrote this poem to commemorate the death of her friend, Charlotte Forten Grimké. Courtesy Mrs. Regia Bronson and Miss Regina Smith.

Charlotte Forten and the Reverend Francis "Frank" J. Grimké were among Anna Cooper's dearest friends. Of her friendship with Charlotte, which began in 1887, Anna said, "we were both lonely and . . . not a part of Washington's oldest cit's club." Courtesy Moorland-Spingarn Research Center, Howard University.

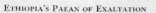

ETHIOPIA'S PAEAN OF EXALTATION   *Harry T. Burleigh*

Come sing us a song of hoeing the corn,
And picking the cotton in bolls,
Where the sweet scuppernong scents the dewy
    morn,
And the mocking bird note trills and trolls,

Oh sing once again the wild plaintive strain,
Of the land of the westward sun;
Songs born of the soil from its children of toil,
Where sighing and laughter are one.

We are rolling through an unfriendly world;
Nobody knows the trouble I see, but Jesus;
Swing low, swing lower sweet chariot,
Come carry me home.

Nay, is't not your home,
O children of song
This land of the sun of the West?
Where new comers roam finding surcease from
    wrong
And a haven of freedom and rest.

Lo, the land of your birth, of your toil and mirth,
Where your forefathers brawn wrought of yore;
Where brave Attucks died and thousands beside
On battle fields red with their gore,
Those graves of your sires,
Those blest altar fires;
Those hearth stones enshrined in your hearts.

Can you leave them for aye?
Will you wander away?
While the tear of old home longing starts?

Sweet land of liberty!
Land of the noble free!
Just God!
Do not mock!
Mote it be!
Sons gird anew; work, fight, live it true;
Till brotherhood reign from sea to sea.

                                        Anna Cooper

This paean of exaltation by Anna Cooper was set to music and performed by Harry T. Burleigh in St. George's Episcopal Church, New York City, in 1942. Courtesy Moorland-Spingarn Research Center, Howard University.

This sampler was a gift to Anna Cooper in 1950. Courtesy Mrs. Regia Bronson and Miss Regina Smith.

186

Anna Cooper, 105, Dies, Negro Writer, Educator

By Kenneth M. Boyd
Staff Reporter

Anna J. Cooper, writer, teacher and school administrator who celebrated her 105th birthday in August, died Thursday in her sleep at her home, 201 T st. nw.

The daughter of George Washington Haywood, a slave, Mrs. Cooper married the Rev. George A. C. Cooper, an Episcopal minister in Raleigh, N.C., in 1877. After her husband's death two years later, Mrs. Cooper moved north to become one of the few Negro women college graduates in the country when she received her master's degree from Oberlin College in 1884.

As principal of the old M Street High School from 1901 to 1906, now Dunbar High School, she was the second woman principal in Washington public schools. A crusader for college scholarships for eligible Negro high school graduates, she won assurances from Harvard, Yale, and Brown Universities that her students would be considered if they could pass the entrance examinations.

"Our two boys accepted at Harvard were the first Negro high school graduates to enter without having to study at an academy first," she recalled five years ago on her 100th birthday.

After teaching Latin for several years at Dunbar, Mrs. Cooper received her Ph.D. in Latin from the Sorbonne in Paris in 1925, also publishing that year, in French, "Le Pelerinage de Charlemagne."

From 1929 to 1941 she was president of Frelinghuysen University, a school for employed Negroes which she located in her spacious home on T st. The school closed three years ago.

Mrs. Cooper is survived by two great-nieces, Regia Bronson and Marion Goodwin, and a nephew, Andrew Haywood, all of the T st. address.

Mrs. Cooper

"Reunited Trio Blazed a Trail," was the headline of the interview in the *Washington Post* in 1952 as these three notable women recounted their pioneer days at Oberlin College. From left to right are Anna Cooper, Ida Gibbs Hunt, and Mary Church Terrell, shown here in the former's home. Courtesy *The Washington Post.*

Anna Julia Cooper died peacefully on Thursday, February 27, 1964. While this *Washington Post* obituary identifies her father as a slave, she had written, more than three decades earlier, "I owe nothing to my white father beyond the initial act of procreation." Courtesy Mrs. Regia Bronson and Miss Regina Smith.

187

Anna Cooper was buried in her native North Carolina after a simple service at St. Augustine's College Chapel. Courtesy Mrs. Regia Bronson and Miss Regina Smith.

In this poem, written by Anna Cooper on her eighty-second birthday, she expressed her thanks to all for the "courage & strength" given "in the Struggle we call Life." Courtesy Moorland-Spingarn Research Center, Howard University.

No Flowers Please.

Oh just a rose perhaps, a few violets
Or even a handfull of wild honeysuckle
Or Star of Bethlehem & sweet alyssum
Which says you remember kindly.
For this I shall thank you, Wherever I am.
And more for the courage & strength
You gave in the Struggle we call Life.
By the touch of your shoulder to shoulder
And the understanding glance of your eye
And the hearty Pull together of a sympathetic heart.
Priceless & undying these as God's gracious bounty.
And I shall thank you, Wherever I am.

But please, please, don't pass the hat for big florist's offerings
Or take up a collection to crowd the room & cover my poor bier
With mute withering symbols of God's eternal love & Christ's unspeakable Prayer
Agonizing that we all should be one & love one another
Even as He & the Father are One in Love.
No flowers please, just the smile of sweet understanding
The knowing look that sees Beyond And says gently & kindly
'Somebody's Teacher on Vacation now - Resting for the Fall Opening' Anna J Cooper Aug 10, 1940

GRADUATES OF THE
WASHINGTON NORMAL SCHOOL NO. 2;
M STREET HIGH SCHOOL;
ARMSTRONG BUSINESS AND MANUAL TRAINING SCHOOL

WASHINGTON NORMAL SCHOOL NO. 2

Blanch Adams
Elizabeth B. Ball
Blanch Butler
Rosa E. Carter
Blanch I. Coleman
Natalie Collier
Eleanor J. Curtis
Adah E. Dale
Josephine I. Dandridge
Gertrude P. Early
Jennie L. Fearing
Mamie E. Fearing
Edith Fleetwood
Emma A. Greens
Millie Hall
Anna M. Jackson
Sarah P. Johnson
Lillian T. Lott
Georgianna A. Lucas

Mary E. Merriwether
Lillian P. Parker
Jessie B. Parks
Ruth Piper
Rachel A. Randolph
Bessie M. Shippen
Katherine C. Thomas
Charlotte M. Wallace
Eva A. Watson
Mabel H. Weaver
R. Blyden Wilkinson
Alice K. Wormley
Mary A. Wright
Elizabeth E. Yates
William A. Fair
J. Parker Gillem
Richard A. Gillem
G. Bernard Key.

M STREET HIGH SCHOOL

Susie Elizabeth Arnold
Evelyn French Baker
Frances L. Bostic
Eleanor Allease Syphax
    Boston [?]
Geneva Braxton
Ernestine Jones Brent
Willis Franklin Brown
Carrie Beaner Carter
Desiree Cornelia Catlett
Susan Estell Clark
Janie Beatrice Cole
Rachel Mae Cornush
Eva Gladys Crutcher
Grace Lillian Daniels
Londonia Louis Denney
Claudia Laura Deveaux
Madonaah Isabel Ease
Martha Virginia Edelin
Harriet Virginia Edmonds
Sarah Alice Fisher
Maude Elizabeth Fleming
Nellie Ford
Lois Esther Geary
Bertha Ernestine Hanson
Eugenia Thompson Hart
Fannie Elmira Holmes
Louise Blanch Howard
Julia Juanita Jenkins
Grace Frances Jackson
Rosa Louisa Keating
Lottie Rachel Lane
Percy Ashford Lawrence
Marie Carnell Lewis
Naond Mollie Lewis
Elizabeth Reed Martin
Julia Elizabeth McKenzie
Helen Lucille McKinney
Helen Uretia Middleton
Esther Mae Middleton
Altonia Maywood Mitchell
Mary Melvina Mitchell
Maria Raven Montgomery

Helen Anne Moss
Lumina Nunley
Josephine Patterson
Audie Mae Perry
Gazelle Surville Plummer
Eva Reid
Mattie Geneva Scurlock
Emma Florence Smith
Addie May Solomon
Marion Ethel Sumner
Marion Anna Sydnor
Gypsy Mae Taylor
Lucy Madeline Taylor
Mattie Jennie Taylor
Louise Stonella Thomas
Lillian Beatrice Tignor
Marie Louise De Vaul
Amanda Norine Wilbern
Emma Jane Williams
Jennie Orrie Winfield
Isabelle Anna Wood
Parthenia Roberts
    Woodson
Frances Elizabeth Young
Alfred Sylvester Bland
James Frances Bowie
Samuel Graye Bullock
Charles Francis Gates
Laurence Archibald Goines
Harry Augustus Harvey
James Blain Hunger
Andrew Franklin Jackson
Reginald Leopold Lynch
Samuel Dozier Matthews
Willis Monroe Menard
William Francis Newman
Robert Harold Ogle
John Morgan Phillips
Wendell Phillips Smith
William Henry Twise [?]
Joseph Edward Smothers
and Benjamin Andrew
    Wade.

ARMSTRONG BUSINESS AND MANUAL TRAINING SCHOOL

Four-year manual training course:

Ada Rebecca Beverly
Marion Grace Beverly
Lucy Beatrice Carroll
Maude Mueller Crump
Laura Helphenstine Early
Gertrude Norman Ewin
Carrie Letitia Gray
Charles Gordon Cooke
Francis DeSales Miller
James Morris Saunders
Richard Alonsita Winslow

Two-year manual training course:

Lula Lena Ball
Ella Annetta Baltimore
Commora Beatrice Carter
Florence Edith Childs
Ella Edmonia Cochran
Blanche Elizabeth Cropp
Geneva Mary Cropp
Blanche Louisa Hollins
Jessie Cornelia Mason
Mary Beatrice Perry
Florence Irene Scott
Eva Estelle Taylor
Carrie Theresa Simpson
Charles Stephen Geary
Robert Watson Day

Business Course:

Blanche Ginnie Carter
Bessie Elizabeth Gibson
Sadie Anna Harper
Lelia Loretta Henderson
Alverta Lynch
Ethel Theordora Peters
Alice Ashby Robinson
Josephine Arnenia Thomas
Arthur Mack Carter
Clarence Monroe DeVelle
David Holmes
Frank Lourey McKinney
Charles Franklin Longus
Charles Frederick Scott
Claude Lorraine Tolson
Reuben Morton West
Thomas Eugene Smith

Special Students [these did not receive diplomas but were given certificates showing the kind and quality of special work done:]

Irene Margaret Bailey
Mary Alice Booker
Janet Mabel Bradford
Agnes Cecelia Brown
Ida Virginia Bronaugh
Neville Helena Bronaugh
Drusilla Edith Byrd
Lelia Virginia Freeman
Edna Lenora Johnson
Pearl Teresa Keys
Ruth Geneva Lee
Minnie Bradford
   McKinney
Tenetta Augusta Taylor
Mary Elizabeth Winters
Mirion Lillian Whitley
Mirian Hunster Wormley
Lola Juleane Lei Brant
Sarah Elizabeth Lomos
Andrew Joseph Thomas*
Eugene A. Dandridge*
Herman A. Wilson*
Arthur Albert
Ulysses Jesse Banks
Isaiah W. Hatton (?)*
William B. Mitchell*.

*Granted engineer's license by the District of Columbia

CONTRIBUTORS OF THE FIRST
COLORED SETTLEMENT HOUSE
IN THE DISTRICT OF COLUMBIA

Givers of Goods:

Brown, Mrs. Edenborough
Cook, Mrs. Coralie
Cook, Mrs.
Gilfillan, Mrs. H. W.
Henry, Mrs.
Hooper, Miss Mary
House & Herrman
Howard University
Jackson, Miss E. C.
Miller, Miss L. K.
Murray, Mrs. Anna
National Plant, Flower and
    Fruit Guild
Neal, Mrs. Charlotte
Neal, Mrs. Jessie E.
Normal School No. 2
Pendleton, Mr. R. L.
Plymouth Congregational
    Church C. E.
Quivers, Mrs. Alice
Weller, Mrs. Chas. F.

Volunteer Helpers:

Adams, Miss Emily B.
Ball, Miss Elizabeth B.
Baltimore, Miss Ella
Beverly, Miss Marion
Beverly, Miss Ada
Boyd, Miss Elizabeth
Butler, Miss Blanche
Campbell, Miss Clara
Carter, Miss Rosa Z.
Costin, Miss Edith
Chisolm, Mr. Sumner
Coleman, Miss Blanche
Collier, Miss Natalia
Curtis, Miss Eleanor J.
Cropp, Miss Blanche
Cropp, Miss Geneva
Dale, Miss Ada
Dandridge, Miss Josephine L.
Dillard, Miss Ritha
Dodson, Mr. B. S.
Duffield, Mr. W. S.
Duffield, Mrs. W. S.
Early, Miss Gertrude P.
Early, Miss Laura
Evans, Mrs. Annie
Evans, Miss Lillian
Evans, Mr. Joseph
Ewing, Miss Gertrude
Fair, Mr. Wm. A.
Fearing, Miss Lubertha
Fearing, Miss M. Estelle
Fleetwood, Miss Elizabeth
Gillem, Mr. J. Parker
Gillem, Mr. Richard A.
Gray, Miss Carrie
Greene, Miss Emma A.
Greene, Miss Minnie B.
Green, Miss Mabel
Green, Mr. Thomas

Green, Miss Clara
Grimké, Miss A.
Hall, Miss Sadie
Hill, Miss Mittie
Harper, Miss Mabel
Henderson, Mr. Wm.
Jackson, Miss Selina
Jackson, Miss Sarah E.
Jackson, Miss Nannie
Jackson, Miss Estelle C.
Jackson, Miss Anna M.
James, Mr.
Jefferson, Miss Iola
Johnson, Miss Sarah P.
Keys, Mr. G. E. Bernard
Lee, Miss Teresa
Lei Brant, Miss Lola
Lewis, Miss Beatrice
Lott, Miss Lillian T.
Love, Miss Lula E.
Lucas, Miss Georgianna A.
Meriweather, Miss Mary E.
Milton, Mr. Samuel
Moore, Miss Lily
Murray, Mrs. Anna
Murrell, Miss Margaret
Newman, Miss
Parks, Miss Jessie
Parker, Miss Lillian
Pendleton, Mrs. Lelia
Piper, Miss Ruther
Queen, Miss Flora
Randolph, Miss Rachel A.
Riley, Miss Clara
Saunders, Mr. James M.
Scott, Miss Florence
Smith, Miss Rose
Storum, Miss Ethel
Thompson, Miss

Thomas, Mrs. E. M.
Thomas, Miss Beatrice
Thompson, Miss Katherine A.
Turner, Miss Jessie
Van Loo, Mr. J.C.
Wallace, Miss Charlotte M.
Watson, Miss Eva
Walker, Miss Fannette
Walker, Mr. J. E.
Weeden, Mr. Henry
Weaver, Miss Mabel H.
Welsh, Miss Mary
Wilkinson, Miss R. Blyden
Wormley, Miss Alice K.
Wright, Miss M. Altoona
Yates, Miss Elizabeth G.

Contributors and Subscribers:

Armstrong Manual Training
    School
Asbury M. E. Church Missionary
    Society
Banneker Relief Association
*Bassett, Mr. U. S. G.
Beason, Miss H. H.
*Brent, Miss Ethel
Brooks, Mrs. O.
*Brooks, Miss Rachel
*Brown, Miss S. W.
Brown, Miss Fairfax
*Brown, Miss M.
Brown, Mr. C. M.
Burns, Mr. Wm. S.
Crescent Aid Circle
*Catlett, Miss B. S.
*Cook, Miss M. A.
*Cooper, Mrs. A. J.
*Craig, Prof. A. U.
Croswell, Mr.
Curtis, Dr. H. S.
*Day Nursery Association,
    Washington, D.C.
Dixon, Miss Rosa
*Duffield, Mr. W. S.
Duncanson, Mrs. A. S. P.
Evans, Mrs. Annie
Evans, Dr. W. Bruce
*Fifteenth St. Presbyterian S.S.
Farso Club, The
Francis, Mrs. B. G.
Georgetown, S.S. (R.
    Howard Supt.)
Gilfillan, Mrs. H. W.
*Grimké, Miss A. H.
*Grimké, Mr. Archibald
*Grimké, Dr. F. J.
Glenartney Club

Howard University
James, Miss Marie
*Jasper, Mr. James L.
Jefferson, Mr. Lewis
*Jones, Miss Virginia A.
*Jones, Miss Mary E.
LaFetra, Mr. E. S.
*Martin, Miss F.
Mayberry, Mrs.
McKinlay, Mr.
    Whitefield
Mead, Miss
Metropolitan A.M.E.
    Church Woman's Club
Metropolitan A.M.E.
    Church Friendly Aid Society
Middleton, Mr. Samuel
Miller, Prof. Kelly
Murrell, Miss Margaret
Mt. Zion M.E.S.S.
Mt. Moriah Baptist Church
Ovington, Miss M. W.
Plymouth Congregational
    Church
Pendleton, Mrs. Lelia
Prudence Crandall
    Association
*Russell, Mr. Aaron
*Ryan, Miss Amelia
Shadd, Miss Marion
*Sinclair, Mr. W. T.
*Sleman,. Mr. John B., Jr.
*Smith, Miss Gertrude F.
Stevens Night School
Stroud, Mrs. M. I.
*Tancil, Mrs. A. W.
*Terrell, Mrs. Mary
    Church
*Thomas, Mrs. E. M.

Thompson, Miss
Tuckerman, Miss J.
Van Trump, Miss Clara
Ward, Mrs. E. T.
*Weller, Mrs. Eugenia W.
*Weller, Mr. Charles F.
West, Mr.
*Williams, Mr. H. J.
Willing Workers Club,
    Armstrong Manual
    Training School
Wormley, Mrs. W. H. A.
Zion Baptist Church
    C. E. Society
*Normal School No. 2

Note: The listing of con-
tributors to the work of the
Colored Settlement House is
presented here exactly as published in the Souvenir booklet, *The Social Settlement for
Colored Boys, Girls and Adults,
1905.*

Those marked with (*)
g[a]ve stated sums of money

APPENDIX III

STUDENTS ENROLLED IN THE M STREET HIGH SCHOOL—1891

A

Adams, Anna
Addison, Grace
Adkins, Caledonia G.
Ages, Katie
Alexander, Mary
Allen, James F.
Armstead, Ada
Arnold, Oliver
Ashton, Ella

B

Banks, Maggie
Beason, Arabella
Beckley, Alice
Beckwith, Addie
Bell, Hattie
Bell, Mary A.
Bland, Fannie
Booker, George
Booker, Olive
Boone, Julia
Bowser, George
Bradford, Nannie
Broadus, Amanda
Brockenburgh, Lottie
Brooks, Arena
Brooks, Eugene
Brooks, Everett A.
Brooks, John
Brooks, Musette
Brooks, Thaddeus
Brown, Ella
Brown, Esquadora
Brown, George
Brown, Hattie
Brown, Ida E.
Brown, Julia
Brown, Robert
Brown, Sarah
Brown, William
Bruce, Ella
Bruce, John C.
Bruce, Louise
Bryant, Ada
Bryant, Maria

Burgess, Ada
Burke, Martha
Burrell, Mary
Burrill, Edmond A.
Burton, Lilian
Burwell, Emma
Burwell, Henry D.
Bury, Maggie
Bush, Anna
Butcher, James W.
Butler, Amelia
Butler, Dina

C

Campbell, Arminta
Campbell, Geneva
Campbell, Grace P.
Cardozo, William
Carroll, Agnes
Carroll, Alice
Carroll, Elizabeth
Carter, Martha
Carter, Nettie
Champ, Ella M.
Chase, Susie
Chisolom, Lottie A.
Churchwill, Charles
Clark, Anna
Clark, Gertrude
Clarke, Percy
Clay, Bessie
Clinton, Preston
Coates, Julia
Colbert, John
Cole, Anna
Cole, Sarah
Coleman, Alexander
Coleman, Benjamin
Coleman, Louise
Colen, George
Contee, Etta
Cook, Ralph
Cooper, Mary
Coquire, Selina
Cornish, Lee
Cornish, Louis A.

Cox, John
Cox, Thomas
Cromwell, Mary E.
Curry, William

D

Dabney, George
Dade, Julia
Darrall, Laurence
Davis, Alberta
Davis, Eugenia
Dawson, Gertrude
Dawson, Mary
Deviele, Lavenia
Dickerson, Lizzie E.
Dixon, Charles
Dixon, John
Dodson, Boynton
Dodson, Eva
Donaldson, Samuel C.
Dorsey, Andrew
Dorsey, Rebecca
Dowling, James C.
Downes, Florence C.
Dyson, Nellie E.

E

Edelin, Emma
Edwards, Bertha
Edwards, Carrie E.
Edwards, James H.
Elkins, William
Ellis, Lulie
Evans, Ella
Evans, Oliver

F

Fauntleroy, Addie
Fauntleroy, Mary
Ferguson, Charles
Ferguson, Emma
Ferguson, Lizzie
Ferguson, Louis
Fisher, Lorraine
Fletcher, Bessie L.
Fletcher, Martha
Fletcher, William
Fox, Lida
Franey, Hattie
Frazier, Annie
Freeman, Florence
Freeman, Harry
Freeman, Jessie N.
Freeman, Sarah
Fuller, Hattie

G

Gaines, Carrie
Gregory, James F.
Gregory, Eugene

Grant, Glovenia A.
Geary, Hattie
George, Blanche
George, Cornelia
George, John
Gibson, Lubelle
Goines, Augustine
Goings, Pauletta
Goodrich, William
Goodwin, Amos
Gorden, Olive
Grady, Ethel
Gray, L'Berta
Gray, Mattie
Green, Maria
Green, Mary
Green, Sarah A.
Greene, Annie
Grice, Alberta L.
Griffin, Georgie
Grimshaw, Eva
Gunnell, William

H

Haithman, Mary
Hall, Bessie
Hall, Edmond
Hall, Judge
Hamilton, Sadie
Hansborough, Winnifred
Hanson, Annie
Hanson, Annie M.
Harris, Esther M.
Harris, Hattie
Harvey, Eva
Harvey, Marietta L.
Hawkins, Annie M.
Hawkins, Estelle
Hawkins, Joseph
Herbert, Mattie
Herbert, Sadie
Hickman, Emma
Hill, Hattie
Hill, Mary
Hite, Mary Addison
Holmes, Lillian E.
Hopson, John
Hudnell, Samuel
Hughes, Bessie
Hunter, Eloise
Hurdnell, Annie
Hurley, Minnie
Hyman, N. Nora

J

Jackson, Alice B.
Jackson, Estelle
Jackson, Rosa
Jackson, Wiletta

James, Samuel
Janifer, Isabel
Johnson, Alice
Johnson, Beatrice
Johnson, Florence
Johnson, Grace
Johnson, Henry
Johnson, Jennie
Johnson, John H.
Johnson, Lillie
Johnson, Minnie
Johnson, Sarah
Johnson, Susie
Jones, Ella
Jones, Filena
Jones, Ida
Jones, Lila
Jones, Nannie
Jones, Ruth

K

Kelley, Lonise
King, Matilda
Kirkland, Minnie

L

Lancaster, Ella
Lee, Anna V.
Lee, Pillanna
Leibsant, Chauncey
Lewis, Harriet A.
Lewis, Jessie
Lewis, William
Lightfoot, Gertrude M.
Love, Lula E.
Loving, Walter
Lucas, Ada
Lucas, Ellen M.
Lucas, Joseph Henry
Lucas, Katie
Lucas, Louise
Lucas, Minnie
Lynch, Arthur*
Lynch, Arthur*
(*Not the same students.)

M

Madden, Edith
Magruder, Layton
Malvan, Beatrice E.
Mann, Mary E.
Manning, Ida
Marshall, Teressa
Martin, Corinne
Martin, Martha
Martin, Roselle B.
Mason, Jessie
Masin, Lillie
Matthews, Florence
May, Mamie

Merritt, Gertrude L.
Miller, William
Milton, Samuel
Miner, Posie
Miner, Rosie
Minor, Josie
Mitchell, Alonzo
Montague, Alexgine
Morris, Hannah
Morse, Maude
Moten, Florence
Moxley, Ella

Mc

McGinnis, Eunice

N

Naylor, Mamie H.
Newton, Celestine
Nugent, Blanche E.

O

Orer, Mary

P

Palmer, Thomas
Pannell, Hyler
Parham, Elizabeth
Parker, Irene G.
Parker, Lula
Payne, Annie
Payne, Mary
Peebles, Louisa A.
Perry, George
Peters, Lula
Peyton, Josephine
Phillips, Mamie K.
Phillips, Marvelline A.
Pierre, Virginia A.
Pinckney, Ermma
Pinkney, Estelle
Pinn, James L.
Piper, Lottie
Piper, Sadie
Plummer, Sadie
Pollen, Lucy

Q

Quander, Annie
Quander, John
Quarles, Annie

R

Randolph, Lenora
Rawles, Mary
Renfro, Daniel I.
Ricks, Henry
Ridgely, Albert
Robb, Susie
Roberts, Urskine
Robinson, Eleanor

Robinson, Lettie
Robinson, Susie
Ross, Hattie
Ross, Henrietta
Russell, Charles

S

Saunders, Mary
Savoy, Georgiana
Sayles, Alice
Sayles, Lillian
Schooler, Medora
Scott, Chaney
Scott, Georgie
Scott, Maggie
Sewall, Elinor
Shelton, Maggie M.
Shephard, Virgie
Shepherd, Lucy
Shepperson, Julia
Shippen, Cyrus S.
Shorter, Charles
Shorter, Geneva
Simmons, Daisy
Simms, Catherine
Simms, Eliza
Simms, James
Simms, Sarah L.
Simpson, Alberta
Smallwood, Ida
Smallwood, Louise R.
Smith, Isabel
Smith, Isabella
Smith, Paul
Snowden, Blanche
Sprauge, Fredericka
Stevenson, Julia
Stewart, Mattie
Stewart, Maud
Storum, Harry
Strachn, Matthew C.
Sydney, Isabel
Syphax, Julia
Syphax, Marcellus

T

Taliferro, Olivia
Taylor, Maggie
Taylor, Martha
Taylor, Matilda
Taylor, Sumner
Terrell, Laura
Thomas, Charles
Thomas, Julia
Thomas, Mary
Thomas, Shermond
Thomas, Sylvester
Thompson, Frances
Thompson, Jennie
Thornton, Addie

Thurston, Mary F.
Tibbs, Julia
Tignor, Annie
Tignor, Charles A.
Tilghman, Maggie
Toliver, Fannie
Tubman, Anna
Turner, James
Turner, Mabel
Turner, Mary
Tyler, John
Tyler, Lillie

V

Vessels, Dola

W

Walker, James, E.
Washington, Benjamin
Washington, Mary
Washington, Mary E.
Watkins, Mary
Wayman, William
Webster, Delaphine
Wells, William, Jr.
Wesley, Anna E.
West, Arthur
West, Clara
West, Emma
West, Harriet
West, Janie
West, Martha
Weston, Josephine
Whipper, Ionia
White, Mattie
Whiting, Elizabeth
Wilder, William
Wilkinsin, Estelle
Wilkinson, Harry
Wilkinson, James
Wilkinson, Jennie
Williams, Emma
Williams, Harry
Williams, Mamie I.
Williams, Sarah
Williamson, Annie O.
Williamson, Jennie
Williamson, Mary
Wilson, Maggie
Winston, Clarence
Woodson, Alphonso
Wormley, Jessie
Wright, Clarence

Y

Young, Julia
Younger, Maggie

Lenders to the Exhibition and Book

Mrs. Sadie T. Alexander
Association for the Study of Afro-American Life and
  History (ASALH)
Barbados Museum and Historical Society
Mr. Charles L. Blockson, the Afro-American Col-
  lection of
Mrs. Regia Haywood Bronson
Mr. William N. Buckner, Jr.
Mrs. Beatrice Christopher
Columbia Historical Society
Dr. Paul Phillips Cooke
District of Columbia Department of General Services
District of Columbia Public Library, Washingtoniana
  Division
District of Columbia Public Schools
District of Columbia Recorder of Deeds
W. E. B. Du Bois Papers, University of
  Massachusetts
Duke University Library
Family of Conard A. and Marion Demby Edwards
Mr. Perry G. Fisher
Hampton Institute, Hollis P. Frissel Library
Mrs. Mary Gibson Hundley
Mrs. C. F. Hunlain
Mrs. Phyllis Terrell Langston
Mr. James L. Lawson
Mrs. Georgia R. Lawson
Mr. and Mrs. Benjamin T. Layton
Mr. and Mrs. Burton Lewis
Library of Congress
Moorland-Spingarn Research Center, Howard
  University
  Anna J. Cooper Papers
  Francis J. Grimké Papers
  Photograph and Prints Division
National Archives and Records Service
  Spanish American War Records
North Carolina Department of Archives and History
  Fabius J. Haywood, Sr., Papers
Oberlin College Archives
Mrs. Ella Howard Pearis
Enoch Pratt Free Library, George Peabody
  Department

Mrs. Anna Rosetta Lawson Prescott
Recorder of Deeds, North Carolina
Dr. Henry S. Robinson
Robert Scurlock, Scurlock Studios
Mr. Paul Sluby, Sr.
Smith College, Sophia Smith Collection
Miss Regina Smith
Smithsonian Institution
  National Museum of American History,
  The Nannie Helen Burroughs Collection, and
  Division of Domestic Life,
  National Portrait Gallery
Mrs. Ann Weaver Teabeau
Virginia State College
The Washington Post
The Washington Star
Miss Hilda Woodford
The Woodrow Wilson House, National Trust for His-
  toric Preservation

Bibliography

Alexander, Charles. *One Hundred Distinguished Leaders.* Atlanta: Franklin Printing & Publishing Co., 1899

Aptheker, Herbert, ed. *A Documentary History of the Negro People in the United States.* New York: Citadel Press, 1969.

Bardolph, Richard. *The Negro Vanguard.* New York: Rinehart & Company, 1959.

Barrett, John Gilchrist. *North Carolina as a Civil War Battleground, 1861-1865.* Raleigh, N.C.: State Dept. of Archives and History, 1960.

Beard, Mary R., ed. *America Through Women's Eyes.* 1933. Reprint. New York: Greenwood Press, 1969.

Blassingame, John W. *The Slave Community: Plantation Life in the Antebellum South.* New York: Oxford University Press, 1972.

Brawley, Benjamin. *The Negro in Literature and Art in the United States.* New York: Duffield & Company, 1918.

Brawley, Benjamin. *A Social History of the American Negro.* New York: Macmillan Company, 1921.

Brawley, Benjamin. *Women of Achievement.* Written for the Fireside Schools under the auspices of the Woman's American Baptist Home Mission Society, 1919.

Brown, Hallie Q., comp. *Homespun Heroines and Other Women of Distinction.* 1926. Reprint. Freeport, N.Y.: Books for Libraries Press, 1971.

Bruce, John E. *Short Biographical Sketches of Eminent Negro Men and Women.* Yonkers, N.Y.: Gazette Press, 1910.

Cederholm, Theresa Dickason. *Afro-American Artists. A Bio-Bibliographical Directory.* Trustees of the Boston Public Library, 1973

Chamberlain, Ernest Barrett. *The Churchills of Oberlin.* Oberlin, Ohio: The Oberlin Improvement and Development Organization, 1965.

The Colored Social Settlement, Inc., 1913-14. Pamphlet. Washington, D.C.: Murray Brothers Press, 1913.

Congressional Quarterly, Inc. *Members of Congress Since 1789.* Washington, D.C.: Congressional Quarterly, 1977.

Cooper, Anna J. *Equality of Races and the Democratic Movement.* Pamphlet. Privately printed. Washington, D.C., 1945.

Cooper, Anna J. *Legislative Measures Concerning Slavery in the United States.* Pamphlet. Privately printed. Washington, D.C., 1942.

Cooper, Anna J. *Personal Recollections of the Grimké Family & The Life and Writings of Charlotte Forten Grimké.* Privately printed. 1951.

Cooper, Anna J. *The Social Settlement: What It Is, and What It Does.* Pamphlet. Washington, D.C.: Murray Brothers Press, 1913.

Cooper, Anna J. *The Third Step (Autobiographical).* Booklet. Privately printed. n.d.

Cooper, Anna J. *A Voice from the South: By a Black Woman of the South.* 1892. Reprint. New York: Negro Universities Press, 1969.

Cromwell, John W. *History of the Bethel Literary and Historical Association.* Washington, D.C.: Press of R. L. Pendleton, 1896.

Cromwell, John W. *The Negro in American History.* Washington, D.C.: American Negro Academy, 1914.

Culp, D. W. *Twentieth Century Negro Literature.* Naperville, Ill.: J. L. Nichols & Co., 1902.

Dabney, Lillian G. *The History of Schools for Negroes in the District of Columbia, 1807-1947.* Washington, D.C.: Catholic University of America Press, 1949.

Dannett, Sylvia G.L., ed. *Profiles of Negro Womanhood.* Negro Heritage Library. Yonkers: Educational Heritage, 1964.

Davis, John P., ed. *The American Negro Reference Book.* Englewood Cliffs, N.J.: Prentice-Hall, 1964.

Directory of Afro-American Resources. Edited by Walter Schatz. New York: R. R. Bowker Co., 1970.

Du Bois, W. E. B. *The Autobiography of W. E. B. Du Bois.* New York: International Publishers, 1970.

Fifth and Sixth Years' Report of the Colored Y.W. Christian Association (May 1909-May 1911). Washington, D.C.: 1911 (?)

Fletcher, Robert Samuel. *A History of Oberlin College from its Foundation through the Civil War.* 2 vols. Oberlin, Ohio: Oberlin College, 1943.

Flexner, Eleanor. *Century of Struggle: The Woman's Rights Movement in the United States.* Rev. ed. Cambridge, Mass.: Belknap Press of Harvard University Press, 1976.

Foner, Philip S., ed. *The Voice of Black America: Major Speeches by Negroes in the United States, 1797-1971.* New York: Simon and Schuster, 1972.

Foner, Philip S., ed. *W. E. B. Du Bois Speaks: Speeches and Addresses, 1890-1919.* New York: Pathfinder Press, 1970

Franklin, John Hope. *The Free Negro in North Carolina, 1790-1860.* Chapel Hill: University of North Carolina Press, 1943.

Fuller, Thomas O. *Pictorial History of the American Negro.* Memphis, Tenn.: Pictorial History, 1933.

Gay, Joseph R. *Self-Educator for a Rising Race.* Nashville, Tenn.: The Southwestern Co., 1913.

Gibbs, Mifflin W. *Shadow and Light, An Autobiography.* Washington, D.C., 1902.

Grant, Joanne, ed., *Black Protest: History, Documents, and Analyses: 1619 to the Present.* Greenwich, Conn.: Fawcett Publications, 1968.

Grimké, Francis J. *The Works of Francis J. Grimké.* Edited by Carter G. Woodson. Vols. 1 & 2. Washington, D.C.: Associated Publishers, 1942.

Haley, James T. *Afro-American Encyclopedia . . .* Nashville, Tenn.: Haley & Floride, 1895.

Halliburton, Cecil D. *A History of St. Augustine's College, 1867–1937.* Raleigh, N.C.: St. Augustine's College, 1937.

Harlan, Louis R. *Booker T. Washington: The Making of a Black Leader.* New York: Oxford University Press, 1972.

Harley, Sharon, and Rosalyn Terbog-Penn, eds. *The Afro-American Woman: Struggles and Images.* Port Washington, N.Y.: Kennikat Press, 1978.

Harrison, Dr. Earl L. *The Dream and the Dreamer.* The Nannie Helen Burroughs School. The Literature Foundation, 1956, 1972.

Hartshorn, William Newton. *An Era of Progress and Promise, 1863–1910.* Boston: Priscilla Publishing Co., 1910.

Hawkins, William G. (Rev.). *Lunsford Lane, Another Helper from North Carolina.* 1863. Reprint. Miami: Mnemosyne Publishing Co., 1969.

Haywood, Hubert Benbury. *Sketch of the Haywood Family in North Carolina.* North Carolina, 1956.

Hilyer, Andrew F. *The Twentieth Century Union League Directory.* Published under the auspices of the Union League of Andrew F. Hilyer. Washington, D.C., 1901

A History of the Phyllis Wheatley Young Women's Christian Association 1905–1930. Booklet. Washington, D.C., 1930 (?).

History of Schools for the Colored Population. Reprint. New York: Arno Press and New York Times, 1969.

Holmes, Dwight Oliver Wendell. *The Evolution of the Negro College.* College Park, Md.: McGrath Publishing Company, 1934.

Howard University Directory of Graduates, 1870–1963. Edited by Frederick D. Wilkinson. Washington, D.C.: Howard University. 1965.

Hundley, Mary Gibson. *The Dunbar Story (1870–1955).* New York: Vantage Press, 1965.

Ingle, Edward, *The Negro in the District of Columbia.* 1893. Reprint. Freeport N.Y.: Books for Libraries Press, 1971.

Klein, Abbé Felix. *In the Land of the Strenuous Life.* Author's translation. Chicago: A. C. McClurg & Co., 1905.

Knox, Ellis O. *Democracy and the District of Columbia Public Schools.* Washington, D.C.: Judd & Detweiler, 1957.

Lamb, Daniel Smith, ed. *Howard University Medical Department: A Historical, Biographical and Statistical Souvenir* (c. 1900). Freeport, N.Y.: Books for Libraries Press, 1971.

Lawson, Jesse, comp. & ed. *How to Solve the Race Problem.* 1904. Reprint. Chicago: Afro-Am Press, 1969.

Leavell, Ullin Whitney. *Philanthropy in Negro Education.* 1930. Reprint. Westport, Conn.: Negro Universities Press, 1970.

Lerner, Gerda, ed. *Black Women in White America: A Documentary History.* New York: Vintage Books, 1973.

Lewis, Helen Matthews. *The Woman's Movement and the Negro Movement—Parallel Struggles for Rights.* A thesis presented to the graduate faculty of the University of Virginia in candidacy for the degree of Master of Arts. Charlottesville: University of Virginia, 1949.

Loewenberg, Bert James and Ruth Bogin, eds. *Black Women in Nineteenth-Century American Life: Their Words, Their Thoughts, Their Feelings.* University Park: Pennsylvania State University Press, 1976.

Logan, Rayford W. *The Negro in the United States. Vol. 1: A History to 1945, from Slavery to Second Class Citizenship.* New York: Van Nostrand Reinhold Company, 1970.

Majors, Monroe A. *Noted Negro Women: Their Triumphs and Activities.* 1893. Reprint. Black Heritage Library Collection, 1971.

Mattingly, Robert N. *Autobiographical Memories, 1897-1954: M Street-Dunbar High School.* Privately printed. Washington, D.C., 1974.

Meier, August. *Negro Thought in America, 1880-1915.* Ann Arbor: University of Michigan Press, 1971.

Montgomery, Winfield Scott. *Historical Sketch of Education for the Colored Race in the District of Columbia, 1807–1905.* Washington, D.C.: Smith Brothers, Printers, 1907.

Mossell, N. F. (Mrs.). *The Work of the Afro-American Woman.* 1894. Reprint. Freeport, N.Y.: Books for Libraries Press, 1971.

Moton, Robert Russa. *Finding a Way Out, an Autobiography.* Copyright, 1920, by Doubleday, Page & Company. Reprint. New York: Negro Universities Press, 1969.

National Association of Colored Women's Clubs, Inc. *A History of the Club Movement Among the Colored Women of the United States of America.* Washington, D.C., 1902. (Reprinted 1978.)

Newbold, N. C. *Five North Carolina Negro Educators.* Chapel Hill: University of North Carolina Press, 1939.

Olcott, Jane. *The Work of Colored Women.* New York: Colored Work Committee War Work Council National Board, Young Women's Christian Associations, 1919.

One Hundredth Anniversary of the Nineteenth Street Baptist Church. Washington, D.C.: Murray Brothers, 1939.

Pendleton, Lelia Amos. *A Narrative of the Negro.* 1912. Reprint. Freeport, N.Y.: Books for Libraries Press, 1971.

Proctor, John Clagett, ed. *Washington Past and Present.* Vols. 1-4. New York: Lewis Historical Publishing Co., 1930.

Public Schools of the District of Columbia. Report. (Submitted by Mr. [A.T.] Stewart, from the Committees on the District of Columbia.) Washington, D.C.: Government Printing Office, 1900.

Richings, G. F. *Evidences of Progress Among Colored People.* Philadelphia: Geo. S. Ferguson Co., 1905.

Sears, Jesse B. *Philanthropy in the History of American Higher Education.* Department of the Interior, Bureau of Education, Bulletin No. 26. Washington, D.C.: Government Printing Office, 1922.

Siebert, Wilbur H. *The Underground Railroad from Slavery to Freedom.* 1898. Reprint. New York: Arno Press, 1968.

Smith, Edwin W. *Aggrey of Africa: A Study in Black and White.* London: Student Christian Movement, 1929.

Spivey, Donald. *Schooling for the New Slavery: Black Industrial Education, 1868-1915.* Contributions in Afro-American and African Studies, No. 38. Copyright by Donald Spivey, 1978. Westport, Conn.: Greenwood Press.

Stolpen, Steve. *Raleigh: A Pictorial History.* Norfolk, Va.: Donning Company, Publishers, 1977.

Taylor, Rosser Howard. *Slaveholding in North Carolina: An Economic View.* 1926. Reprint. New York: Negro Universities Press, 1969.

Thornton, Mary Lindsay, comp. *A Bibliography of North Carolina, 1589-1956.* Chapel Hill: University of North Carolina Press, 1958.

Todd, Charles Burr. *The Story of Washington, the National Capital.* New York: G. P. Putnam's Sons, 1889.

U.S. Advisory Committee on Education. *Special Problems of Negro Education.* Washington, D.C.: Government Printing Office, 1939.

U.S. Congress. Senate. *Report of the Schoolhouse Commission. . . . Document No. 338.* Washington, D.C.: Government Printing Office, 1908.

U.S. Office of Education. *Report of the Commission of Education for the Year 1900–1901.* 2 vols. Washington, D.C.: Government Printing Office, 1902.

Washington, Booker T., with N. B. Wood and Fannie Barrier Williams. *A New Negro for a New Century.* 1900. Reprint. New York: Arno Press and New York Times, 1969.

Washington, Booker T., W. E. B. Du Bois, et al. *The Negro Problem. . . .* New York: James Pott & Co., 1903.

Washington Post. *A History of the City of Washington.* Washington, D.C.: 1903.

Waugh, Elizabeth Culbertson. *North Carolina's Capital, Raleigh.* Chapel Hill: University of North Carolina Press, 1967.

Who's Who in Colored America. Vol. 1. Edited by Joseph J. Boris. New York: Who's Who in Colored America Corp. Publishers, 1927.

Who's Who of the Colored Race. Vol. 1. Edited by Frank Lincoln Mather. Chicago, 1915.

World's Congress of Representative Women. *The World's Congress of Representative Women: A Historical Resume.* Vol. 11. Chicago and New York: Rand, McNally & Company, 1894.

Writer's Program of the Work Projects Administration in the State of North Carolina. *Raleigh: Capital of North Carolina.* 1942. Reprint. New York: AMS Press, 1975.

Documents, Articles, and Periodicals

"Alumni of M Street," *Washington Post,* September 9, 1905.

"Anna Julia Cooper." In *A Study of Historic Sites in the District of Columbia of Special Significance to Afro-Americans.* HUD Study, 2. (Prepared by the Afro-American Bicentennial Corp.) Washington, D.C.: Afro-American Bicentennial Corp., 1974.

"Anna Julia Cooper." *The Southland* 2 (April 1891). Winston-Salem, N.C., 1891. [Editors: S. G. Atkins and Anna J. Cooper.]

Bassett, J. S. "Suffrage in the State of North Carolina." *Annual Report of the American Historical Association for the Year 1895.* Washington, D.C.: Government Printing Office, 1896.

Bassett, John Spencer, "Anti-Slavery Leaders of North Carolina." *Johns Hopkins University Studies in Historical and Political Science,* series 16, no. 6 (June 1898): 8–74.

Bassett, John Spencer. "Slavery and Servitude in the Colony of North Carolina." *Johns Hopkins University Studies in Historical and Political Science,* Fourteenth Series (April–May 1896): 11-75.

Bureau of Refugees, Freedmen, and Abandoned Lands, District of Columbia: Superintendent of Education. Selected School Reports 1865–1870. Washington, D.C.: National Archives, Record Group No. 105.

Caliver, Ambrose. "Education of Negroes." *Biennial Survey of Education, 1928-1930.* Bureau of Education Bulletin no. 20 (1931): 559–618.

Caliver, Ambrose. "Negro Education in the Depression." *School Life.* February 1933, pp. 111-12.

"Charged with Malice." *Washington Post,* October 3, 1906.

Chase, Enoch Aquila. "Doctor William Tindall." *Records of the Columbia Historical Society of Washington, D.C.* (1935): 182-91.

Collins, Carolyn B. "Mayor Sayles J. Bowen and the Beginnings of Negro Education." *Records of the Columbia Historical Society of Washington, D.C.,* vols. 53-56 (1959): 293–308.

"Colored High School." *Washington Post,* September 19, 1905.

"Colored Schools of Washington and Georgetown." U.S. Congress. 41st, 3rd Session. *Senate Executive Documents,* pp. 1-53. (Doc. no. 20.)

Colored Woman's League of Washington, D.C. *Fifth Annual Report*. Washington, D.C.: Smith Brothers, 1898. (Library of Congress, Mary Church Terrell Papers.)

Compilation of Laws Affecting the Public Schools of the District of Columbia, 1804 to 1929. Washington, D.C.: Government Printing Office, 1929.

Cook, George F. T. "Historical Sketch of the Colored Schools, Past and Present." *First Report of the Board of Trustees of the District of Columbia, 1874–75*. Washington, D.C.: M'Gill & Withebow, Printers, 1876.

Cooper, Anna J. "Angry Saxons and Negro Education." *Crisis*, May 1938, p. 148.

Cooper, Anna J. "College Extension for Working People." *Journal of the (Oberlin) Alumnae Club*. Washington, D.C., n.d., pp. 34–38.

Cooper, Anna J. "The Higher Education of Woman." *The Southland*, April 1891, pp. 186–202.

Cooper, Anna J. "The Humor of Teaching." *Crisis*, November 1930, p. 387.

Cooper, Anna J. "The Negro Exhibit at the Paris Exhibition." *National Capital Searchlight*, February 1901, pp. 2-5.

Cooper, Anna J. "Souvenir: Xi Omega Chapter, Alpha Kappa Alpha Sorority." Washington, D.C., December 29, 1925.

Crummell, Alexander. "The Black Woman of the South: Her Neglects and Her Needs." Address before the Freedmen's Aid Society, August 15, 1883. New York Public Library, Schomburg Center for Research in Black Culture. Microfilm no. 6551-001.

Crummell, Alexander. "Charitable Institutions in Colored Churches." Pamphlet. Washington, D.C.: R. L. Pendleton, 1892.

"D. C. Scholar Looks at 100 Years of Living." *Washington Evening Star*, August 10, 1958.

"Dismissal of Mrs. A. J. Cooper, Colored . . ." *Washington Post*, September 15, 1906.

Du Bois, W. E. B. "American Negro at Paris." *American Review of Reviews*, November 1900.

Du Bois, W. E. B. "Heredity and the Public Schools." A lecture delivered under the auspices of the Principals' Association of the Colored Schools of Washington, D.C., Friday, March 25, 1904. Washington, D.C.: R. L. Pendleton, Printer.

Du Bois, W. E. B. "The Negro Since 1900: A Progress Report." *New York Times Magazine*, November 21, 1948, p. 24.

Du Bois, W. E. Burghardt. "The Study of the Negro Problems." *Annals of the American Academy of Political and Social Science* 11 (January-June 1898): 1–23.

Du Bois, W. E. Burghardt. "The Burden of Negro Schooling." *Independent* (magazine), July 18, 1901, pp. 1667–68.

Enck, Henry S. "Black Self-Help in the Progressive Era." *Journal of Negro History* 41 (January 1976): 73-87.

Ferris, William H. "Alexander Crummell, An Apostle of Negro Culture." American Negro Academy, Occasional Papers, no. 20. Washington, D.C.: American Negro Academy, 1920.

Frelinghuysen University. Pamphlet. Washington, D.C.: Murray Brothers Printing Co., n.d.

Frelinghuysen University. *Annual Catalogue of the Frelinghuysen University, 1926–27*. Washington, D.C.

Frelinghuysen University. *Courses of Study in the Frelinghuysen University of Washington, D. C.* Catalogue. 1920–21. Washington, D.C.

Harris, Abram L. "The Negro Problem as Viewed by Negro Leaders." *Current History* 18 (June 1923): 410–18.

Haycock, Robert L. "Sixty Years of the Public Schools of the District of Columbia—1885 to 1945." *Records of the Columbia Historical Society of Washington, D.C., 1946–1947*. Vols. 48–49 (1949).

"Hearing Brought to Close." *Washington Post*, October 7, 1905.

Johnson, Guy B. "Some Factors in the Development of Negro Social Institutions in the United States." *American Journal of Sociology* 40 (July 1934–May 1935): 329–37.

Lindsay, Inabel Burns. "The Participation of Negro Women in the Development of Some Post Civil War Welfare Services in the District of Columbia." *Women in the District of Columbia: A Contribution to Their History*. Washington, D.C.: International Women's Year Coordinating Committee, 1977.

Logan, Rayford W. "Educational Segregation in the North." *Journal of Negro Education* 2 (January 1933).

"Lone Graduate Hears Vicar at Frelinghuysen." *Washington Afro-American*, June 7, 1947.

Miller, Kelly. "The Negro and Education." *Forum* 30 (February 1901): 693–705).

Miller, Kelly. "The Negro and Education." *Report of the Commissioner of Education, 1900-01* Washington, D.C., 1902, pp. 731-859.

"Miss Cooper's Defense." *Washington Post*, Oct. 18, 1905.

Mossell, N. F. (Mrs.). "The National Afro-American Council." *Colored American Magazine* 3 (August 1901): 293–95.

"Mrs. Mary [sic] J. Cooper Defended." *Washington Bee*, September 30, 1905.

"Negro Education." *Crisis*, August 1925, pp. 166–80.

"Negro Educator Sees Life's Meaning at 100." *Washington Post*, August 10, 1958.

Oak, Vishnu V. "Higher Education and the Negro." *Education* 53 (November 1932): 176–81.

"Official Compilation of the Proceedings of the Afro-American National Conference, 1890." *The Southland*, June 1890.

"Our High School." *Washington Bee*, September 30, 1905.

"Our Schools." *Washington Bee*, May 21, 1904.

"Our Schools." *Washington Bee*, September 22, 1906.

"Pay Teachers Oct. 10." *Washington Post*, October 5, 1906.

"Proceedings of the 9th Annual Session of the National

Afro-American Council . . . 1906" (Louisville, 1907). *AME Zion Quarterly Review* 23 (January 1907).

"Protests from Teachers." *Washington Post*, September 19, 1906.

Record, Wilson. "Negro Intellectuals and Negro Movements in Historical Perspective." *American Quarterly* 8 (1956): 3-20.

"Retains Mrs. Cooper." *Washington Post*, October 31, 1905.

Scarborough, W. S. "The Negro and the Higher Learning." *Forum* 33 (May 1902): 349–55.

"School Board Estimates." *Washington Post*, Oct. 12, 1905.

"School Board Violates Law." *Washington Post*, September 21, 1906.

Sims, Edgar R. "Dunbar High School: The Crack in the White Wall, 1870–1974." Unpublished manuscript.

"Sociological Body Picks New Officers." *Washington Evening Star*, September 22, 1923.

"Superintendent Chancellor." *Washington Bee*, September 29, 1906.

"Support Mrs. Cooper." *Washington Post*, September 29, 1905.

Taylor, Genevieve. "The Observance of the Seventy-fifth Anniversary of Public Education for Negroes in the District of Columbia." *Negro History Bulletin* 3 (1939): 37–41.

Terrell, Mary Church. "The History of the Club Women's Movement." *The Africamerican Women's Journal*, 1904 (Summer and Fall), pp. 34–38.

Thompson, Charles H. "Introduction: The Problem of Negro Higher Education." *The Journal of Negro Education* 2 (July 1933): 257–71.

Thompson, Charles H. "75 Years of Negro Education." *Crisis*, July 1938, p. 202.

Thornbrough, Emma Lou. "The National Afro-American League, 1887–1908." *Journal of Southern History* 27 (November 1961): 494–512.

"Trying to Embarrass School Management." *Washington Post*, September 16, 1906.

U.S. Congress. House of Representatives. Commission . . . Investigating the Public School Buildings of the District of Columbia. *Public School Buildings in District of Columbia*. 47th Congress, 1st sess. (1882). Misc. Doc. no. 35.

U. S. Congress. Senate. Committee on the District of Columbia. *Public Schools of the District of Columbia*. 56th Congress, 1st sess. (1900). Report no. 711.

U. S. Congress. Senate. "Letter of The Secretary of the Interior, Communicating . . . Reports of the Board of Trustees of Colored Schools of Washington and Georgetown." 41st Congress, 3rd sess. (1871). Ex. Doc. 20.

Walters, Alexander (Bishop). "The Pan-African Conference." *The AME Zion Quarterly Review*, 1901.

Ware, Edward T. "Education of Negroes in the United States." *Annals of American Education* 49 (September 1913): 209–18.

Washington Record Books for the Public Schools: Division Number 7 & 8; Section High School, 1891–1892. *Teachers:*
Henry L. Bailey
P. N. Bailey
Laura F. Barney
Percival D. Brooks
F. L. Cardozo, *Principal*
Anna J. Cooper
J. W. Mason
Mary E. Nalle
Mary Jane Patterson
Hattie E. Riggs
James Storer
D. R. Thompson

Waugh, Irene M. "Frelinghuysen Meets a Need in D.C." *Washington Tribune*, September 14, 1946, p. 20.

"What I Saw and Heard." *Washington Bee*, Nov. 18, 1905.

Williams, W. T. B. *Report on Negro Universities and Colleges*. John F. Slater Fund, Occasional Papers 21 (1922).

Wilson, J. Ormond. "Eighty Years of the Public Schools of Washington, 1805-1885." *Records of the Columbia Historical Society* 1 (1897).

Wormley, G. Smith. "Educators of the First Half Century of the Public Schools of the District of Columbia." *Journal of Negro History* 17 (1932): 124–40.

Index

Page numbers refer to illustrations as well as text.

No Flowers [

Oh, just a rose perhaps, a f[
Or even a handfull of wild [
Or Star of Bethlehem & sweet [
Which says you remember ki[
  For this I shall thank you [
  And more for the coura[
  You gave in the Struggl[
  By the touch of your shou[
  And the understandin[
  And the hearty Pull togethe[
  Priceless & undying these [
    And I shall thank y[

But please, please, dont pass [
Or take up a collection to crowd the [
With mute withering symbols of God's eter[
Agonizing that we all should be one & lo[
Even as He & the Father are One in Love.
    No flowers please, just the sm[
  The knowing look that sees Beyond And s[
'Somebody's Teacher on Vacation Now - Resti[